I0135407

Chiefs, Priests, and Praise-Singers

WYATT MACGAFFEY

Chiefs, Priests, and Praise-Singers

History, Politics, and Land Ownership in Northern Ghana

University of Virginia Press *Charlottesville and London*

University of Virginia Press
© 2013 by the Rector and Visitors of the University of Virginia

All rights reserved

Printed in the United States of America on acid-free paper

First published 2013
9 8 7 6 5 4 3 2 1

LIBRARY OF CONGRESS CATALOGING-IN-PUBLICATION DATA
MacGaffey, Wyatt.
  Chiefs, priests, and praise-singers : history, politics, and land ownership in
northern Ghana / Wyatt MacGaffey.
    p.   cm.
  Includes bibliographical references and index.
  ISBN 978-0-8139-3386-3 (cloth : alk. paper) — ISBN 978-0-8139-3387-0 (e-book)
  1. Dagbani (African people)—History. 2. Dagbani (African people)—Politics
and government. 3. Dagbani (African people)—Land tenure. 4. Chiefdoms—
Ghana—Northern Region. 5. Local government—Ghana—Northern Region.
6. Land tenure—Ghana—Northern Region. 7. Dagomba (Ghana)—Historiography.
8. Dagomba (Ghana)—Politics and government. I. Title.
  DT510.43.D34M33 2013
  966.70049635—dc23   2012030531

Contents

From 1996 to 2012 I visited Tamale, in northern Ghana, for about two months each year. Because my wife, Dr. Susan Herlin, who was given the chiefly title, or "skin," Tamale Zo-Simli Na in 1995, is from Texas by way of Kentucky, and because she decided to take her title seriously rather than to treat it as the equivalent of an honorary degree, we needed and benefited from the constant advice of her elders, which amounted to an extended education in traditional conduct, a life known to few foreigners and increasingly unknown to educated townspeople. As a chief "enskinned" by the Ya Na, the king of Dagbon, she respects her customary obligations to the hierarchy of her fellow chiefs and has several times paraded with them through Tamale on horseback during the annual Damba festival. Because her skin is an honor conferred jointly by the traditional hierarchy and the Tamale Metropolitan Assembly, she is also in frequent contact with the chief executive (the mayor), with elected members of the assembly, and with the administration of the Northern Region. Her work in education and development projects, in collaboration with her elders and supporters, helped us to know politicians, chiefs, schools, schoolchildren, and villages both urban and rural; it built such a reputation for her that wherever I went in remote parts of Dagbon I could count on a warm welcome as Zo-Simli Na *yidana,* her husband. Later, the chief and people of the village of Foshegu gave me an identity of my own, the much lowlier title Saba Na, which people always prefer to use rather than a proper name and for which I am grateful.

I did not set out to "do research" or to question the history of Dagbon, but gradually that history revealed itself as the ideological foundation of what was happening around me, as people constantly made reference in contemporary disputes to events and conjunctures in the past. I do not speak Dagbani and was therefore dependent in some contexts on translators and assistants. I am well aware of the limitations of this kind of research, but I was able to become familiar with people and events over a long period of time, to visit and revisit, developing a sense of the issues that seemed important. Arriving each year after a lapse of time made clear the pace of "modernization" and the rapid decline of all things "traditional."

I have done my best to follow the advice of E. F. Tamakloe, who wrote that researchers will do well if they are "conversant, liberal, kind, unbullying, affable, patient and neither friends nor foes to anyone." For explaining matters and for opening doors for me I am indebted to, among many others, the late Dulogulana Ebenezer Adam, the late Dakpema Richard Alhassan, Vo'Na the Honorable M. B. Bawa, Alhaji Mohammed Haroon, Alhaji Abdulai Haruna (sometime district chief executive of Savelugu, later metropolitan chief executive of Tamale), Zubwogu Na H. Abukari Kaleem, Alhaji Ibrahim Mahama, Prince Mohammed, Hajia Fati Munkaila, Ahmed Rufai (then municipal coordinating director of Tolon-Kumbungu), the late Gulkpeogu Ngwo Na Musah Sugre, the staff of the Public Records and Archives Administration Department (PRAAD) in Tamale, my *wulana,* Samson Adam, and especially my assistants, Alhassan Iddris Gallant, Zo-Simli Lun'Na Issa Yakubu, Yusif Saïd, and Choggo Zi-Sung Na Abdul-Somed Shahadu. Like all who wish to think about Dagbon today, I owe a great deal to Martin Staniland's *The Lions of Dagbon,* in his own words "a disquieting mixture of history, political science, and anthropology," and wonderfully so. I thank Allegra Churchill and Lindsay Cameron for photographs; Professor Justin McCarthy, of the University of Louisville, for making the maps; and David Locke for introducing me to the late Alhaji Abubakari Lunna. In revising my manuscript I was greatly aided by the reports of the University of Virginia Press's readers and by the hard work of my editor, Joanne Allen (none of my previous books was ever so thoroughly edited). The remaining mistakes, ambiguities, and omissions are my own. I am grateful to Haverford College for occasional help with travel expense and for the support of its computer center.

PRAAD Accra and especially PRAAD Tamale provided indispensable resources. Unfortunately, in Tamale the classification system cited by Staniland, for example, as "NAG, ADM," and so on, has been replaced; the new system uses "NRG," and it is very difficult, if not impossible, to establish correspondence between the two. Moreover, the files in Tamale, heavily used, are in very bad condition. Old paper is disintegrating, file numbers may be illegible, documents have been misplaced, and some material is missing. A project of the British Library to digitize the records and thus save what we have, initiated by Professor Ismael Montana, of Northern Illinois University, was being carried out in 2010. Quotations from unfiled letters are taken from copies in my possession.

Tamale, June 2012

A Note on Dagbani Orthography

I have used both Ibrahim Mahama's *Dagbani-English Dictionary* and the "provisional" *Dagbani Dictionary* prepared by Roger Blench. The first was written and published in Tamale by a native speaker; the second is the product of a progressive collaboration begun by H. A. Blair and E. F. Tamakloe in 1940 and continued since then by scholars and professional linguists but still unfinished in 2004. It is readily available online at http://www.rogerblench.info/Language/Niger-Congo/Gur/Dagbani%20 dictionary%20CD.pdf. The two dictionaries use different orthographies. According to Knut J. Olawsky, one of the linguists, "Orthographic standards are not even consistent within publications by one and the same author, since the writing rules are not fixed and writers cannot be sure about how to write certain words." Blench adds that present writing systems do not accurately represent the sounds of the language.

My compromises may please nobody. In this book, as a rough guide to pronunciation certain words of particular interest are written using three special letters:

/ɣ/, for the voiced velar fricative /ɣ/ in Gur languages, is produced in the back of the throat and sometimes written /gh/; in Dagbani it is a positional allophone of the plosive /g/, occurring between vowels.

/ŋ/ represents a velarized /n/; for example, the second syllable of *Dagbon* is pronounced approximately as in the French *bon* and is often written as *Dagbong*.

/ʒ/ is pronounced approximately as in English *leisure*.

Mahama recommends that vowels be pronounced as follows: /a/ as in *arm;* /e/ as in *ten;* /i/ as in *see;* /o/ as in *got;* /u/ as in *too. Tamale* is pronounced with equal emphasis on all three (short) syllables.

Dagbani words that occur frequently in this book, such as *bugulana*, appear on the first occasion in italics, followed by a phonetically improved version, *buɣulana*, but thereafter appear only in roman. In the glossary both the singular and plural, if any, are given: *buɣulana*, pl. *buɣulanima*.

Chiefs, Priests, and Praise-Singers

Introduction

The primary source of the received history of the founding of the kingdom of Dagbon in the fifteenth century and its subsequent development is E. F. Tamakloe's account, published in 1931:

> After the enstoolment of Na Nyagse, his father Sitobu remained in Bagale as chief of that place; he died and was buried there. His tomb was encircled by a compound and a house was built on it. Into this house all the departed souls of the Kings of Yendi are said to resort even unto this day. Na Nyagse now took the field against the Dagbamba people; first he went to the West and then to the East, fought with and massacred all the Dagbamba fetish priests, and appointed his sons, brothers and uncles as chiefs in their stead.[1]

This book is a critique of this story, evaluating it in relation to other sources of information, assessing the colonial context of its composition and publication, finding out what happened to the "fetish priests," comparing Dagbon with other kingdoms and other peoples in northern Ghana, and following the political career of the received history in colonial and postcolonial times. Since 1900, chieftaincy in the north has evolved in step with the changing significance of land ownership and its progressive transfer from fetish priests to chiefs. The fetish priests, the *tiŋdamba*, s. *tiŋdana* (hereafter *tindana*, pl. *tindanas*), were not in fact eliminated; everybody in Dagbon knows that they still exist and that some of them play important roles in the kingdom. This is a paradox to be explored.

The truth of history is not simply an antiquarian, local, or even northern issue. It is animated by the competition over land and over the control of land that gives rise to conflict all over Ghana between chief and commoner, "landowner" and "stranger"; it is the topic of much research, public discussion, and proposed legislation. Is the chief or some other traditional figure the "landowner"? What about incomers who want land for agricultural, residential, or commercial purposes but owe no traditional loyalty to the chief? Should any traditional authority have a role in the administration of land, and if so, what role? What should be the role of chieftaincy itself in a modern state? Most of the discussion assumes that chieftaincy is the same all over Ghana, a national institution, but that is a mistake, as northerners know.

Historiography and Anthropology: Sorting the Data

This book also illustrates the evolution of African historiography since the 1960s, when it was an exciting new field of study. Before that, it was generally supposed that Africa had little history besides the activities of intruders—Hamites, Phoenicians, Europeans. Until about 1960 Africa was therefore relegated to anthropology and students of primitive customs. At first, historians concentrated on what they thought were states and empires and sought to understand them primarily in instrumental and progressive terms that assimilated them to models familiar from European history. More recently, other social and political forms and distinctive organizational modes and values have come into focus.

In the early colonial period, say, 1902–35, the anthropology of the north was founded on nineteenth-century concepts of social evolution and racial classification. R. S. Rattray, the dominant ethnographic authority after the publication of his *Tribes of the Ashanti Hinterland* in 1932, was trained at Oxford University, but district commissioners also saw their African world in terms of evolutionary perspectives derived from C. G. Seligman and J. G. Frazer, influential anthropologists of the day. In the 1930s the social anthropology of A. R. Radcliffe-Brown, B. Malinowski, and their students rejected the conjectural history of the evolutionists and substituted functionalism, showing that "primitive societies" might have no rulers but nevertheless had rules and were organized in ways that made sense, that worked. Meyer Fortes's study of the Talensi in what is now Ghana's Northern Region became a classic of the new anthropology that was widely copied even though the model of segmentary lineage systems that constituted its theory was fatally muddled.[2] All this seems quaintly past, but much of it is still explicit in the political discourse of northern Ghana.

Although Fortes, for example, discounted evidence of political activity as irregular, in the 1950s anthropology began to take notice of agency as well as structure.[3] In 1954 Edmund Leach, in his *Political Systems of Highland Burma,* caused something of a scandal in British social anthropology by suggesting that the pursuit of power by individual actors was a factor in social process. Two other ideas from the same book are important in the present study: his pioneering use of a regional rather than a "tribal" approach, and his demonstration that social structure consisted of models followed and manipulated by social actors rather than sets of rules that constrained their actions. Similar revisions of orthodoxy were advanced by Raymond Firth, who distinguished between social structure and social organization. Both of these new perspectives led anthropologists to think more closely about both agency and history.[4]

Political independence in Africa created the need for a usable past, which liberal historians undertook to provide. The results too readily accepted the European model of the state and of historical progress; African states were represented as similar to those of late medieval Europe, on their way to becoming "modern." In common with the historians of Europe itself, historians of Africa selected their data, preferring those that suggested rational choices on the part of historical actors and setting aside ideological factors, religion, and ritual—with which, as Finn Fuglestad put it in his well-known critique, "historians feel uncomfortable."[5] Such historiography establishes comparability with the "modern" world at the expense of the traditional concerns of anthropology, which are marked off as given, irrational, and therefore ahistorical. T. C. McCaskie, himself a historian, puts the matter bluntly in his critique of Ivor Wilks's account of Asante. The history of Asante has been distorted, he says, by analyses of the political hierarchy without reference to the society that supports it and by the materialist, universalist assumption that actors are motivated by rational self-interest rather than, for example, social values or religious belief.[6]

Political anthropologists of the 1960s and 1970s did not do much better, attempting unsuccessfully to isolate the political sphere and to define the state by means of descriptive models. Misled by Maquet, Balandier, and others whom he cites, Martin Staniland concludes (mistakenly in my view) that Dagbon was justifiably called a state because it had a centralized machinery of government that maintained law and order, a specialized, privileged ruling group separated from the rest of the population, and a sovereign leader who could delegate authority to those in charge of territorial subdivisions.[7] The following chapters show that none of this is straightforwardly true of Dagbon. Despite this inflection, Staniland's book is not just excellent but indispensable for an understanding of Dagbon since 1900.

The division between social structure and culture (ideological commitments, religion, ritual, mythology, material culture) was precisely the one upon which social anthropology's success in the 1930s and 1940s was founded. In the 1950s, partly because of an influx of American ethnographers, this narrow perspective was abandoned in African studies; still, quite recently several anthropologists have found it necessary to insist on the historicity of religion, especially religious movements. Steven Feierman notes that historical narratives are weighted in favor of "stable, ordered and linear accounts of masculine authority," and Matthew Schoffeleers deplores "the continuing neglect of the historical study of African religion."[8]

Many other scholars have questioned the common use of the term *religion* and its identification as a discrete domain of human activity. Much of what is now referred to as African religion was once simply African culture, which became "religion," an alternative to Christianity and Islam, as a product of the liberal trend in twentieth-century anthropology to make African "beliefs" respectable. For most people in Dagbon, however—or in Africa generally, as many observers have remarked—paganism is radically unlike Islam or Christianity, and therefore there is no contradiction between being a Muslim or Christian and being at the same time a "traditional person," a pagan. By the time we have noted the absence from African "traditional religions" of a founding event, a creed, a scripture, an orthodoxy, an authorized clergy, and the possibilities of conversion or heresy, we are left with little besides "belief in spiritual beings," in which belief is identified as that in which we do not believe and the spiritual is that which is, to us, immaterial and imaginary. J.-P. Olivier de Sardan deplores the resulting exoticism: "Spontaneous western concepts of magic, of possession and sorcery, in contrast to African concepts, are linked [in the minds of Westerners] with the supernatural, the extraordinary, the mysterious and the fantastic. These phenomena are beyond comprehension, whilst in Africa they form one of the pillars of the most elementary understanding." K. A. Appiah adds, "For the modern Westerner . . . to call something 'religious' is to connote a great deal that is lacking in traditional religion and not to connote much that is present."[9]

Realistically, even without a definition we cannot expect to abandon religion entirely as long as we are speaking European languages, in which many activities cannot conveniently be described except with the vocabulary of religion.[10] Nevertheless, we should be aware of the distortion entailed by the use of such terms as *worship, spirits,* and *sacred.* Pagans want results: they ask at shrines for what they need and respectfully bring an appropriate gift ("sacrifice") if they get it. They make their requests to the dead because their invisible grandfathers shaped the lives they lead and are ever-present in it; their needs and their beliefs are eminently realistic rather than spiritual.

A new willingness to rethink "the political" and to recognize it in unfamiliar guises is exemplified by Jan Vansina when, describing the role of collective imagination in early Angolan kingdoms, he writes that "in some ways, politics and the political establishment are a theater, a make-believe world in which real power can be derived from imagined majesty."[11] Major challenges to the segregation of religion and "theater" from politics and history have come from research in East Africa. A recent example is Neil Kodesh's *Beyond the Royal Gaze,* which reviews the problem, but another, of direct relevance to Dagbon, is *Tongnaab,* by Jean Allman and John Parker.[12]

Although historians are increasingly ready to pay attention to religious factors, they have generally taken for granted the traditional picture of genealogical kinship as a static regulatory system characteristic of stateless societies and therefore as "social," apolitical, and marginal to history. This book gives support to the generalization that kinship systems always admit of and indeed require choice and therefore make room for political agency; there is no boundary between kinship and kingship. A long line of anthropologists from Lewis Henry Morgan through A. R. Radcliffe-Brown and G. P. Murdock has been responsible for reifying kinship and descent as structures, independent of the motivated human activity that takes place in and around them. In fact, patrilineal and matrilineal descent are, as J. C. Miller says of slavery, "outcomes of the strategies of interested historical parties to the struggles of their own times," not agencies.[13]

Dagbon in Context

The ethnographic picture of life in Dagbon has been updated by only a few narrowly focused studies, such as Bierlich's work on gender relations, healing, and money in Savelugu. Oppong's study of domestic life is similarly limited in scope and is now out of date.[14] We have inherited a picture that dates from the time when research, with some exceptions, amounted to listing the cultural traits and normative rules of particular societies, findings that now have the status of accepted fact. What is required is not just an updating of the cultural inventory but a critique of the anthropology that created it and the role it has played in misrepresenting history.

Dagbon is one of the two traditional kingdoms, the other being Gonja, that dominate the Northern Region of Ghana. Dagbon has been noted since at least 1948 for political turmoil in which contending factions of the royal family base their claims on what they consider to be historical truth. The precolonial history of Dagbon can be divided into two parts—the first two centuries, from about 1500 to 1700, and the second, from 1700 to 1900—because of changes in the basis and organization of power and in the nature of the related historiographic problems. Under colonial rule (1900–1957), Dagbon was incorporated into the Northern Territories of the Gold Coast, and the sources of power changed once again. In independent Ghana, Dagbon came to be part of the Northern Region, one of ten administrative districts in the country, while the rest of the north was divided into two new regions, the Upper West and the Upper East (see map 1).

The received history of Dagbon combines the history of the dynasty, as recorded in "drum chant" recited by the praise-singers of chiefs, with early-twentieth-century anthropological assumptions about social evolution.[15] The indigenous people, it tells us, succumbed to socially more advanced invaders from the northeast because the concerns of their leaders, the tindanas, were spiritual rather than political. The tindanas were replaced by chiefs, elements of a new, hierarchical and military political system.[16] The conquered disappear from the narrative; it is not even clear who makes up this element of the population. Modern critiques of evolutionary anthropology and recent research in Dagbon call its received history into question and suggest a new perspective on both the remote past and the present constitution of Dagbon.

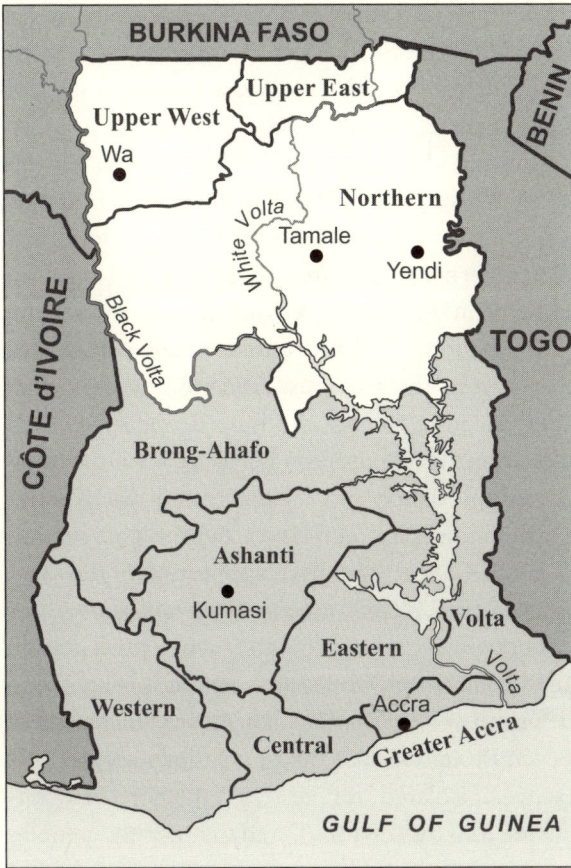

Map 1 Administrative regions of Ghana

Revising the history of Dagbon, this book examines differences among the available versions of drum chant and the contexts in which they were set down instead of accepting them as more or less congruent and therefore probably reliable. It seeks to understand the origin and original character of the kingdom by comparing it with the related kingdoms, Mamprugu and Nanun, which came into existence at much the same time but evolved differently. It investigates social structure, kinship, descent, and religion to provide contexts for the dynastic story. It shows that the supposed contrast between two social strata—invaders and aborigines—was not original but developed over time, that chiefs and tindanas in the kingdoms were and still are components of a single system of government that has its roots in the culture of the north as a whole, even though kingdoms are located almost exclusively in the Northern Region. Though the received history, generally accepted by scholars, speaks of two civilizations of different origin and composition, close ethnographic attention dissolves the supposed contrasts between religion and politics, kinship and kingship, matrilineal and patrilineal descent, tindana and chief, states and the stateless, invader and aborigine. These oppositions are morally loaded, implying relations of superiority and inferiority to which northerners today are sensitive.[17]

Part of the historical revision depends on broadening the focus from a limited concern with the kingdom, its heroic founders, and subsequent leaders to the regional context of their actions. Fernand Braudel's masterly study of the Mediterranean in the age of Philip II was specifically directed against accounts of history focused on heroic action; it showed how the interweaving of multiple factors in a region created spaces of opportunity for political and economic entrepreneurs, but the state no longer framed the analysis. James C. Scott's modern application of the same perspective to Southeast Asia, *The Art of Not Being Governed,* shows how much historiography has bought into the ideological self-representation of the state as the home of civilization, while those whom it is unable to incorporate are labeled "primitive," "barbarians," or "slaves," incapable of governing themselves, even though in fact the populations are not discrete.[18] Despite the presence of isolated "refuge areas," the northern population did not clearly divide into the "civilized" and the "unruly" peoples fleeing forced labor, as in the political dynamics of Southeast Asia, but the fluid, "symbiotic" relations between political orders are similar.

Given certain technologies of production and destruction, a region offers specifically limited opportunities to entrepreneurs: climate and soil fertility, the distribution of wildlife and mineral resources, access to trade routes, defensible hills in certain places, rivers as barriers.[19] In northern Ghana, states were anchored not by lowland rice agriculture, as in Southeast Asia, but by urban centers on international trade routes, where literate Muslims (Mande, Hausa) provided commercial services (credit, accounting, information, Islamic law). T. E. Bowdich's mapping of the north in terms of trade routes and the number of days it took to traverse each route amounts to a diagram of the regional system in the eighteenth and nineteenth centuries. In what Scott calls a symbiotic, or contrapuntal, relationship with surrounding areas that they raided for slaves, the states established outposts among groups they did not incorporate (Mamprugu among Kusasi; Gonja and Dagbon among Konkomba); those subject to raiding took to the hills or fled, but some could "join" a kingdom by accepting a ritualized relationship with the center, and intermarriage afforded individuals and families the opportunity to shift their identities. (In the bloody 1994 Konkomba war, many people in eastern Dagbon, products of intermarriage between Konkomba and Dagbamba, did not know which side to join, or rather, of which to be more afraid.)

Inadequate ethnography and reliance on traditions that he described as mythical but nevertheless had to use as historical data hampered Peter Skalník's pioneering effort to understand the emergence of the Voltaic states as a group (the Mosse states in Burkina Faso as well as Dagbon, Nanun, and Mamprugu). His conclusion, that "the original dichotomic opposition between the immigrant concept of naam (power, office) and the autochthonous concept of tenga (earth, land), most probably reflecting original violent conflicts between the two groups, became transformed with time into a dual unity, bolstered by the interconnected ideology and political system," is the reverse of the one I put forward here but like the one that he himself later adopted: that the duality of the system emerged from an original unity, not of Dagbon or Mamprugu but of the political culture of the region.[20]

Tamale, the administrative capital of the Northern Region and the site of the largest concentration of population in the north, is also the major population center of the traditional kingdom of Dagbon and the principal site of its political activity, although the capital is at Yendi, sixty miles east. The British created the town, now a city of at least four hundred thousand, in 1907 to be the headquarters of their administration of the Northern Territories. The rapidly developing problems in the administration of land that exist all over the north are most acute in Tamale, which is therefore a good place in which to study relations over time between "traditional" and "modern" and between chief and tindana.

The book is organized as follows: The first chapter offers a critique of historiography, the political contexts in which historical narratives are constructed, and the legacy of colonial anthropology. It argues for a regional approach rather than one focused on the states and other discrete units, but it summarizes what is known of their history, precolonial and colonial, dwelling on that of Dagbon. Chapter 2 discusses the ideology, performance practice, and content of drum chant and relates it to other forms of oral tradition and to its evolving political context. Chapter 3, after a theoretical discussion of problems associated with both "conquest" and "religion," provides an ethnographic sketch of the similarities and differences between chiefs and tindanas, focusing on ceremony and on rules of succession. Chapter 4 argues against the prevailing assumption that chiefs and tindanas belong to two different social orders, one imposed on the other, and represents them as complementary elements of a single cultural foundation, common to the north, which developed into states in certain circumstances. Immigrant bands of horsemen were instrumental in the development, but we should allow for the aggrandizement of "indigenous" men of ambition, a process of which we find examples in the twentieth century. One such is the Dakpema of Tamale, a "tindana" whose long conflict with the Gulkpe'Na, officially regarded as the divisional chief of Tamale, is the main topic of chapter 5, in the context of the changing meanings of land and land tenure in colonial and postcolonial times. Chapter 6 follows the movement of northern chiefs, particularly those of Dagbon, into the national arena, in which reconstruction of law and practice related to the control of land is contributing to an increasing differentiation of social classes at the expense of traditional ideals.

1

Colonial Anthropology and Historical Reconstruction

The assumptions upon which the colonial practice of government was based are built into the political discourse of the north, in association with ongoing conflicts that threaten at times to engulf in warfare all three administrative regions into which the north is now divided.[1] One of those assumptions is that there is a radical difference between the Northern Region, in which the major kingdoms are located, and the other two, the Upper East and the Upper West, where other forms of political order prevail. It is more consistent with the available facts and with modern political anthropology to treat the north as a single region in which the boundaries separating states from the stateless were permeable, political structures were in constant reorganization, and identities were fluid and situational. Most of the population speaks languages of the Gur group (Guan, the language of the Gonja aristocracy, is the major exception), and I argue here that whatever their language, they shared a common political culture and responded to the opportunities and limitations of a common regional resource base.

The image of Dagbon as an integral state is probably a projection from modern times, a simplification of a much more amorphous situation, as David C. Davis suggests for Mamprugu also.[2] An alternative, albeit speculative history of Dagbon and neighboring states would say that they grew slowly over many generations in the unsettled conditions after the expansion of the Songhai Empire in the fifteenth century. There were no doubt invaders and migrants, but it may be that in the history of a given kingdom, instead of a single invading group at a single time, there were, as R. S. Rattray suggested, different bands of horsemen, whose stories have been reduced to that of a single dynasty. Dagbon grew over a period of time during which alliances were formed and the territory expanded to its present outline, beyond that of Na Nyagse's murderous

tour and shaped by competition with Gonja for control of economic resources—salt, gold, iron, the kola trade, located primarily on the eastern
or the western frontier.

Local investigations reveal inconsistencies in the heroic narrative and
suggest alternative stories. The picture of Dagbon to be gleaned from
the many tindanas—known as "fetish priests" in colonial English, also
called "Earth priests"—still independent today is not that of a unified
kingdom but a mosaic of chieftaincies subordinate to the Ya Na at Yendi,
interspersed with the territories of tindanas, who are thus also "chiefs"
(*nanima*, s. *na*). Their stories of what allegedly happened in the fifteenth
century are no less political than history as recited by the praise-singers
of the chiefs, but they fit with other evidence that Dagbon was always a
work in progress rather than a direct product of conquest; that the relationship between chiefs and tindanas was always intimately complementary; and that some of the chiefs were originally tindanas. It is even
possible that the kingdom was created, at least in part, "from below"
rather than simply by invasion.

The Region

The knowable history of the precolonial north extends for about four
hundred years, from the late fifteenth to the late nineteenth century. It is
shaped by the development of trade along two principal routes and the
social changes associated with that development: a western route followed the Black Volta to link the Songhai Empire (in modern Niger and
Burkina Faso) to the gold-bearing regions of the south; an eastern link
ran through the Oti valley between the Hausa states of the Middle Niger
and Kumasi.[3] The goods transported from the south included cloth, gold,
kola nut, and commodities imported from Europe, such as guns and
gunpowder; from the north came iron, talismans, horses, luxury goods
from the Mediterranean, and, above all, slaves. Although the western
route was not regularly developed until the late nineteenth century, there
is evidence that slaves were taken both north to Songhai and south to the
coast by the early sixteenth century.[4] Slave raiding and trading intensified
as demand increased from the Asante Empire and from the European
forts on the Gold Coast, especially between about 1722, when Asante
conquered Gonja, and the mid-nineteenth century.

For the first two centuries little definite information is available; archaeology is of little help, and the primary sources are oral traditions

of questionable validity. The names of people and places begin to take historical form as long-distance trade increases in volume. The traditions of the kingdoms of Dagbon and Gonja, recorded in drum histories, tell of invasions and conquests by raiders from the northeast and the northwest, respectively, disturbances that may have provoked indigenous communities to migrate to less accessible territories.[5] For the eighteenth and nineteenth centuries, some correlations can be established among local traditions, Arabic and Hausa manuscripts, travelers' accounts, and events elsewhere in West Africa.

The north was clearly a frontier area, perhaps a backwater, separated from the largely Akan-speaking south by a belt of almost uninhabited country and marginal also to the Sahelian states, such as Songhai. But it was also an area of contested internal frontiers, in which the multiplication or expansion of states was limited by the agricultural potential of the region, the carrying capacity of the major trade routes, the reluctance of marginal communities to accept overlordship, and the fact that once incorporated in states, communities were not available for slave raiding. The soils of the generally flat, undulating savanna are gravelly and the rains unreliable, offering small rewards to the farmer and no surplus for the ready formation of states.

Only the interregional trade routes could support stable hierarchies through tolls and looting; elsewhere, scattered villages were organized by kinship networks. Trade itself depended on demand from elsewhere, which varied over time; in the early period, gold and salt, both found in the west, were more valuable than slaves, which is probably why Gonja was stronger than any of the eastern kingdoms. First Dagbon and then Gonja controlled the north-south trade in kola and salt through Daboya, on the west side of the White Volta. From 1700 on, slaving became relatively more important, increasing the demand for iron, which came mostly from Bassar country, east of the Oti River. The balance of power shifted in favor of Dagbon, particularly after Asante conquered Gonja in 1722 and raided Yendi, the capital of Dagbon, in 1744. These kingdoms were required to provide Kumasi with thousands of slaves every year; the chiefs raided the rest of the north to satisfy these demands but raided and traded for their own profit as well, absorbing slaves into their own communities. The courts of princes required slave attendants, and the major trading depots, such as Salaga, required the support of plantations worked by slaves.[6] Kola from the forested south, imported guns, and northern goods such as horses, leather, and cloth paid for the movement of slaves south to Kumasi and north to Hausaland in increasing volumes of trade. Yendi flourished because the major routes from the Hausa states passed through it on the way to Kafaba, which until the early nineteenth century was more important than Salaga. Merchants paid taxes and gifts to the Ya Na to secure safe passage.[7]

Horses do not breed in most of the north, but they could be acquired in exchange for slaves and in turn helped to generate more slaves (the "horse-slave cycle").[8] As slaving increased and horses became readily available, small communities raided by cavalry from Dagbon, Gonja, Mamprugu, and elsewhere fled to the west or sought refuge in fortified villages and scattered outcrops of rock, such as the Tong Hills, famous in anthropology as the habitat of the Talensi. "Stateless" peoples defended themselves, but leaders among them also raided and sold slaves. The frontier between states and the stateless reflected the dynamic of slaving: to the extent that marginal groups were incorporated in the state, they were no longer available as a source of captives, some of whom might well be needed as soldiers for the raiding armies of the state.[9] Claude Meillassoux writes of the Sahelian slave trade: "Its internal organization is necessarily linked to the historical and social context in which a society is situated and to the nature of its external relations. These relations, being essentially of two kinds, war and trade (rendered inseparable by slavery), the circulation of slaves among raided societies, the raiders and the purchasers, constitutes a system which represents the true economic dimension of slavery. Here too the scope of a monograph is too limited; it should open onto social and economic history on the scale of the region."[10]

The typical frontier situation was, and still is (e.g., in eastern Dagbon), one in which princes affiliated with the state attempted to keep marginal communities in subordination, subject to intermittent and arbitrary forms of extraction, but were unable to incorporate them. In the twentieth century, colonial officials accepted the claims of the states to have ruled marginal communities in the past and "restored" their authority, but resentments against this imposition fuel conflicts to this day, between Gonja and Nawuri, Mamprugu and Kusasi, Dagbon and Konkomba, among others. In modern times, in the Northern Region as in the rest of Ghana, the parties to the conflicts accuse one another of being immigrants or "strangers" rather than firstcomers and "landowners."[11]

In 1898 and 1899, British, French, and German expeditionary forces overcame local resistance and divided the savanna region of West Africa into their several colonies. In 1902 the British annexed to their Gold Coast Colony an area falling roughly between longitude 8° and 11° north, bounded on the west by the Black Volta and on the east by the Oti River, calling it the Protectorate of the Northern Territories. The political boundaries of the Northern Territories were finally settled in 1919, when the kingdom of Dagbon, partitioned in 1899 between Britain and Germany, was reunited as part of the protectorate.[12] As a protectorate, the Northern Territories were ruled differently from the Gold Coast Colony and Ashanti, with which they were united only in 1951. In 1960 the "Northern Region" of 1951, with its capital at Tamale, was divided into the Upper and Northern Regions, the first of these being itself divided into the Upper West and the Upper East in 1983.[13]

When British officials arrived in the north, like the representatives of other imperial powers worldwide they regarded the states, founded, according to tradition, by immigrants like themselves, as superior to village networks, which they saw as primitive. Nineteenth-century anthropology took for granted the essentially different qualities and capacities of discrete races, arranged on an evolutionary scale from primitive to advanced. Primitive promiscuity supposedly led to matrilineal descent (succession passing from a man to his sister's son), then to patriliny (sons succeeding their fathers). Primitive people were passive, anarchic, and religious, or merely superstitious. Advanced races had an inherently greater political capacity, evident in centralized government and in acts of conquest. These alternatives are linked and ranked, so the received story tells us that Dagbon and other states were created by a superior, politically competent patrilineal group that conquered a disorganized, matrilineal people whose leaders had merely religious capacities. This anthropology thus legitimated British rule as the next stage in a natural sequence.

In going about the business of administration, colonial officials classified the people into tribes, which were supposedly stable cultural entities, and sought to encourage social evolution and make administration easier by incorporating unorganized societies into neighboring kingdoms that had once ruled them, or so officials believed.[14] The invidious distinction they imposed between politically competent peoples organized into states and acephalous societies, whose leaders were merely religious, infuriates modern spokesmen for the latter.[15] The states, on the other hand, cite it in asserting their claims: in 1993 the king of Dagbon wrote that as an "aucefuloss" society the Konkomba could have neither chiefs nor central authority.[16]

The Ghanaian historian Benedict Der blames Fortes and Evans-Pritchard for introducing the distinction, although it has very old roots in European political philosophy and was meant to be much more benign than he supposes. Their celebrated *African Political Systems* was a relatively late, liberal, and romantic attempt to show that acephalous societies, or "tribes without rulers," were not anarchic but had their own form of government, one that could even be admired for its freedom from the despotic potential of centralized rule.[17] Der, who is from the Upper West, proceeds to dispute Carola Lentz's statement that there were no chiefs in that area in precolonial times. The issue is partly semantic: by *chief* do we mean one exercising leadership and public responsibility or the occupant of a perpetual office with regular succession and control of a definite territory?[18] But the issue is also political: in the northern context today, to have or to have had "chiefs" is to associate oneself and one's group with superior status; those who supposedly had none are at risk of being called "slaves" by others. To finesse issues of boundaries and political structure, the Ghanaian government prudently uses the vague name Traditional Areas.

The States

The kingdom of Gonja (Ngbanya) is said to have been founded in the fifteenth century by raiders who moved down the Black Volta from Mande country on the upper Niger River. They conquered a band of territory that stretches across the southern edge of the north, thinly inhabited by speakers of several different languages (map 2). The conquerors adopted one of these, Guan, a language of the Kwa group spoken in southern Ghana. It is difficult to know what to make of this early history; the stories relate all events to a hero called Jakpa, who probably stands for a number of military figures active over a period of time. His reputed descendants in the male line constitute the ruling estate, eligible for the highest titles. Jakpa is said to have owed his success to the supernatural powers of a Muslim cleric whose descendants constitute a separate estate in the kingdom, exercising important ritual and political functions.[19] The Gonja link all their traditions to the name of Jakpa, creating "a skein of stories impossible to untangle."[20] In the nineteenth century the paramount, the Yagbumwura, had little physical force at his disposal; his authority was limited to ritual. The revenues of the chiefs came from slaving, taxes on trade, and some servile agricultural labor.

The history of Wa, on the Black Volta, is the most complex and the most difficult to make sense of. According to Ivor Wilks, the Wala "make constant reference to a past, embodied in oral and written texts [but not drum histories], in terms of which they construct reality as they see it."[21] This constructed past is self-contradictory and cannot all be true. It indicates that at different times warlords who came from Dagbon and Mamprugu, probably in the late seventeenth century, contributed to the formation of the kingdom of Wa and to its heterogeneous population. As in Gonja, Muslim lineages of Mande descent play a considerable role in public affairs. Wa only became an important commercial center, trading in slaves, guns, and gunpowder, in the second half of the nineteenth century.

The founders of Mamprugu, Dagbon, Nanun, and the closely related Mosse kingdoms in modern Burkina Faso are traditionally said to have

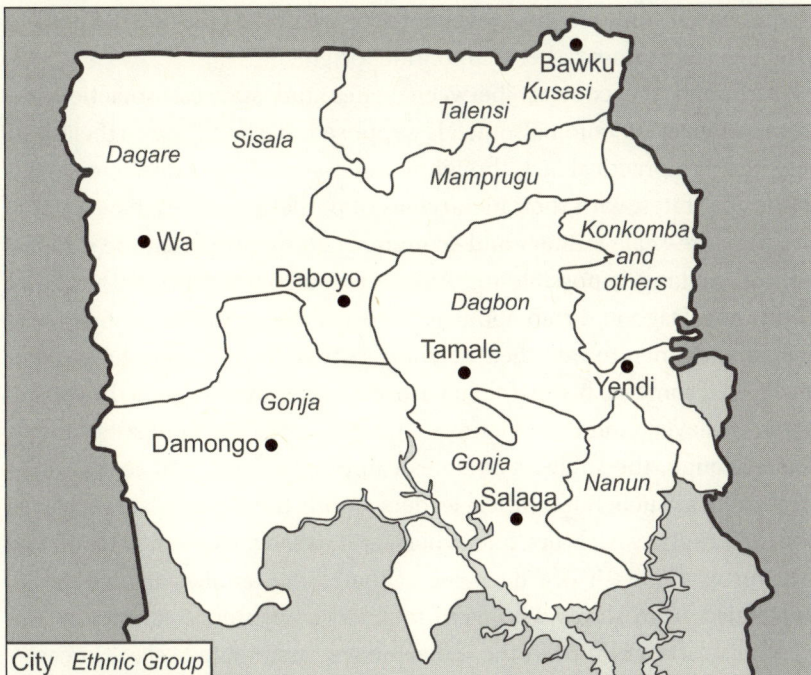

Map 2 Northern Traditional Area

come from the northeast, from what is now northern Nigeria. The drum history, stories told to the accompaniment of drumming by the praise-singers of chiefs, begins with Tohazie, "the Red Hunter," a mythical figure resembling the "kings from elsewhere" in the traditions of Central Africa.[22] His great-grandson Gbewaa migrated into the northeast corner of modern Ghana as the founder of a kingdom that Gbewaa's sons later divided into those of Dagbon, Mamprugu, and Nanun, whose peoples all call themselves Dagbamba. Sitobu is described as the founder of Dagbon, but he left it to his son Na Nyagse to conquer the indigenous people, whose only leaders were tindanas. In African foundation stories a shadowy immigrant father is often followed by an energetic warrior son who consolidates the polity.[23] In Mamprugu and Nanun, as we shall see, the story is somewhat different. Local historians push the date of these events to as far back as the early fifteenth century or even earlier; the best scholarly estimate for Na Nyagse's conquest is 1476.[24] So much for the official history of kingdoms. But perhaps half of the population of the north were not centrally organized, did not have official histories, and have not received as much attention from historians because their traditions tell only of the movements of small groups—stories told to establish rights now rather than remote origins.[25]

Although the contrast between states and stateless societies was never as clear as colonial officials supposed, it should nevertheless be retained as a practical fact, though not of essential, let alone "racial," difference.[26] States, with their hierarchies of perpetual offices, have capacities for large-scale military and economic coordination that the stateless do not, making it possible for Asante to outsource slave gathering to Gonja and Dagbon. From about 1670 to the 1880s, the states mobilized armed horsemen to raid their neighbors for captives whom they sold or enslaved. From this historical fact arose another oversimplified contrast, between slavers and their victims, which grounds much hostility today; often enough, the subjects of states call others slaves and seek to mistreat them as such. But political leaders among the stateless also enslaved and sold captives, debtors, and others, and in the states—in Dagbon and Wa, for example—it is a deep secret that some families are (allegedly) descended from slaves who were retained as fighters, servants, or agricultural laborers.[27] Even the Talensi have "assimilated" slave lineages, thought it took Fortes a year to discover them.[28] In Tamale, Dagbamba avoid the use of the word *dabili* (slave) when discussing, or hinting at, somebody's questionable pedigree, but they are happy to use it as an insulting label for the "stateless."

Historiographic Problems

For lack of much other data, and from an inclination to respect the self-representations of authority, historians of the 1960s, eager to endow newly independent African countries with a respectable political past, generally accepted invasion stories at face value.[29] Invasion and conquest seem historical because they are irreversible and thus seem to create history by establishing a caesura between time past and time future. (The arrival of a mysterious hunter serves the same narrative function.) Indigenous invasions seemed also to prefigure the colonial occupation. The same myths of origin thus served, in different political contexts, three different ideological functions: as charters for states, as legitimation for colonial rule, and as certification of the indigenous political capacity of independent Ghanaians. In the historiography of Europe itself the assumption that change normally resulted from the influx of better-endowed peoples was seriously challenged only in 1966, partly because carbon dating made better chronology possible and partly because in the aftermath of World War II a new generation of historians grew up who did not share the myths of race and the mystique of empire.[30] Historians are now less inclined to isolate and ennoble African "states" and "empires." As Jack Goody writes, "The reality of social relationships . . . demands that each 'society', each tribe, each settlement, be treated as part of a field of interaction that takes account of neighboring peoples, the mutual influence of town and village, the nature of long-distance trade and wider religious affiliations."[31]

The invasion model, as it appears either in colonial anthropology or in drum history, silences commoners and the "conquered," who are no longer part of the story after the conquest. Rattray, in his *Tribes of the Ashanti Hinterland,* supposed that the invaders, exclusively male, were obliged to marry local women, so that their descendants all spoke the local language (Dagbani in Dagbon). Ibrahim Mahama, in a polemical account of the Dagbon-Konkomba war of 1994, uses this argument to assert that Dagbani speakers were aboriginal and therefore the sole landowners.[32] In 1930 H. A. Blair, a knowledgeable official, thought the autochthons were Guan-speaking Kpareba (Gonja); the term *Kpareba* is problematic, but there is much evidence from local history to support it.[33] One scholarly opinion holds that they may not have been Dagbani or Guan speakers but Konkomba, like the Talensi a classical example of a "tribe without rulers," who speak a somewhat distant language of the same group. If that was so, the invaders brought Dagbani with them. David Tait, an ethnographer of the Konkomba, persuasively argues the case, pointing out that near Tamale, in western Dagbon, many toponyms are of Konkomba origin.[34] When the kings of Dagbon moved their capital east to modern Yendi at the beginning of the eighteenth century to escape Gonja pressure and to be nearer the trade route between northern Nigeria and Asante, they overran Konkomba, whom they partly assimilated, and dominated other peoples with whom they are frequently at war to this day.

The trouble with these questions and with the answers is that they presuppose essential ethnic identities that may not have existed until colonial officers used the concept of tribe as an administrative tool. In the precolonial north, identities seem to have been multiple, situational, and fluid, as Fortes repeatedly emphasized.[35] Whole villages can change their "ethnic" identities within one or two generations. In the neighboring kingdoms of Mamprugu and Nanun diversity is explicit; their peoples refer to themselves collectively as Dagbamba, as do the people of Dagbon, but they have no concept of identity based on common origins. The common identity of immigrant segments is based on loyalty to the royal throne, the Nam.[36]

The population of Dagbon now seems homogeneous, but colonial officials noted in the 1920s that there were partly assimilated outsiders everywhere. There is a ruling estate, the *na bihi* (princes), whose members claim descent ultimately from Na Nyagse, but those members who fail to attain one of the royal titles effectively merge over time with commoners. The spokesmen of the modern state apparatus insist that all its members are of royal, immigrant descent. Princes and their drummers may recite up to sixteen generations of their forebears, but there is evidence that slave and client lineages attach themselves fictitiously to royal lines into which they have married. Genealogy is remembered insofar as it is useful; it represents political claims that have been established in the course of history but may not be historical records.[37] There is in fact no ethnic division in Dagbon and no ruling class, as some scholars have supposed; all are much intermarried. The term *tiŋbia*, "child of the soil," often translated as "aborigine" or "native," can also describe a royal, who is necessarily a native somewhere.[38] There is no definite category of aborigines except in parts of eastern Dagbon where Konkomba and other linguistically distinct communities resist Dagomba overlords, but even there the boundaries are contested and uncertain.

The three "Dagbamba" states—Mamprugu, Nanun, and Dagbon—are traditionally linked and culturally similar, but Dagbon stands apart from the others in its supposed origin in the conquest of the indigenes and the extermination of their leaders; it is also larger and more centralized. In Nanun, a small kingdom southeast of Dagbon and almost an appendage of it, tradition has it that the immigrants were welcomed by the local people, with whom they set up a kingdom based on mutual respect. It thus offers an alternative story of the relationship between chiefs and tindanas. Nevertheless, the power of the written word being what it is, in Nanun, in the course of a dispute in 1975 over land rights, a witness cited "an authoritative work, History of the Dagomba People by Tamakloe," to support his assertion that in the beginning Ngmantambu had conquered the land and appointed chiefs to rule it.[39] The population is ethnically diverse, but the people paid little attention to ethnic categories until their recent confrontations with Konkomba and Gonja. Traditionally, access to the kingship alternated between the Lion House and the Bangle House; *nam*, the special power of chieftaincy, can only be renewed with the sanction of the tindanas. Chiefs had very little authority over the people; each had his own armed force, and they only collaborated when confronted by an external enemy.[40] In Mamprugu also the king is installed by tindanas, but the details of the tindana role must await consideration in later chapters.

Although social science has traditionally assumed that the state would be a political organization in control of a bounded territory, these kingdoms were mobile, oriented toward a "king" who had little direct authority over his subjects but was the source of the special power, called *nam* in Oti-Volta (Mole-Dagbani) languages, that characterized chiefs after their ritual investiture, or "enskinment." "It is possible to imagine," writes Susan Drucker-Brown of Mamprugu, "how the entire system, not being based on control of land, might have moved over the ground in the past."[41] Gonja and Dagbon competed for access to the eastern and western trade routes, their boundaries shifting accordingly. In the seventeenth century the kingdoms fought repeatedly (though never as unified organizations) until Gonja captured Daboya, killed Na Dariziegu, and

crossed the White Volta. From then until after Na Andani Sigili killed the
Gonja king Kumpatia in 1713, the Dagbon capital was a mobile war camp.
A successor of Na Andani settled at Yendi, formerly a Konkomba village,
and Dagbon began to recover the lost territory in the west.[42] Chieftaincies were created in western Dagbon during the eighteenth and nineteenth centuries as Yendi-related chiefs reoccupied it, the most recent
only in 1930.

In Dagbon, the office of Ya Na in Yendi was reserved to the sons of
previous kings. To be a candidate, a prince had also to occupy one of
the three chieftaincies of Karaga, Savelugu, or Mion, to which in turn a
hundred other titles, reserved to descendants of Na Nyagse, ultimately
gave access. To be royal was prestigious and offered the possibility of
advancement to Yendi, but individual royal titles were often of small importance. (A chief is called "Na" or "Lana"—the choice is simply a matter of euphony—preceded usually by the name of a place or function of
which he is the "owner.") Commoners holding titled positions such as
the military chieftaincies of Tolon and Kumbungu; court elders such as
Kuga Na and Zohe Na; independent ritual authorities such as Gushie'Na;
and descendants of Na Nyagse who had opted or been pushed out of the
line of succession to Yendi, such as the chiefs of Sunson and Nanton, all
exercised different functions in the political system, which was not the
single, inclusive hierarchy of divisions and subdivisions that colonial rule
sought to make of it. The gate skins to Yendi were not the equivalent of
vice-presidencies through which the Ya Na could delegate responsibilities.

In fact, these states were never very statelike. The kingdoms of Gonja,
Dagbon, and Mamprugu probably came into existence over time as the
leaders of multiple raiding parties, attracted by mineral deposits and
the vulnerability of trade networks, formed alliances among themselves,
the better to protect their territories and looting opportunities from
one another. Early Mamprugu, before the emergence of Nayiri Atabia in
about 1690, may have been only a confederation of independent chiefs
acknowledging one among them as *primus inter pares.* Like his contemporary Na Zanjina (fl. 1700–1714) in Yendi, Atabia was a reformer connected with trading interests. In both Mamprugu and Gonja, sectional
chiefs exercised more effective power than their overlords, the Nayiri
and the Yagbumwura, respectively.[43] Dagbon is different in having had, at
least since about 1715, a concentration of real power at the top, in Yendi;
this concentration is attributable to the use made of Muslim scholars and

experts by Na Zanjina and his immediate successors, and it did not extend to the rest of the kingdom.[44] Yendi was situated at a particular point,
an intersection of east-west and north-south trade routes unmatched
elsewhere in the region; although Atabia played a similar role in Mamprugu, he did not have the same access to trade. After the war between
Asante and Dagbon in 1744, both parties benefited from their connection. Gonja had no similar concentration of power; Salaga, the essential
link between Kumasi and the northern trade, although located in Gonja
territory, close to the capital, Kpembe, was controlled by Asante.[45]

With only weak central control, the kingdoms were held together
to some extent by force (cavalry), but more by the marriage alliances of
princes (with one another and with members of the other estates) and by
the illusion that since almost anyone could obtain a title of some kind,
everybody participated in the pomp of chieftaincy. That horses and other
means of destruction did not suffice for state building is shown by the
history of the Zabarima, Muslim horse traders and raiders from the
north, who operated from movable bases near what is now the northern
frontier of Ghana in the latter half of the nineteenth century. Lacking
direct access to the principal trade routes, they served the kings of Dagbon as mercenaries; as the European powers moved in, the last of the
Zabarima settled in Yendi.

Dagbon: Writing the Received History

In his Informal Diary for July 1930, Commissioner Duncan-Johnstone
wrote, "In writing up the history of this country it must be remembered
that there are two histories running side by side, that of the invading
ruling class and that of the plain folk."[46] The history of the kingdom of
Dagbon was known to European travelers and Hausa scholars in the
nineteenth century and to the first British administrators of the Northern Territories of the Gold Coast. It is memorized and authoritatively
recited by the praise-singers of the chiefs, who tell of invaders from the
northeast, led by Na Sitobu, founder of the kingdom, and his brothers,
who founded the neighboring kingdoms of Mamprugu and Nanun. Sitobu's son Na Nyagse conquered the space that became Dagbon by killing off the Earth priests and replacing them with his own relatives as
chiefs. How do we know this? In fact we do not, but that does not mean
that something like this did not happen. The consistency of traditions
reported from the three kingdoms suggests that they shared a common

origin. Na Nyagse probably existed; it is the details that are in question, but insufficient questions have been asked, because the story is both plausible and politically foundational. Nevertheless, the story deserves to be questioned because the tindanas are still there and their functions are intimately related to chieftaincy.

The alleged primordial slaughter is effectively an assertion of exclusive political control by representatives of the authority of Yendi, the capital. The message of the foundational myth sets the royal family apart and legitimates their right to migrate from one royal title to another in hopes of advancing to that of Ya Na. They are the mobile element of the population, perpetual strangers. Besides the inclination of historians to restrict their inquiries to dynastic events, the secrecy attaching to the rituals of *nam,* and therefore to the role of tindanas, contributed to the bias of the received history. Since 1960, modern "enlightenment" and secularization have reduced—and for some people entirely eliminated— the significance of these secrets; competition over control of land and the chiefs' interest in building up their own importance in modern terms have produced new reasons for not talking about tindanas.

The principal source of the received history is oral tradition in the form of drum chant recited by praise-singers on special occasions. It is known to scholars only through prose versions stripped from the history as sung and endowed by their narrativity and their availability in the library with an authority that deflects skepticism. Three such versions, all collected in Yendi in about 1928, are the basis of the history of Dagbon as it is publicly known today, yet they differ in interesting ways. The most widely cited version is that of E. F. Tamakloe, a southerner in German and, later, British service who had learned Dagbani and, with H. A. Blair, published a dictionary of the language as well as a *Brief History of the Dagbamba People.* He heard much of the story from a Namo Na, the chief drummer of Yendi, in the 1920s. His version is the most bloodthirsty: "Na Nyagse took the field against the Dagomba people; first he went to the west and then to the east, he fought with and massacred all the Dagomba Fetish Priests and appointed his sons, brothers and uncles in their stead."[47] (The term *sons* is not to be understood literally; every chief's subordinate is referred to as his son.) Yet even Tamakloe goes on to describe the role of fetish priests in the enskinment of a Ya Na.

District Commissioner H. A. Blair appended a "History of the Dagomba" to the report of the constitutional conference of Dagbamba chiefs convened by the British at Yendi in November 1930. Most of it he learned from Malam Halidu, "a very cultured Hausa" who had heard the chant many times and served as an interpreter for the conference. Blair, who spoke Dagbani, had heard the chant several times himself but could only partly understand its esoteric language. His summary dwells at length on the clearly mythical and folkloric incidents that make up the story of Na Gbewaa, but it says very little about Na Nyagse other than that he made war and died in battle, and it mentions no tindanas killed.[48] In the same report a different summary of the story, by Duncan-Johnstone, is closer to what became the received history.

The government anthropologist Rattray, fresh from his studies of Asante, elaborated the traditional story in his ethnography of the north, published in 1932. He prided himself on his skills as a field ethnographer: "Were the anthropologist to confine his researches to the doings and sayings of those Natives whom he finds invested with minor authority under the local Government, real anthropological history would never be written." He had discovered, he said, that the conquerors and the conquered belonged to different races, something that had not been noticed before. The present societies had been formed when small bands of patrilineal conquerors, "better armed, better clothed, familiar with the idea of kingship or chieftainship in our modern sense," overcame indigenous matrilineal peoples with Earth priests and introduced the "new and unheard-of" idea of territorial and secular leadership in place of the immemorial institution of a ruler who was the high priest of a totemic clan and dealt only in "spiritual sanctions." They thus had interrupted what would have been "a natural process of evolution, from the Priest-King to the Territorial ruler." Since the invading bands were made up only of men, they married local women; their descendants adopted the local language and customs. "The result was that among many of these tribes, before our advent, there had been evolved a kind of dual mandate."[49] The phrase *dual mandate* comes from the title of Lord Lugard's book *Dual Mandate in British Tropical Africa*, recommending "indirect rule," published in 1922. Since the chief dealt with administrative and secular matters and left religious welfare to the tindana, "quite a workable and satisfactory Native Administration was thus evolved by a blending of old and new."[50] Lord Lugard was therefore indigenous to Africa, so to speak.

Summarizing the story of the origin of Dagbon, Rattray tells us that his information came from the elders of Yendi; he himself spoke Hausa and had some fluency in what he called "Mole." The elders said that Na Nyagse had killed the indigenous rulers "because they would not run away and because they declared that the land belonged to them." Rattray noted, however, that two of the priest-kings were spared, including the Dakpema of Tamale, whom we will encounter shortly, and the one at Tampion. The term *priest-king* was taken from J. G. Frazer's *The Golden Bough,* the most popular anthropology book of its day (the third edition was published in twelve volumes from 1906 to 1915); as Goody remarked, the book provided a glimpse of the Golden Bough in the orchard bush of the savanna, although in fact Frazer's priest-kings were quite unlike tindanas.[51] Having thus decided that he was dealing with two different civilizations, one original and the other intrusive, Rattray wrote them up in separate chapters of his ethnography.

By the time of Rattray's research, the idea of a conquering race was already accepted by colonial officials, who used it to distinguish between native states, in which "a Paramount of alien blood rules by right of conquest a collection of tribes," and tribes, collections of families held together by religious sanctions. In the view of the acting chief commissioner of the Northern Territories, "The opinions of Captain Rattray, who has only spent a day or two in Dagomba, and does not speak its language, should be disregarded."[52] Rattray's report, claiming the authority of fieldwork, reifies in Dagbon the evolutionary assumptions of mid-nineteenth-century anthropology and specifically borrows the language and perspectives of not only Frazer but C. G. Seligman, whose book *The Races of Africa* was published in 1930, the same year as Rattray's original report to the government.[53] Similar assumptions, characterizing peoples who are marginal in relation to the state as backward and in need of civilizing, are typical of state ideologies worldwide.[54]

In the part of the received history that is drawn not from drum history but from Rattray, the "aborigines" practiced matrilineal descent, befitting their primitive evolutionary level, as opposed to the patrilineal descent practiced by the invaders. Supposedly, the succession rules for the office of tindana are relics of this primitive condition. In fact, the basic social unit anywhere in Dagbon is a bilateral descending kindred with a patrifilial bias. The founder is a relatively important grandfather or great-grandfather to whom most members trace descent in the male line, but others are attached through women, especially in important families to which others would like to be linked. Exclusive patrifiliation is found only at the highest levels of the aristocracy, where a candidate for a title who bases his claim on a uterine link is least likely to succeed. Even there, certain skins (titles) are reserved for the sons of daughters of kings. Succession rules and descent are discussed in detail in chapters 3 and 5, where it will be shown that there is a single kinship system, not two.

Drum chant tells us the names of the early kings and usually gives no more information than that they reigned and then they died, with an occasional anecdote that invents an incident in order to explain the alleged etymology of a name. Because the several versions of the drum history are generally congruent, their truth has been accepted. No one has looked closely at the discrepancies between them, interrogated the milieu in which they were written, or talked to any tindanas. Blair was one of the principal architects of the new policy of indirect rule being introduced in the Northern Territories at the time. That policy called for inquiries into the traditional constitutions of the various northern kingdoms that were to be co-opted on the assumption that there were in fact "constitutions," bodies of rules that only needed to be written down. Rattray was not enthusiastic about hierarchy, or at least not this hierarchy; he thought that Na Nyagse and his ilk, whose dominion was endorsed by the Dagomba constitutional conference in 1930, had inter-rupted what could have been a natural process of evolution. He believed that the peaceful, matrilineal, and egalitarian social order of the tindanas would have developed into something like Asante, on which his own first book had just been published and whose civilization he admired for its decentralization. He recommended that a sound native administration should be based on this aboriginal social order, that is, precisely on the tindanas that he was proud to have "discovered" in the northeast and the northwest but whose survival in Dagbon he overlooked, with the excep-tions noted.[55]

Blair, known as *daybonbia* (a son of Dagbon) for his knowledge of Dagbani language and culture, believed in traditional order and there-fore in the truth of tradition. According to him, drum chant is handed down from generation to generation by the drummers; because the in-habitants of any big chief's town know it, even though they may not tell it, they guarantee the accuracy of the story. In fact, Blair thought, oral tradition is probably more reliable than written documents, which, as in the case of the Bible, may include copyist's errors. No modern student of folklore and oral tradition would share this opinion.[56] Nevertheless, although scholars have described the story of Na Nyagse as a myth, nobody has seriously challenged it or offered an alternative. Somehow it has seemed reasonable to suppose that oral tradition reliably reports events that took place several centuries ago. Oral tradition, praise-singing, and drum chant are discussed in the next chapter.

Ibrahim Mahama, a modern historian of Dagbon, quotes Tamakloe and Rattray but offers a more complex version of the origins than theirs because he needs to account for certain realities they overlooked, notably that the tindanas are still there. Following Rattray, he calls them "priest kings" on account of their "dual role" as spiritual leaders and administrators of land and asserts that at first relatives of the conqueror took over both parts of the dual role. In due course, however, the royal family relinquished the spiritual function to "certain fetish priests" whom they appointed from the original priestly families.[57] Female tindanas, however, are priests by hereditary right, since Na Nyagse's descendants appointed only men. This version of the story solves problems arising from the earlier versions, because it recognizes that there exists a separate estate of tindanas, some of them women, and explains why their succession rules differ from those for chiefs but still clearly divorces their role from the political one reserved to the descendants of Na Nyagse (Rattray's "dual mandate"). It does not explain why it should have been necessary to kill them in the first place, or why only "certain" fetish priests were reinstated; and it does not admit that many tindanas are independent. Mahama mentions that the tindana of Tampion was spared but does not mention the Dakpema of Tamale, although he and the modern Dakpema were personally well acquainted.

Mahama introduces a further modification of the story when, in listing the high officials of the state, he draws attention to a group of them, overlooked by Rattray, whose origins antedate the building of the state by Na Nyagse. They are the Yani Kpamba or Yogu Kpamba, the "Original Elders," who, though few, are "the most powerful in the affairs of State. They are literally feared and revered by the Ya Na and the Nabihi [royals]."[58] They are persons of royal descent who have given up rights to the Yendi skin; tradition traces their origin to a time before Na Nyagse and the building of the kingdom. Successors are appointed to each office from its own lineage. This picture of ritual figures who were in place before Na Nyagse's rampage, were not exterminated, and occupy powerful positions in the structure of the state strongly resembles the organization of the Dagbon-related kingdom of Nanun, according to modern ethnography. We shall explore this issue in chapter 4, after looking more closely at tindanas today.

Indirect Rule: Yendi and Tamale

Mahama's 2004 revision of the invasion story recognizes the existence of tindanas but explicitly excludes them from control of land: "The Tindana lost his land and temporal power to those who conquered him." By this date, land had taken on a new significance as commodity as well as territory, and tradition was being called upon to justify intensely competitive land claims. At the time when the canonical redactions of drum history were being written down, the control of land as between "landowners" and strangers was already of concern to the chiefs of Dagbon; land, though not yet a commodity, was becoming a source of revenue. It is difficult to know just what was going on in Yendi in 1930, but a study of the documents generated at the constitutional conference in that year is rewarding. The documents indicate that the Ya Na and his elders fully understood that British policy would greatly strengthen the Ya Na's power and authority in the name of restoring a supposed status quo ante and were eager to play along. A major issue that the conference had to settle was the status of Tamale, a cluster of villages in western Dagbon that had been taken over by the British in 1907 as their headquarters for the Northern Territories. Their principal go-between with the local population was the Dakpema, whom in 1905 Major Morris had named king of Tamale. In February 1930 the Reverend A. H. Candler, recently appointed superintendent of education, had written a long memorandum in which he said that despite the literal meaning of his title, "market elder," the Dakpema was the descendant of a line of influential local leaders. He had in fact ruled all of the Tamale area, which was now being called Gulkpeogu, until under the changed conditions of British rule jealous chiefs eroded his prerogatives and took over some of his powers. Seeing what was happening, Dakpema Nsungna, the original king of Tamale, went to Yendi to protest; unfortunately, he died on his return. His successor, Busagri, who himself died in 1929, had been advised by the British not to fight the claims of the local chiefs.[59]

Replying to Candler in September 1930 in another long memo, written after he had consulted elders in Yendi (as though they were impartial authorities on tradition), Blair said that the only authority in Tamale/

Gulkpeogu was the Gulkpe'Na, the "divisional chief," although he lived in Yendi, sixty miles to the east. The Dakpema was nothing but a tindana whose unscrupulous partisans had misled Candler. The late Dakpema Nsungna had died, Blair said, of hubris, of his temerity in violating the traditional order by his insubordinate trip to Yendi. (*Hubris*, which he usually wrote in Greek letters, was a favorite word of Blair's when describing those who in his opinion flouted established order.) The Gulkpe'Na, although he had a base in the village of Zagyuri, a short distance north of Tamale town, to which he returned from time to time, lived in Yendi because the capital of Dagbon had been moved there from the west at the end of the seventeenth century. Blair was well aware that from the beginning certain tindanas were important figures in the rituals that governed succession to the position of Ya Na and that the Gulkpe'Na himself was one of these. This knowledge did not incline him to modify his view of Dagbon as an early modern state that with a little tinkering could be incorporated into the colonial regime as "a microcosm (mutatis mutandis) of our own administration of the colony." Or as Duncan-Johnstone put it, "The divisional Chiefs are to be taught to govern the primitive pagan as they themselves are governed."[60]

Two months later, at the constitutional conference, the "jealous chiefs" mentioned by Candler all swore that the Dakpema was nobody in particular and certainly subject to the Gulkpe'Na and to Yendi. The British said it was important that the Gulkpe'Na, as chief of a division, should actually live in it; the Ya Na thought that could be arranged but wanted time to discuss the matter with his elders. He also wanted particulars of what his representative in Tamale would be expected to do. The provincial commissioner, Duncan-Johnstone, a principal architect, along with Blair, of the policy of indirect rule in the Northern Territories, said that the Gulkpe'Na would travel with the district commissioner and that he would issue all instructions in the name of the Ya Na, who would be kept fully informed. The Ya Na said that he was very satisfied with this arrangement and that he wished to thank the provincial commissioner for the turn affairs had taken. As well he might. We shall learn more about the Dakpema and the Gulkpe'Na in subsequent chapters.

Postcolonial Chiefs

In the 1960s a new generation of historians sought to provide a usable political past for Ghana and other newly independent African countries.

John Fage, Ivor Wilks, and Wilks's student Phyllis Ferguson revisited the kingdoms of the north; they accepted the general outline of Rattray's story, although they substituted *ethnic group* for *race*, and confirmed the image of Dagbon as an early modern state.[61] By then, as a result of colonial policy, Dagbon and the other kingdoms had become more like administrative structures than they had been at any time in the past. Fage focused on dynastic events; he corrected Tamakloe's dates but commended him as a reliable reporter without ever questioning the story as a whole. Ferguson, after extensive research in Yendi, divided the history of Dagbon into the First and Second Kingdoms. Dagbon, she showed, had been essentially refounded at the end of the seventeenth century by Na Zanjina, a wealthy trader and convert to Islam who made extensive use of Muslim experts to organize Yendi as a trading state.[62] A late-nineteenth-century Hausa text says that "now when the Dagomba people enumerate their kings, they just start from Zangina. They do not take into account the ones before [him] who were living in Bagale [the shrine to past kings] because they consider them as if they were village heads."[63] The route of Na Nyagse's conquest, as reconstructed from tradition by Ferguson, followed a counterclockwise path from the north around Dagbon, but such a raid does not establish a kingdom. It was likely carried out by horsemen, although traditional histories do not mention horses before the seventeenth century, but the settlement of the domain required a distribution of horses throughout the country over a period of time.[64] This in turn required sources of wealth, since horses do not breed in Dagbon and must be imported from further north at considerable expense; the stateless peoples were too poor to acquire them, and the agricultural economy did not offer an extractable surplus to conquerors. The First Kingdom was a less bounded entity than Dagbon eventually became; both ambitious princes and "refugees," that is, people who did not care to submit to the exactions of chiefs, fled west. The dates are uncertain, but Dagomba warriors are said to have founded dynasties in Wa and Bouna, although Bouna tradition describes the Dagomba founder as a wandering hunter rather than a prince.[65]

The Second Kingdom's history is relatively well known because other sources can be correlated with drum chant, which is itself much more detailed than for the First Kingdom; the reconstituted state required a more elaborate history. For the First Kingdom one has little to rely on besides general knowledge of what was happening in West Africa in the sixteenth and seventeenth centuries, but we still have to ask why the story of Na Nyagse, which Ibrahim Mahama had to modify even though he preserved its ideological message, was so readily accepted. Invasion stories appeal to historians because, first, they appear to make history; but that, of course, is the ideological function of the story in the context of its original telling. Second, it has always been difficult for European thinkers since Aristotle to imagine a political order that is not centralized. Third, scholars have only recently begun to acknowledge that political power in Africa is not reducible to what the modern world regards as its rational, secular elements. That is the burden of McCaskie's critique of Wilks, among others.

The first critique of the supposed opposition between "religious" priests and "political" chiefs and of the idea that the latter were introduced from elsewhere is apparently attributable to Kunz Dittmer, who found that in modern Burkina Faso the two roles were so similar that they seemed to replicate each other.[66] There is even a Dagbani maxim that says that all chiefs are tindanas.[67] Peter Skalník, revising his own, earlier view of Nanun, deplores the logic that isolates politics from economics and separates religion and kingship, which has too facilely led to the conclusion that African leaders and the institutions they personified were comparable to Western political institutions, although in fact, he argues, they were fundamentally different.[68] In Dagbon, tindanas have been dismissed as religious figures of no constitutional or historical importance; conversely, the religious or metaphysical nature of chiefly power has been underplayed.

These complexities tend to be obscured in modern times by the weight of colonial models of chieftaincy. Public discussions on the future of chieftaincy in Ghana today divide on the question whether chiefs should play a greater or a lesser role.[69] The administration and control of land is one of the principal issues, already looming in 1930 when the Ya Na and the elders of Dagbon collaborated with the district commissioners to their mutual benefit. St. J. Eyre-Smith, a colonial officer who opposed indirect rule, pointed out that "land is now assuming economic values, and sometimes the chief may take the best land for himself."[70] By 1930, foreshadowing development to come, Yendi was little more than a large village, but Tamale had begun to fill up with strangers—Hausa and Yoruba traders, Mosse and other military veterans, southern clerks in British employ. Farms were being taken over by housing, and rents provided income to the administration and to the chiefs. By 2004 the population of Tamale had risen to 350,000; the uses and rents of land had come to dominate local politics (see chapter 5). The story of Na Nyagse's slaughter of the tindanas asserts not only the unchallengeable authority of the Ya Na over an integral kingdom but also his claim to control land, which is newly becoming a commodity.

From 1902 until 1979 the government in Accra controlled land in the north; under the constitution of 1992, all northern lands were returned to their traditional owners (see chapter 6). The constitution, in a reaction against Kwame Nkrumah's high-handed treatment of chiefs, guaranteed chieftaincy "as established by customary law and usage" and denied Parliament the power "to confer on any person or authority the right to accord or withdraw recognition to or from a chief for any purpose whatsoever."[71] The result is a political pluralism more radical than any that obtained in colonial times. The National House of Chiefs was charged with discovering and encoding the appropriate customary laws and usages, that is, of reducing chieftaincy to its administrative aspect and eliminating politics, as the British tried to do in 1930.

The power imbalance between north and south throughout the twentieth century and continuing today has meant that the southern, or Akan, model of chieftaincy has dominated policy discussions, to the exclusion of tindanas, who are either overlooked entirely or still confined, for the most part, to the "religious" role assigned to them by Rattray.[72] The 1992 constitution vests land in "chiefs" and makes only indirect allowance for tindanas. In so doing, it has the support of northern chiefs, well aware of their own interests. Among the educated, all accounts of early Dagbon, popular and scholarly, rely on Yendi tradition as mediated by Tamakloe and Rattray, who are routinely quoted, and less often Blair. Almost all of the recent scholarly literature on tradition, chiefs, and the control of land in the north recognizes that in the Upper West and the Upper East there are tindanas actively asserting claims to control of land but accepts, in effect, the story of Na Nyagse as defining the situation in the Northern Region, specifically in Dagbon.

Although there were no doubt invaders and other immigrants, all the early kingdoms were networks of distributed *nam* rather than states and as such probably amounted to developments of the relationship between "chief" and "landowner" that existed all over the north, even where there was no centralization. Anthropology, historiography, colonial policy, and

the canny enterprise of chiefs themselves combined to entrench a historically misleading model of chieftaincy. Though chieftaincies are the
same in name, the nature and sources of the power of chiefs changed under colonial rule and have changed again since 1970. It is not advisable to
multiply historical "periods," but serious modifications of chiefly power
occurred with the shifts away from warfare and slave raiding to indirect
rule in 1930 and from indirect rule to district councils in the early 1950s;
with Kwame Nkrumah's attack on chieftaincy in the early 1960s; and
with the guarantees provided for the institution in the constitution of
1992.

2

Drum Chant and the Political Uses of Tradition

This chapter traces the role of tradition in the politics of succession to the Nam of Yendi, the kingship of Dagbon. It necessarily focuses on chiefs, but the issue of *nam*, the essential quality of chieftaincy conferred by ritual, obtrudes from time to time. The ritual administration of *nam* is conducted by tindanas, a function described in chapter 4.

The First Kingdom, from the mid-fifteenth to the late seventeenth century, is known to history almost entirely through oral tradition, especially drum chant. The Second Kingdom, from 1700 to 1900, is better known because, in addition to drum chant, we have other sources of information, some of them independent of events in Dagbon itself. Over the course of the twentieth century, drum chant and tradition in general took on new functions as "tradition" came to be the defining characteristic of a social system opposed to the "modern" and the "political" in Ghana.[1]

Dagbamba describe their tradition as the way of life that distinguishes them from other Ghanaians. Somewhat more narrowly, it is the story of the origin of that way of life in the creation of the kingdom of Dagbon and the institutions of chieftaincy by Na Nyagse and his descendants. Tradition (*Dagbon kali*) is embodied in at least three kinds of activity: the recitation of drum history, the performance of ceremony at chiefs' courts, and the performance of sacrifices and other rituals at family, dynastic, and local shrines, the last being in the charge of tindanas (see the appendix and chapter 3). Although tradition itself distinguishes chiefs and tindanas as conquerors and aborigines, respectively, all three loci of tradition are elements of a single complex that Dagbamba speak of as essential to the continued moral and political integrity of Dagbon.

Tradition as historical account is in the charge of drummer praise-singers (*lunsi*, s. *luŋa*, hereafter *lunga*), known elsewhere in West Africa as griots. Drum chant, or praise-singing (*salima*), a form of epic poetry, together with the complex repertoire of rhythms and dances and the ceremonies of chieftaincy, is the primary art form, closely associated with Dagbamba identity. In performance on special occasions at the palace of an important chief it continues for hours. Phyllis Ferguson was present in 1970 at the maiden performance of a gifted *lunga* that went on for five hours without stopping, a remarkable feat.[2] As political ideology it is compelling. Drummers are often described as the historians of Dagbon, but drum chant is not really history at all, though educated men with scholarly inclinations today follow the example of British scholars to draw from it history in the modern sense, complete with highly questionable dates stretching back to 1400 or even further. The received history of Dagbon, as one meets it in the writing or more often in the conversation of intellectuals, combines elements of drum chant with material derived from colonial anthropology and a limited number of publications that are themselves colonial products, whose contents have to some extent entered oral tradition.

History as presented by tradition is politically salient at two levels. The myth of Na Nyagse supports the exclusive right of his descendants to govern and to control land, not only as territory but, in modern times, as a productive and saleable resource. As Ibrahim Mahama succinctly puts it, "The kingdoms can all list their kings from the beginning; the Konkomba can not, therefore they have no knowledge of the past on which to base their claims to land."[3] The story of events in the Second Kingdom, especially from about 1800 on, supports the current rights of chiefs, royal and commoner, as determined by the outcome of past struggles. In principle, tradition is single and true, but in fact it may be multiple and contested, as opposed factions invoke and manipulate different accounts of the past. This use of tradition is central to the conflict between the descendants and supporters of two sons of Na Yakubu (1832–1863), Na Abudulai (1863–1875) and Na Andani (1875–1899). As the twentieth century progressed, this conflict between "the Abudus" and "the Andanis" became more and more bitter and more productive of violence until in 2002 it resulted in the death of Ya Na Yakubu Andani and made Dagbon a byword for political disorder in Ghana.

Fig. 1 The late Ya Na Yakubu Andani. (Photo by the author)

The Truth of Drum Chant

No extended transcription of the chant is readily available; scholars have relied on selections and reduced "prose" versions. The anthropologist David Tait, working in Yendi in the 1950s in collaboration with the historian John Fage, collected drum history by using intermediaries, literate scribes who wrote and translated histories in different parts of Dagbon under the supervision of local chiefs. The results, known as "Tait A" and "Tait B," were filed at the University of Ghana, Legon.[4] A decade later, Ferguson made extensive use of Hausa texts and Muslim informants in Yendi, writing a doctoral thesis on the role of Muslims in the development of what she called the Second Kingdom, since Na Zanjina. The musicologist David Locke has written down major episodes from the history in interviews (in English) with the drummer Alhaji Abubakari Lunna, the only published version that includes the rhythms that are essential to the chant. All these versions are in general agreement, despite minor differences with respect particularly to what Ferguson calls the First Kingdom. All of them are reductions from what drum chant may be in actual performance. Birgitta Benzing is the only scholar to have undertaken a systematic comparison of multiple versions of the drum history.[5]

The folklorist Abdulai Salifu, a native of Tamale, has written a doctoral thesis focusing especially on the praise-names of chiefs as they appear in drum chant. The work includes transcriptions and translations of recent performances that show how the narrative is formed around praise-names, supported by expressions both heroic and elliptical that call for some level of interpretation. The names and the family relations among them form both the mnemonic of the recitation and the skeleton of the organization of the state; this, rather than the document drawn up by the British in 1930, is the "constitution" of Dagbon. Even more informative is an insider's description of drumming in a thesis by Zablong Zakaria Abdallah, a drummer by heredity and training who teaches at Legon.[6]

The drum history is considered by drummers and chiefs to be unquestionably true, but like similar traditions in Gonja, Mamprugu, and elsewhere in Africa, it is a political document whose function is to praise the dynasty and its current chiefs; it silences commoners and the "conquered," who simply disappear after the conquest. Historians no longer regard such recitations as reliable historical accounts. John Thornton expresses the modern consensus when he writes, "Traditions of origin provide fascinating insights into the political philosophy of the people who tell them, but they have not proven to be as helpful for reconstructing the earliest history of African polities." M. Schlottner, writing about Mamprugu, agrees: "The past as revealed in the official oral traditions of the [drummers] reconstructs the history of the rulers rather than that of the segments that constituted the bulk of the population." Drum chant stresses the continuity of chieftaincy; "whatever is said in such a context is intended to strengthen the position and authority of the ruling dynasty."[7] Carola Lentz has shown how clan histories in the Upper West have changed during the twentieth century and describes "the mutual constitution of oral traditions and political interests." Stefano Boni, showing how tradition is constructed to meet political ends, usefully distinguishes between history "intended as a narrative concerning the past" and "history intended as past events." Such critiques cannot show that the drummer's recitation is historically incorrect, though they encourage the search for complementary evidence.[8] The truth of drum chant lies not in its correspondence with evidence derived externally but in its tautological self-presentation as "the truth" of a heroic story.

There may have been no drummers until the formation of the Second Kingdom in about 1700, when they were imported from Hausaland and then introduced to Mamprugu from Dagbon only in the mid-eighteenth century. David Davis suggests that Mamprugu would have had no need of drummers until it reached a certain level of hierarchical organization. A. A. Iliasu reaches an opposite conclusion, that Dagbon has more history because its drummers constitute an "elaborate, accessible and efficient machinery" whose function is to propagate it.[9] Originally, memory of important events was handed down, in both Dagbon and Mamprugu, by professional historians called *baŋsi*, a class of hereditary eulogists also called *daŋbelanima*, literally "holders of walking stick," based on the sign of their function. The *baŋsi* were always few in number, rarely performed, and in fact may no longer exist. Tradition as told to me in Yogu, where they say Na Nyagse lived, says that his son Bizung, neglected as a child, drew attention to himself by banging on a calabash. He became Na Nyagse's first *lunga* and was given land, Namogu, near Yogu, through which ran a river, so that he could both farm and fish. That is a prose version; here is a transcription of the story from a recitation performed in Yendi in 2006:

> The Namo Na Bizung's father, Na Nyagse,
> My ancestor Bizung was a prince of Dagbon
> But turned himself into one who entreats
> Entreats at dusk and entreats till daybreak; beseeching the king will not
>   go unrewarded.
> He precedes the king to the royal pavilion
> Amid the morning thunderclaps of his lead drum
> And the supporting drums drone like mosquitos,
> And all say that it is Prince Bizung.
> Bizung describes how the king burns grass and how he fishes . . .
> And the king watches the horn-players blowing

And the king watches the lute players

And when the king rides his horse Malimali, Bizung rides Malimali's tail
    (is right behind)

Then when the king rides Fast-horse-with-a-mane

My grandfather follows behind the maned one.[10]

Bizung thus became the first Namo Na, the chief drummer at Yendi, but Mahama, after telling the story, says that it was only after Na Luro's defeat of Gonja (ca. 1670) that he chose drummers over other musicians to celebrate his victory, and all important chiefs added drummers to their courts.[11] There are seven families of drummers. Their members, like the families of the chiefs to whom the drummers are attached, are scattered all over Dagbon. Chiefs are said to "woo" drummers to their service, and a drummer is the chief's "wife."

Despite the confidence of scholars and Dagbamba alike, there is in fact no such single thing as drum chant. Drummers, while assuring you that they personally know the true story, recognize that some of their colleagues are less well informed or perhaps politically biased and that different circumstances call for different versions. Zablong says that the teaching method is so strict that no apprentice drummer would dream of changing anything he had been taught, but he admits that in any drummer family (as in other families) some lines may be descended from slaves and therefore are "not to be trusted."[12] Since 1885, when the split between the Abudu and Andani branches of the royal family originated, there have been histories favoring one or the other version of events, and there is no reason to suppose that histories were less partisan before then. In Mamprugu, "in theory, the corpus of traditional knowledge remains intact from generation to generation; in practice, only relevant material is retained."[13]

In 2008, just before his death, Alhaji Abubakari Lunna, the chief drummer of Kasuleyili, told me that in 1974, when the Supreme Court was trying to settle the royal dispute, it summoned important drummers to Accra to tell the history, but they refused, lied, or accused one another. The Namo Na performed an enormous sacrifice of "all the animals, male and female," at Abubakari's own house in Accra. (Sacrifice is necessary to avert danger associated with telling secrets; the more danger, the larger the appropriate sacrifice.) Either because the rituals were not performed correctly or because of the lies, on their return home several drummers found that a family member or a horse had died; moreover, as part of the fallout, "everywhere in the north we now have two chiefs" and continuing conflict. Abubakari's sympathies were clearly Abudu. He did not regard the Namo Na as the historian of Dagbon, but merely as the Ya Na's *lunga*. He made it very clear that there was no single history, for because of ignorance or politics different drummers tell different stories, but he clung to the notion that his own teachers (his father, the Nanton *lunga*, and another one) told the truth. To David Locke he said, "My father always told, 'Don't take one teacher's idea to be the correct meaning. Compare many people's ideas and *see which is best.*'"[14]

Differences between versions are not usually about matters of historical fact, however, but about levels of "danger," the most dangerous incidents or versions being therefore the most secret and the most "true." Dangers are clearly related to the political context of the practice of drum chanting, as Abubakari's story suggests. Drum chants are performed on three sorts of occasion, involving increasing degrees of danger: entertainments, as at weddings, funerals, and market days; chiefly events, such as receptions on Mondays, Fridays, and other days; festivals and other special occasions when *sambanluŋa* performances take place, notably the annual Damba festival, which nominally commemorates the birth of the Prophet but is in fact a pre-Islamic celebration of chieftaincy itself. These three sorts of performance are not sharply distinguished; each may be more entertainment or more history; the more history, the more danger. At festivals and entertainments the drummers focus on the rich and powerful, accompanying and stimulating them as they dance to display their honorable heritage, their wealth, and the wealth of their family and supporters, distributing money generously among the musicians. Drummers flatter the dancers by playing the praise-names and rhythms associated with the most distinguished of the dancers' real or supposed ancestral lines; therein lies a possibility of giving offense to someone. When many chiefs are gathered, it is important that the drummer know their order of precedence, an extremely touchy subject.

Dangerous Secrets

Drum storytelling is always a coded reference rather than an explicit narrative; the references themselves recede into ever more dangerous levels of secrecy. Of Na Gbewaa, "the great ancestor-fetish of Dagomba and Mamprusi and Nanumba alike," Commissioner Blair wrote in his version

Fig. 2 Drummers at Yendi. (Photo by Allegra Churchill)

of the drum history, "The mode of Gbewa's attaining the chieftainship, indeed everything about him, is terribly Tabu; but there were great deeds and bloody ones done at that time, of which few Dagombas know, and those who know the most least like to speak of them."[15]

Reciting a given story is more dangerous if the story relates to origins, for example, to the first incumbents of a given title; if it describes particularly bloody events or a family quarrel; if it is discreditable to the protagonist; or if it may be considered derogatory by some of the audience, especially when many are gathered together—triumphant chiefs often adopted praises that insulted and challenged others.[16] The danger is diminished when one or more sacrifices on a scale appropriate to the danger are carried out; when recitation is private, as when a drummer instructs his son or a visiting anthropologist; when the drummer performs a euphemistic version; or when the drummer is not affiliated to the skin to which the story relates and therefore cannot know the real story. A story may turn out to be a screen for a more dangerous one; a drummer may be able to play a dance without knowing its meaning, or knowing only a false one. Abubakari recommended that since a drummer never knows which stories are dangerous, he should be careful to ask.

Drummers asked to tell the story of some event obviously have the "poetry" in their heads as their source, but they present their "prose" versions as though they were dramatic reports by an eyewitness; Tamakloe and others offer such reports, recollections of famous wars. The following dangerous story cost me a chicken; it illustrates not only "danger" but the genealogical complexities that a drummer keeps in mind and the typical wealth of cultural details.

Na Zoligu's son Zombilla had a son Dariziegu, who was exceptionally beautiful. Finding the child amidst his admirers, the Ya Na praised him extravagantly. This was not wise, because it meant that when Zoligu died and Zombilla, his regent, also died, Dariziegu replaced him, becoming his own grandfather's regent. But Zombilla, because he was regent when he died, was buried as a Ya Na. Na Zoligu's second son, Yanzo, succeeded him, but he also died, and his nephew Dariziegu became Ya Na. As such he felt, as other big chiefs do, that he should make a name for himself by going to war. Now, his mother's people were Gonja from Kwalon, near Daboya. Fearing his ambition, they placed a curse on him, that he would die if he attacked them, but he went ahead anyway. The Gonja king Kalosidajia killed him at Yapei and cut off his arm. His uncle Na Luro [the third son of Na Zoligu] became Ya Na. After his enskinment, Na Luro's mother's people came to greet and congratulate him. He gave his young wife, his *komlana*, guinea fowl and yams and told her to prepare food; meanwhile he retired to his room. After two hours and no food, he sent messengers and then went himself to ask why. He found the woman spinning cotton; she said, "All you can think of is food, and yet you are a man who does not even know where his father's grave is." By his father she meant his nephew Dariziegu, who had been Ya Na before him and therefore deserved this title of respect. Na Luro was furious and beat her with his whip *barazum*, but he prepared for war, to find his father's grave, which is in Daboya, although it was the rainy season [and the rivers were full]. He consulted diviners as to the route his forces should follow. When he came to the river Namkambiem, "Chief should not be bad," he saw a fisherman in a canoe and asked him how he might cross. The fisherman advised him to send for blacksmiths, which were unknown there at that time. So Na Luro sent for So Na Famoro and Yidan Borogo, who made tools with which they built a bridge so that Na Luro could cross the White Volta. He raided Daboya and killed many. When Kalosidajia heard of it he said, "If only I had been there I would have done something." He confronted Na Luro. Na Luro gave him a javelin that his blacksmiths had made, but it was one that swerved in use. Kalosidajia used it anyway. He threw it once, and it missed; a second time, and it hit a tree; a third time, and it wounded Na Luro (though we drummers, in singing the story, substitute that it hit his horse). Na Luro killed the Gonja king and cut off his head. After the battle he felt the need for praise, so there came *akarmanima* drummers with *timpana,* which are played on Mondays and Fridays when a chief holds court; but these are "talking drums," which means that the drummer speaks his message as he plays, and Na Luro thought that was uninspiring. Then came *baŋsi,* eulogists who use no drum but hold a forked stick to their mouths when they recite; Na Luro did not like that either, so he gave *kola* to a diviner, asking, "Where can I get good praises?" The diviner said, "Go to Diare [Yogu], to Bizung's son Lunziegu." So *lunsi* came with their wives and children, they were many. They hailed Na Luro as *Sampiemo tindanpaɣabia,* that is, as a son of his mother's village, which is near Karaga. Na Luro gave them a ram, that food might be prepared, which they ate from calabashes in the manner of those days. But the food was so good that they broke some of the Ya Na's calabashes, an offense for which you have to pay. They excused themselves, saying, "The food was so good!" Na Luro declared that in future drummers would not have to give *kola,* or pay for food, or be charged in any way. Then he headed for home, but in Kpung Tamale he died.[17]

After a victory, the drummers play "Bangumanga," which is the rhythm associated with this battle and with bloody and victorious events generally. It is said that when Na Yakubu Andani was killed in 2002, the killers played Bangumanga to make the Andani family angry, "and that is why the issue will never be settled."[18]

Drummers, vulnerable to the professional jealousy of others, who may try to cause a poor performance, wear protective talismans under their clothes. Such talismans should not be seen by others and must not be polluted. Besides drummers, the troupes that perform certain dances are at risk either because the dances originated in bloody events or because when they are performed as entertainment at funerals, witches may congregate; then the dancers also wear talismans. These days, however, the origins of dances are unknown to young people, and the sense of danger has largely disappeared.

Except for the witchcraft and sorcery of malicious people, the sources of danger are not clearly defined, nor is the rationale for protective sacrifices. Cynics who consider themselves enlightened hold that the danger is all "politics," meaning simply the hostility of people who hold to a different version of the history recited. That view does not account for the sacrifices, since a dead sheep or chicken will not assuage offended political sensibilities. One might argue that sacrifice enhances the mystique or "mystery" of drumming in that the more esoteric the knowledge, the more dangerous it is and the more spectacular the sacrifice, reflecting credit on the minority of drummers who are instructed to this level. In some situations the sacrifice, which may take the form of a libation, with the rest of the bottle to be consumed later, or of the cash with which to buy an appropriate chicken, can be considered a drummer's royalty, an acknowledgment of his proprietary rights over the knowledge he has laboriously acquired. That, however, explains neither the element of anxiety nor the sacrifice that the drummer may perform privately and at his own expense. One drummer, an observant Muslim, told me that he must sacrifice because his fathers did so before him, but that is not explanatory either. He went on to say that the ancestors, meaning both past chiefs and past drummers, will have his blood if he does not provide that of an animal, although it is still not clear what provokes their anger or how it is assuaged. It is said that they do not like to be talked about, but why not, since their praises are being sung and since in any case the history, which is performed in public, is generally known?

The grandest sacrifice on record, besides that recollected by Abubakari Lunna, was occasioned by a campaign in 1958 to unseat (deskin) Ya Na Abudulai on the ground that because he was physically defective, he should not have been enskinned. The State Council called on the Namo Na, the chief drummer in Yendi, to say whether a prince with bodily defects had ever been made Ya Na. He said that he would risk his life if he did so, but he was induced to respond after being provided with a white cow, a white ram, a white goat, a white cock, two white doves, honey cakes, and milk to sacrifice.[19] In this instance the danger was clear, since the topic was both the shocking possibility of physical defects in Ya Nas past and the political tensions related to the equally shocking possibility of deskinment in the present. The white color of the sacrificial objects called for peace and goodwill, but clearly, in this as in all other instances of sacrifice related to chieftaincy, blood is the essential factor. Commenting on West African animal sacrifice in general, William Pietz writes: "The visible shedding of blood is itself the realization and dynamization of an otherwise invisible spiritual power. Such blood is the material form of the power of life, of living existence, understood as the real substance of a society whose members include the living and the still active ancestral dead."[20] It also, of course, dramatically materializes an otherwise abstract power of death.

Pointing to the religious element ("belief") in tradition enriches the description but does little to account for the passions and the sense of danger that attach to it. As the story of Na Luro shows, force itself is not thought of or represented primarily in what we would call real or histori-cal terms, but as the effect of a metaphysical or magical quality inherent in *nam,* in the person of any king or chief worthy of the name. Although several early colonial officers recognized the "supernatural" component of *nam,* none insisted on it as much as St. J. Eyre-Smith did in order to attack indirect rule's reliance on chiefs. But he understood *nam* in purely Frazerian terms; magic, he said, was adopted by invaders as a means to gain control over credulous and more primitive peoples.[21]

For the nearest equivalent of *nam* in English we have to go back to the Renaissance word *virtù* (virtue), from the Latin *virtus* (manliness), the quasi-divine ability of military princes to transcend the usual restric-tions and ordinary levels of achievement.[22] All discussions of the meta-physical powers of chiefs, princes, and princesses tend to evoke stories of marvelous events in the past, which serve as templates for understand-ing the present. Yo Na Yakubu, who became Ya Na in 1832 after a civil war in which his predecessor, Na Zoli, died, defied his rivals by taking the praise-name Nantoo Nimdi (*nantoo nimdi, bilsi-bilsi, nje,* "Anthrax meat, turn it over, reject it"), paraphrased as "Poison to Princes." When Na Abudulai took the name Nagbiegu, "Dirty Cow," meaning "I will foul your drinking water" or "Don't mess with me!," in 1863, it was at the same time a boast, an oath, and an invocation of *nam* against the Bassar, a neighboring people whom he was raiding for slaves.[23] The epithet *bieɣu,* "bad, ugly, mean," can be applied to any of the higher chiefs invested, as the Ya Na was, in the Katin'du, one of the compounds of the palace at Yendi where former kings also are buried; in that sense it signals the possession of dangerous powers, although no one can say just what they are. Discussing old battles, people describe the occult maneuvers of the antagonists and attribute victory to superior magic. This metaphysical quality, or deficiency in it, is encoded in proverbs and praise-names but is dangerous to speak of explicitly. The closer one gets to the essence of *nam*, by naming old chiefs and telling of their victories and defeats, the greater the danger. The point of a drummer's recitation is not the event as such (Na Luro defeated the Gonja leader) but the evocation of the extraordinary power that made the deed possible. The secrecy of drumming is the same as that which surrounds the work of the tindanas in conferring *nam* on chiefs.

Everybody participates at least potentially in this virtuous violence and is at risk from it, although to judge by their own statements the "enlightened" (educated) set much less store by its metaphysical aspect. Tradition is a hierarchy in which everyone finds his or her place, but it is also intensely competitive and looks to the future as much as to the past. Even in ordinary social situations men are alert to the nuances of rank and the risk of offending a senior person. "Beneath their passions, complaints, and contradictions, the two sides [Abudus and Andanis] were united by an untarnished devotion to the status and authority of chieftaincy, the pursuit of which still seemed to be the consuming preoccupation of all Dagombas of appropriate age and rank."[24] In Dagbon almost any adult male, and some women, can aspire to a chiefly title, since every village has its own hierarchy of them. Each such hierarchy, subordinate to and a reflection of the hierarchy of the whole, produces reality, produces rituals and regimes of truth. To become a chief, no matter how minor, is instantly to be qualified to compete for a higher title. Studies show that the Dagbamba, in contrast to such neighboring people as the Konkomba, who have no chiefs but are formidable fighters, generally favor an aggressive attitude; they "multiply aggressive strategies for achieving higher status, power and economic control."[25] The nature of competition for titles is such that losers are likely to disqualify not only themselves but their descendants from ever competing again at the same level. Only the son of a former king may become king himself; most of his brothers, of whom there may be fifty or more, will have to content themselves with a chance at some lesser title.

The possibility of having one's line eventually reduced in status produces bloody conflicts even today, but the fighting is partly metaphysical.

When a new Nayiri is being chosen in Mamprugu, during the divination process the rival candidates are in such competitive tension that actual warfare is a possibility, but "sorcery battles seem now to be regarded as more significant." Contestants for important skins reportedly spend large sums on magical aids, sacrifices, and Islamic prayers to strengthen their cause. Those at risk from the medicines employed are not so much the rivals as innocent bystanders, because powerful men have powerful protection.[26] The Damba festival is dangerous because ambitious princes and lesser chiefs test the strength of their "medicine" against that of others like them and against that of the higher chiefs; it is said that in the old days many deaths might follow.[27] The praise-name of Na Andani (1875–1899), Naanigoo, "Don't trust," when spelled out in an allusive text that is both history and advice in the present says:

> It is he who knows you, who kills you
> Surely it is your trust that destroys you
> Your uncle's son—he is your assailant
> Give false (misplaced) trust and die,
> beware of the thorn.[28]

It is not surprising that drummers describe all other musicians as good for entertainment but not useful in war. As Mahama writes, "The praise-singer's job in battle is to remind the chief of his heroic ancestors, to fight valiantly, not like a woman, so that even if he dies his family will be proud."[29]

Besides the stories told by drummers, which relate mostly to chiefly families, oral traditions are preserved by people who take an interest in them. Commenting on a tradition concerning the celebrated Muslim scholar Pu'Samli, who became Yo Na, a drummer said, "It is also true, but this is the story of old men, not drummers."[30] Drummers themselves keep in their heads volumes of information constituting the backstories to the cryptic formulae of the chant itself. In this field discrepancies and even contradictions are more evident, and there are no "authorities" to whom one might appeal, but the sheer volume of information about ancient alliances and disputes is impressive. Most chiefs and drummers are illiterate; nowadays, a few educated people take written notes or use recorders, but this is a new development. The literacy rate in the Northern Region, including Dagbon, is the lowest in the country, 23 percent, and that figure conceals the vast difference between the rates for urban and rural adults, 62 percent and 13 percent, respectively.[31] With reference to their own local family histories, such researchers may not hesitate to assert that the drummers are wrong. The educated, though aware of the authority of written documents in the modern world, generally are not trained in the critique of texts and sources. When it comes to the history of Dagbon, dogma reigns.

In practice, the researcher, in Dagbon as elsewhere, discussing tradition with drummers and other persons claiming knowledge of tradition, often encounters situations such as the following. The chief, chief drummer, or family head summons elders to support him, one of whom will do most of the telling. Also in attendance are younger men interested in learning history. When the principal speaker falters, they may chip in with their own version, which they have heard elsewhere or which they advance to fill a gap or resolve an inconsistency. On occasion the elders will declare that they must adjourn to consult the ancestors, or as I might say, to sleep on it. In such interactions one can see the components of tradition being shaped and reshaped to a narrative that is comfortable in the here and now. Even in the same milieu, two versions of a story are rarely identical. Such discussions are casual, unrelated to political disputes, where there is no room for uncertainty. In politics much is at stake, and the outcome determines the "traditional" allocation of rights and also the authority of those acknowledged as qualified to pronounce upon the truth of tradition.

On occasion I met with evasions and even outright lies. Knowledge is valuable; why should one give it away to inquiring strangers? Who knows what they might do with it? I would be assured that something I was asking about was profoundly secret or could only be known to drummers, not elders, although I knew, or subsequently discovered, that the secrets in question were common knowledge. In Tamale I found, especially in 2010, in the context of an open dispute to be discussed in chapter 5, that conflict broke open the fiction of a single, correct and secret tradition. Parties in dispute offered alternative traditions and in some instances clearly fabricated them. Yet it also became apparent that a purely cynical, rationalist, and instrumental view of tradition is inadequate; elders hesitated at the edge of an answer even though they knew it, and probably suspected that I also knew it, because it was "dangerous." Even though certain facts, like the story of Na Luro, are well known, only drummers should utter them because only drummers can offer sacrifices, only drummers have "protection" against the wrath of the dead. Drummers thus function, in a sense, as a priesthood of chieftaincy. In that sense there is a parallel between drummers and the mediums of Malagasy kings: "For spirits whose lives were associated with excessive acts of violence, their mediums are precisely the people who cannot tell their stories, because to tell them would be somehow to suffer them. The sign of the truth of the story is not its retelling but its silence or the punishment that accompanies narration."[32]

Political History, Tradition Adapted

The history of Dagbon is largely the history of incessant struggles to achieve the Nam of Yendi and to reserve the succession to one's own patriline, if possible. Before 1900, tradition as recorded in drum chant served mostly to glorify the deeds of the princes and to explain the structure of the kingdom as it emerged from succession struggles. The aim of colonial rule was to eliminate violent conflict and, after 1928, to encourage the development of a proto-bureaucratic structure. The function of tradition, particularly drum chant, came to be to provide a constitutional record in which entitlements were more significant than heroic deeds. At the same time, parties to succession conflicts that could no longer be carried on by violence used a reified Tradition to confront and manipulate government, comparably misrepresented as Politics.[33] Despite Tradition's supposed fidelity to historical truth, it provides endlessly regressive possibilities for argument; the dispute between the Andani and Abudu royal factions that began in the 1880s remains unresolved.

Na Nyagse, having killed off the tindanas, is often said to have made his headquarters at Yenn'dabari, but it is likely that the site known by this name was a Muslim trading caravansary on the route between the Mande (Wangara) trade in the west and Hausaland and that the king's palace was nearby at Yogu (Yenn'Yogu), where his grave is, not far also from Yiwogu, the reputed village and site of the grave of his father, Sitobu. The sixteenth century was filled with wars against the emergent state of Gonja, rival of Dagbon for control of trade. Gonja pressure was sufficiently strong that Na Dariziegu was killed, and according to the drum history, "it was many years before we had a new paramount," Na Luro, who himself died after a successful battle. Dagbon had lost control of the kola and salt route from Gbuipe through Daboya to the north, as well as the revenues to be derived from it in the form of taxes and the gifts that merchants offered to be sure of safe passage. The other principal sources of income were labor performed on a chief's farm by his subjects, prescribed portions of large wild and domestic animals killed, and the contributions expected on the occasion of funerals, weddings, enskinments, and other festivities; a chief owed similar contributions to his own superiors. Subsequent kings were forced to move east, but for a while the "capital" was a temporary camp.

About 1700 the succession was in such dispute that the princes asked Atabia, the Nayiri of Mamprugu, to arbitrate. Na Zanjina, the youngest son of Na Tutugri, a convert to Islam, had Muslim advisers and had become wealthy in the eastern trade. By a strategic distribution of wealth and by besting his brothers in a contest to recite apt proverbs, he was chosen to be Ya Na, whereupon the losing princes renounced the right of their descendants to compete for the paramountcy. At the same time, the Nayiri announced that in future only the holders of the gate skins—Karaga, Savelugu, or Mion—could contest for the Nam of Yendi; in fact, however, this "rule" was not followed in any of the next four successions, and in the 1930s other candidates argued that they were entitled to compete.[34]

As king, Na Zanjina camped close to his Muslim adviser, near the Oti River. The capital did not settle permanently at Yani (a Konkomba village formerly called Kyale or Chare and now known in English as Yendi) until after his death in 1713, during the reign of either Na Andani Sigili or Na Ziblim Bimbiegu. Na Andani Sigili was victorious in war, killing the Gonja king Kumpatia, his father-in-law. But in 1744, during the reign of Bimbiegu's successor, Na Gariba, the refounded kingdom was defeated by the expanding Asante state; Na Gariba was captured, and Asante demanded a ransom of one or two thousand slaves (the sources differ), to be paid annually. More an alliance than a tributary relationship, the link with Asante gave Yendi access to Kumasi and the coastal markets through Salaga. Yendi, described as a "Mahomedan kingdom" because of the number of Muslim scholar-merchants there, sent to the south northern cotton cloth, shea butter, tobacco, leather goods, livestock, slaves, and war shirts loaded with protective amulets, together with paper, silks, and other luxury goods from the Mediterranean, in exchange for cloth, iron, gold, guns, gunpowder, and other goods imported at the coast. Cowries were the principal means of exchange and were paid as gifts and taxes.[35] Yendi became a city larger and more impressive than Kumasi itself.[36] The chiefs bought horses from further north on credit and paid for them by raiding for slaves; they acquired expensive harnesses, gowns, trousers, burnouses, swords, and spears. The army added a corps of gunmen (*kambonsi*) on the Asante model. Muslims were not allowed to take royal skins, but many married into the dynasty and were active in politics. Asante helped to keep the western princes in order but treated Gonja less favorably, requiring a tribute in slaves but also raiding it from time to time and controlling the Salaga market.

In the nineteenth century, as Blair's version of the drum history has it, "Na Mahama died. And Na Kulunku [ca. 1820–27] reigned. And in Na Kulunku's time, the troubles of Dagbon started, for he drove out the [other] sons of Na Andani and succeeded his younger brother [cousin] Mahama. This deed of his roused the wrath of the dead chiefs, and they sent discord amongst the Dagomba. And Na Kulunku died, and Na Sumani Zoli reigned."[37] Na Sumani Zoli, son of Na Mahama, was chosen by the oracles and enskinned, but that choice threatened the descendants of Na Andani with exclusion from Yendi. So Yidantogma, also known as Lagfu ("Cowries," referring to his wealth), who as a *malam* and a son of one could not himself be king, made war on Na Zoli on behalf of Lagfu's mother's brother Yakubu, killed him, and made Yakubu Ya Na, probably in 1832. Na Yakubu took the praise-name Nanto Nimdi, "Poison to Princes." His rivals, the supporters of Na Zoli—Tolon, Kumbungu, and Diare—were all westerners. Known as Nabihi Kura, the War of the Princes, this struggle marks the beginning of a political division within Dagbon between the east and the west.

The role of Lagfu is an example of the political engagement of Muslim chiefs in dynastic politics; he was Yelzoli Lana, holder of an eastern title, but he went on to demand more and more skins. Later, his uncle Na Yakubu went mad, and the princes, worried that Lagfu had become so powerful that he might take the opportunity to make himself king, made war against him and killed him. After that, Na Yakubu alarmed them once more by appointing his brother Sunson Na Yahaya to succeed Na Kulunku's son Mahami as Karaga Na (a gate skin), because Yahaya had supported Lagfu and because this move diminished their own chances of reaching Yendi. So Na Yakubu's sons Andani and Abudulai joined with others to kill Yahaya. The king and his allies were defeated, though he was allowed to continue his reign until he died in 1864. As Ibrahim Mahama

```
                           Na Gariba
                              20
                            1733–72
                               │
        ┌──────────────────────┴──────────────────────┐
Na Ziblim Gbandamba                              Na Andani I
        22                                            23
    ca. 1778–97                                   (Jenbariga)
        │                                          1802–20
        │                                               │
        │                 ┌──────────────┬──────────────┴──────────┐
    Na Mahama       Na Ziblim Kulunku  Na Yakubu              sister
       24                  25              27                 Kpatu Na
      1820              1820–27         1832–64                   │
  (Nakworanga)       (Nanto Nimdi)                               │
        │                                                        │
  Na Sumani Zoli                                            Yidantogma
       26                                                   Yelzoli Lana
     1828–32                                                  (Lagfu)
                                                               malam
```

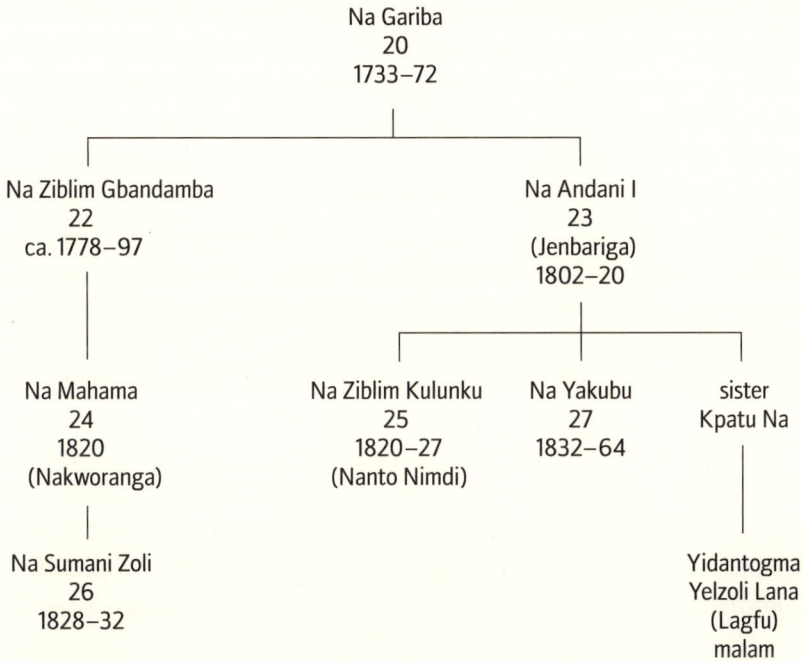

Fig. 3 King list. Succession numbers, given under the Ya Nas' names, are taken from Staniland, *Lions of Dagbon*, table 1, the most accessible source. Dates are from Ferguson, "Islamisation in Dagbon," table 3. Authorities disagree on the list of kings. Na Gariba was succeeded by a cousin, Ziblim Nasa (21). Praise-names and epithets are given in parentheses.

writes, "Having thus eliminated all opposition to their bid for the Nam, the sons of Na Yakubu had a field day on the death of their father. Abudulai and Andani, now occupying the Gate Skins of Mion and Savelugu, respectively, whose former occupants they had defeated, could ascend to the Yendi Skin one after the other."[38]

The sequence of dynastic events in the nineteenth century illustrates the predominant succession pattern, based on the political fact that to the extent that members of a single royal line succeed one another, collateral lines risk permanent exclusion; they therefore are likely to react with violence. The pattern became the basis for the claim made in the mid-twentieth century that there was a traditional rule of alternation. The rivalry between the descendants of Na Abudulai and those of Na Andani is the central theme of twentieth-century politics in Dagbon. But for British intervention, the issue would have been settled by violence, as in the past. Instead, the struggle was carried on by manipulating the British and, after independence, by alliances with national political parties and hearings before national courts and commissions. Arguments on both sides took the form of citations from tradition as to historical events and to rules allegedly revealed by such events, presented as necessary constitutive factors in the past and future of Dagbon. Tradition came to be a political instrument in confrontations not only between the Abudu and Andani factions but also between Dagbon as a Traditional Area and the government of Ghana.

Andani and Abudu traditions began to diverge in the late nineteenth century. After the British defeat of Asante in 1874, Asante influence declined in the north. Political turmoil on the upper Niger River had encouraged the migration of armed Muslim raiders, traders, and malams known as Zabarima, a group of whom settled in the Dagbon chieftaincy of Karaga in the 1860s, greatly adding to its prosperity by their service as mercenaries. By 1875 this relationship with Dagbon had deteriorated to the point that Ya Na Abudulai (1864–1876) sent his brother Andani (then Yo Na, chief of Savelugu) into the northwest to bring back the Zabarima, who apparently wanted to be elsewhere. At first, according to J. J. Holden, the Zabarima were forced to withdraw. They attempted to negotiate with Yo Na Andani at Biyuu (the name of the shrine in Savelugu from which comes the title Yo Na) but eventually gathered their forces and defeated the Dagbamba, killing thousands. "Dagomba tradition is silent about this war," writes Holden.[39]

Apparently Andani did not get support from other princes (the many sons of Na Yakubu who were jealous of Andani), hence his sobriquet Naanigoo, "Don't trust." In 1887, after Andani had succeeded his brother Abudulai as Ya Na, the new Yo Na, Mahami, first son of Abudulai, once again fought the Zabarima under their leader, Babatu, but was defeated and killed. His state drum was captured and, according to the Yo Na interviewed in 1964, never recovered.[40] In 2001 I heard a different version of the story in the village of Yenn'Yogu, once the seat of Na Nyagse himself and also the place where drumming originated, according to tradition. Not only Yo Na Mahami but his chief drummer was killed. Later, the village began to suffer calamities, and a diviner said that to avert them the lost drum must be recovered. Agents went to explain the problem to the Zabarima; the chief said he would make inquiries when his

```
                         Na Yakubu
                            27
                         1832–64
                      (Nantoo Nimdi)
                              |
     ┌────────────────────────┼────────────┬──────────────┐
  Na Abudulai              Mahama       Na Andani       Darimani
     28                   Kworle Na        29            Yo Na
  1864–76                 Karaga Na     1876–99       Ya Na? 1899
 (Nagbiegu)                  |          (Nanigoo)    (Kukra Adjei)
     |                       |              |
 ┌───┴──────┐                |              |
Yo Na Mahami  Allasani   Bukari Narkaw   Yiri (Iddi)
 d. 1887    Tampion Lana   Kworle Na     Tugu Lana
            Karaga Na      Karaga Na      Yo Na
            Ya Na 31      (Zambalanton)
```

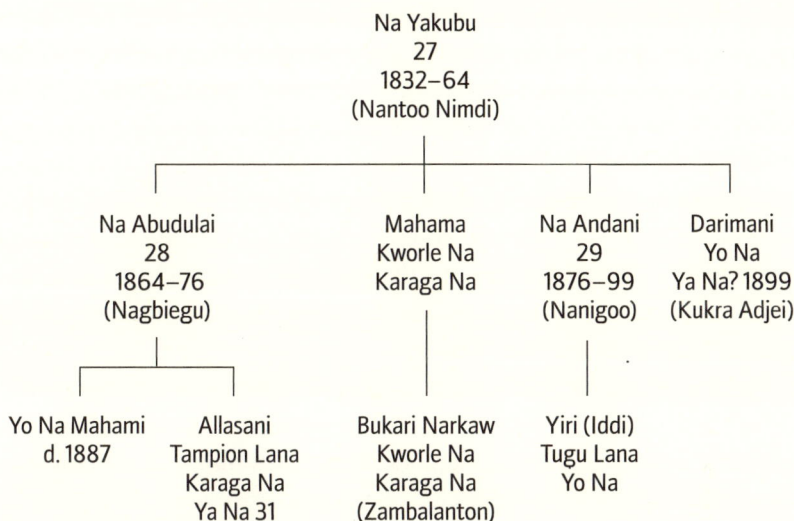

Fig. 4 Some descendants of Na Yakubu.

people returned from their farms at the end of the day, but just at that moment the drum began to play by itself, saying, "These are my people," and so it was returned to Yogu, where it hangs on a wall. It is an ordinary *lunga.*

An Abudu version of the story is that Na Andani, remembering the hostility of the princes, deliberately allowed his nephew Mahami to fight alone; already he was planning to restrict the succession to his own side of the family. He and Abudulai, sons of Na Yakubu, were of different mothers. According to an Andani version, the Yo Na failed to inform the Ya Na officially of his war plans. A version given to me by the drummer grandson of Mahami's own drummer, who was killed with him, is that Andani had sworn to keep the peace with the Zabarima but that Mahami, newly enskinned as Yo Na, wanted to make a name for himself and disregarded the treaty. Whatever the truth of it, according to the drummer Abubakari Lunna, "Because of the death of Savelugu Na Mahami, the Abudu-Andani matter is strong in Dagbon; drummers do not want to talk about it."[41]

The following year, 1888, a German expedition penetrated Dagbon and persuaded the chiefs to accept German "protection." This intrusion meant little, but in 1896 the Germans defeated the Ya Na's army at Adibo and burned Yendi. The Ya Na, however, favored the British, with the idea of keeping open his trade with Kumasi, which the British controlled, although the western princes, less connected to trade, opposed him: the Pigu Na, the Tugu Lana, the Tampion Lana, the Bamvim Lana, and the Sanieri Na, aided by Zabarima, rebelled against the British but were defeated. The British, the French, and the Germans divided this part of West Africa among themselves, drawing up frontiers in 1899 such that Yendi and eastern Dagbon fell to the Germans, while the British took Gonja and the rest of Dagbon. In that year, Ya Na Andani died. In the ensuing struggle over the succession, the anti-British faction tried to put Pigu Na Bukari on the skin, but he lacked traditional qualifications, so they settled for Yo Na Darimani, "apparently with the understanding" that in return Tugu Lana Yiri would become Yo Na at Savelugu. Regarding Darimani as pro-British, the Germans drove him into exile after a "reign" of a few weeks and killed the new Yo Na, Yiri.[42]

Tradition tells a different version of these events, in fact at least two versions, making it clear that dynastic rivalries underlay pro- and anti-British politics. According to an Abudu version, Tampion Lana Alassani, son of Na Abudulai and brother of Yo Na Mahami, who died fighting the Zabarima, pretended to be a bad character. He asked for Karaga, and Na Andani II gave him the skin, saying, "He drinks, he will die soon." Later, Abudus say, Na Andani realized that this move was a mistake, because Alassani at Karaga was in a position to become Ya Na and Andani wanted his own brother, Yo Na Darimani Kukarijee, to succeed him. When Andani died in 1899, his son and regent Tugu Lana Yiri put Darimani in the Katin'du, the compound in which kings are enskinned, and gave him the royal walking stick but could not find the rest of the regalia. Then Yiri had the new king appoint him to Savelugu as Yo Na, because he did not want Karaga. His father, Na Andani, had killed the Karaga Na and destroyed the town, so Yiri had good reason to believe that the people he was supposed to rule would kill him. This was too much for the princes, led by Korli Na Bukari Narkaw, who enlisted the help of "the British" and killed Yiri on his way to Savelugu. The Dagombas were glad, because Yiri had tried to enskin the Ya Na all by himself. Darimani ran away, and the drummers do not record him as Ya Na but only as Yo Na.[43]

Andanis tell yet another story of the same events: Alhassan, son of Na Abudulai, was rescued from slavery in Niamey by Na Andani II (his uncle on both his father's and his mother's side) and groomed for kingship by giving him first Tampion and then Karaga. The king declared that he wanted his nephew to succeed him and that he wanted Yiri, the regent, to take Karaga. Despite his generosity, at his death Alhassan and other Abudus failed to come to the burial as custom required. Andanis point to Na Andani's alleged desire as evidence that he respected tradition and that the conflict originated with the misbehavior of the other side. Some Andanis allege that this sort of "immorality" on the part of Abudus explains why there are so few of them. Later, the Abudus did appear, not at the burial but at the funeral, armed and apparently intent on seizing the Nam. Realizing, however, that he did not have sufficient force, Alhassan sent his cousin Bukari Narkaw to enlist the help of the Germans, not the British. The Andanis, having performed the funeral in all decency, left Yendi. The Germans invaded, killed the regent, Tugu Lana Yiri, on his way to his new place at Savelugu and then enskinned Alhassan. The new Ya Na appointed Bukari Narkaw to Karaga and removed from office the sons of Na Andani who had sided with Yiri.[44] This version does not mention Darimani or say who appointed Yiri to Savelugu. There are other, mutually exclusive traditions as to who conspired with whom in these events.

All this exemplifies what Staniland, following Goody, calls "the Shakespearian pattern of uncle versus nephew or cousin."[45] For subsequent political conflicts, an issue in the stories is whether Darimani was or was not a Ya Na. If he succeeded his brother Andani, his enskinment does not support an alleged rule of alternation between the houses; if he "ran away," as no "real" Ya Na would do, he does not count. As Ibrahim Mahama justly says, "It is always difficult in cases of this nature to assess the accounts and to say which story is true."[46]

The Third Kingdom, 1905–1957

The Second Kingdom (1700–1900), unlike the first, was supported by an administrative structure, both commercial and political, "a complete Islamic system" provided by resident Muslims who married into the royal family, although Islam itself remained weak among the Dagbamba. During the civil wars of the late nineteenth century this system broke down as the Muslim scholars, the malams, retreated to local mosques. Through these mosques the Sufi-related Tijaniyya brotherhood became strong in Yendi, and it remains so today.[47]

Dagbon in colonial times can be described as the Third Kingdom because the functions of chiefs and the basis of their power had entirely changed. Warfare and raiding were no longer possible, the caravan trade died, succession disputes could no longer be settled by force, and a foreign power took over responsibility for the functions of government. British officials were not impressed by the statelike qualities of the kingdoms. Cardinall thought that but for the superstitious belief in the supernatural powers of the kings, the states would long ago have disintegrated. Commenting in the proposed Northern Territories Administrative Ordinance of 1930, the chief commissioner declared that the known chieftaincies of Gonja and Dagomba were to be called divisions, "the whole to be known as States." Mamprusi was to be treated in the same way and "will become a State."[48]

Chiefs became Native Authorities, "tribute" became taxation, judicial matters were dealt with under British supervision, and chiefs, called upon to promote agricultural development, were paid salaries; in 1934 the Ya Na's annual salary was £180. Yet the chiefs were not rendered impotent; on the contrary, the understaffed and underfunded administration relied heavily on the chiefs to carry out its policies and thus, as Staniland puts it, "let itself be made hostage to the processes, crises, and defects of Dagomba royal government." The king's control over the great princes had been strengthened; British authority could be invoked in support of chiefly goals but could also be obliged to take responsibility for difficult decisions.[49] The spirit of indirect rule eluded the chiefs, and the initiatives of district commissioners "triggered the well-trained reflexes of avoidance, compliance and straightforward abdication."[50] As Kwame Arhin Brempong says of Ghana as a whole, "By the 1930's it had become clear that the traditional rulers' authority derived not from the consent of the governed but from colonial ordinances."[51]

The division of Dagbon into east and west under separate colonial authorities created a bizarre situation made no less bizarre by Major Morris, the British commissioner, informing the western chiefs in 1901 that he, not the Ya Na, was now their head chief. In the absence "abroad" of the Ya Na, the Savelugu Yo Na and the Karaga Na assumed nontraditional importance, and members of the Andani branch acquired many of the important western titles. The British occupied Yendi at the outbreak of war in 1914, but it was not until 1919 that a settlement was reached with respect to a new boundary between the British Protectorate of the Northern Territories and Togoland, now controlled by France. Na Alhassan had died in 1917; it was time to find a new Ya Na for a reunited Dagbon. District commissioners argued about the succession, and while the chiefs were publicly refusing to take the initiative, privately they were lobbying for their preferred candidates. The candidate with the best title was Yo Na Bukari, son of Na Andani, but Bukari, being old and blind, was induced by the chief commissioner to cede the skin to Abudulai II, son of Na Alhassan, who had proved satisfactory as the interim "Chief of Yendi." "The elders did not, in fact, take part in the selection of the new Ya Na, and there was no attempt to comply with traditional procedures." Abudu strength in Yendi and Andani strength in the west intensified the existing tension between the two parts of the kingdom. Bukari in Savelugu was supposed to be accorded the title and honors of a Ya Na despite his "abdication," but it is important, in view of later assertions that only a man properly enskinned by the appropriate rituals at Yendi could be considered a true Ya Na, that Bukari was not enskinned in Yendi.[52]

In the early years of their administration of the Northern Territories the British tried to use local "chiefs" as their agents, designating as such anyone who came to hand or offered himself. The unsatisfactory results of this policy have been detailed by a number of scholars.[53] In 1929 a new policy of indirect rule was announced, which required, as shown in chapter 1, that efforts be made to discover the true constitutions of indigenous polities such as Dagbon. Peoples who lacked centralized structures were to be incorporated into neighboring kingdoms whose rulers claimed to have governed them in the past, meaning that they had raided them from time to time. In fact, only the administrative features of kingdoms were to be "restored" to their pristine form; political processes were excluded. As Ferguson and Wilks put it, the British assumed that "a necessary condition of the establishment of full control was the de-politicization of what by then had become 'local government.'" The factional conflicts essential to the processes for determining succession were described pejoratively as "succession disputes" and regarded as aberrations, a breakdown of traditional procedures, incompatible with good government.[54]

In this new political situation, the uses of tradition were directed away from the celebration of feats of *nam* (politics) toward the codification of rules (administration). Oral tradition was treated as equivalent to documents, providing evidence of fact for the use of district commissioners and eventually courts of inquiry, which presuppose a literate environment. Thus, in 1974 the Ollenu Committee, appointed to resolve the Yendi dispute, declared that "whether or not a system of rotation exists [between the Andani and Abudu houses] is a historical and traditional fact and a question of law," thus presupposing rather than examining the facticity of tradition and law.[55] Though transcribed from time to time for forensic use, tradition retained the presumption that its truth resided in its orality, meaning in effect that it could not be challenged by documents or contradictory traditions, which must necessarily be "corrupt." Writing in 2007 to the Asantehene, who had been asked to mediate between the Abudus and the Andanis, the Kuga Na (or his amanuensis) complained about "Foreign Researchers." "Researchers in the history and customs of Dagbon," he wrote, "are sometimes dependent on incompetent traditionalists and local drummers who do not scruple to mislead a foreigner and may tell him what they think he wanted to hear." The chief dismissed colonial writings as reflecting British policy objectives and quoted from Staniland's book a Yendi elder who said to him about his research, "This business has nothing to do with writing and you keep trying to put it down and ruin it for us."[56]

Na Abudulai II reigned until his death in 1938. To cut short the resulting intrigue, "the white man handed Yendi to Mahama," as drum chant put it. Mion Lana Mahama was the son of Na Andani, so the paramountcy returned to the Andani side for the first time since 1899, but once again customary rules had nothing to do with it. The son and regent of Na Abudulai put forward an equally uncustomary claim to succeed his father and attempted to prevent the new Ya Na from entering the palace, but the British stopped him.[57] When Na Mahama II died in 1948, the political situation had changed once again. World War II had exhausted the British and given Africans a much broader sense than they had previously had of the world at large. In the Northern Territories the administration had lost faith in chieftaincy and begun to introduce local councils as the primary administrative instrument. In western Dagbon, where education had made more progress than in the east, educated members of chiefly families were impatient with the rule of illiterate old men.[58] During the interregnum, the State Council, with the collaboration of the administration, put forward sweeping changes in the succession rules. Chiefs were to be elected, and the Ya Na was to be chosen by majority vote of a new Selection Committee and not by divination and a committee of court elders known as "the kingmakers."

The validity of this change has always been denied by the Andanis, who see in it no more than a plot by Abudus to guarantee their own success. They say, among other charges, that the State Council, with a majority of chiefs appointed by Na Abudulai, was incompetent to reach any such decision in the absence of a sitting Ya Na. The Informal Diary of I. W. Bennett, the acting district commissioner, Yendi, which he was required to keep, indicates a situation much more obscure than either side recognizes. Bennett seems not to have been paying much attention to the politics around him, being more interested in the charitable activity of the ladies of the Assembly of God mission, but he regarded it as settled that elections were now the way to go.[59] In fact, the choice of the new Ya Na, Mahama III, son of Na Alassani, was made by the old procedure rather than the new. Or was it? Ferguson writes that "as in 1938, the British intervened to prevent a long struggle and 'the Commissioner', as the drum chants say, 'gave the chieftaincy to Mahama.'"[60] Over the next three weeks Bennett repeatedly found it necessary to explain to the new Ya Na, himself (as regent) a signatory to the decision, what it meant and to dissuade him from abrogating it. Meanwhile, several chiefs wrote to the commissioner recommending that he himself appoint them to the skins they wanted. In fact, in June 1948 there seem to have been three different opinions as to the prevailing succession rule. Since then the Abudu position has been that the traditional rules could be, should be, and were changed to suit modern conditions; the Andani position, that the change was an illegal violation intended to destroy the nature of Dagbon to benefit Abudus.

Since 1948, therefore, tradition has become what indirect rule intended it to be, a timeless, prescriptive record—if only everyone could agree on which tradition. By 1948, as Anamzoya accurately puts it, "Dagbon could not boast of a single criterion acceptable to all as the mode of selection of a Ya Na which could be called custom."[61] Abudus argue for flexibility, but they will also decry violations of tradition, as they see them, on the part of Andanis. Meanwhile, chieftaincy itself had lost any traditional raison d'être except ethnic loyalty and nostalgia, at least at the higher levels, although village chiefs continued to function as leaders and arbitrators.

Mahama III died in 1953. Mion Lana Andani announced his candidacy and claimed, for the first time, that there existed a rule of alternation that entitled him, as representative of the Andani house, to the skin of Yendi. In a scene of intense political excitement, the Selection Committee (popularly called the "1948 Committee") chose Abudulai III, son of Mahama III, as Ya Na, even though he did not occupy one of the qualifying gate skins to Yendi, had not gained experience by moving up through the hierarchy, and was physically defective (reportedly he had a damaged eye and six toes on one foot and was not physically imposing). The Andanis were furious; having had one of their own on the skin for only seven years since 1899, they risked exclusion altogether. They began a campaign to have Na Abudulai deskinned (deposed), although in 1930 the mere suggestion of such a thing at the Constitutional Conference had "shocked the chiefs so profoundly that it was deemed inadvisable to bring up the subject."[62] One can always argue, however, citing "rules," that a particular Ya Na should not have been nominated; that if nominated, he should not have been enskinned; or that if enskinned, he had not been properly so, because some item of procedure had been ignored. Or with equal expediency one could argue that whatever errors had been made, enskinment was a sacred and transforming procedure, conferring *nam,* that could not be undone.

Yendi Enters National Politics, and Vice Versa

The campaign to depose Na Abudulai was largely waged in an entirely new arena, the internal politics of Kwame Nkrumah's Convention Peoples Party (CPP), which needed to pick up votes in the north and therefore became unavoidably entangled in the politics of chieftaincy. In 1960 Nkrumah, as head of the government of independent Ghana, attempted to settle the Yendi situation by means of Legislative Instrument 59, abandoning the indirect-rule approach altogether and laying down a pragmatic solution: that the succession should alternate between the Andanis and the Abudus; that only sons of Ya Nas occupying the gate skins should be eligible; that at least one of those skins should be occupied by a representative of each house; and that since the Abudus had held the Nam twice running, the Andanis should have two turns after the death of Na Abudulai III before succession proceeded in "the normal way."[63] The solution raised as many problems as it appeared to solve: it was not clear that alternation was the normal way, and this time it threatened the Abudus with exclusion, since after the Andani turns it might have been ninety years since an Abudu had held the Nam and there might be no Abudu sons still alive.[64] Legislative Instrument 59 did, however, keep the peace until in 1966 a military group that became the National Liberation Council overthrew Nkrumah.

In this connection, and in relation to the nonrational elements of *nam*, the wording of an official "statement of custom" in the name of the Dagomba State Council in May 1961 deserves attention. Signed by Na Abudulai III, it defied Legislative Instrument 59 by reiterating the succession rules of 1948: that the succession should not be by rotation of any type but by majority decision of the State Council and that eligible candidates included the regent (the oldest son) of the late Ya Na. "The necessary customary performances will then be done. But whether all performances are done or not the Selection Committee's appointment is final and the appointee becomes the recognized Ya Na as from the date of the appointment. . . . [The] custodians or Kingmakers can be represented in the performance of their customary duties and can be present themselves. In the absence of any of the above custodians at the installation ceremony the installation is still valid. . . . It is here emphasized that these Kingmakers have no power to choose or appoint a Ya Na. . . . The Selection Committee's decision appointing the Ya-Na is what makes one the Ya-Na." Succession to the office was thus reduced to rational-legal principles; the mystical content of *nam* and the function of ritual in creating it were abolished (see chapter 4). On the other hand, "destoolment of a properly appointed Ya-Na is *a taboo in the Dagomba constitution.* He is only said to be deposed when death takes him away. He cannot also abdicate."[65] In short, Abudus may rationally appoint their own king, but for religious reasons nobody can remove him; deskinment (of Na Abudulai) had first been proposed by the Andanis.

In 1967 Na Abudulai III died, opening the way for the resumption of old arguments. Meanwhile, it was clear that the chiefs had acquired a new role as representatives of their communities in the ethnic politics of the nation, new power as brokers of votes, and new economic opportunities as "owners" of land. By now the power of the higher chiefs in Dagbon derived less from the support of the government as such than from their relations with the national political parties: in exchange for rounding up votes, chiefs could count on the support of the party in power in succession disputes, influence in the award of government contracts, and freedom to control the disposal of land (see chapter 6). The factions lined up in alliance with the dominant political parties, each in the expectation that when its patron rose to power in Accra its interests in Yendi would be taken care of: the Andanis with the CPP, later the National Alliance of Liberals (NAL) and eventually the National Democratic Congress

(NDC); the Abudus with the Progress Party, later the New Patriotic Party
(NPP).

In the midst of close interference by the government, the police, and
individual Dagomba politicians in public office, and to the accompaniment of numerous apparent violations of custom, each faction's fortunes
rose and fell. Mion Lana Andani succeeded Na Abudulai III, but he died
four months later, and his enskinment was declared by a government
commission to have been "repugnant to Dagomba custom" and therefore null and void. The son of Na Abudulai, though not the holder of
a gate skin, was endorsed by the Selection Committee and installed as
Na Mahamadu Abudulai in 1969 with the support of armed soldiers and
police, causing a number of deaths. In 1974 the new government of Colonel (later General) Acheampong published a white paper based on a report by the Ollenu Committee, which found that Na Mahamadu had not
been properly selected or enskinned, so that his appointment too was
null and void. The commission accepted the Andani argument that in all
the murk of Yendi politics since 1752 a principle of alternation could be
discerned, violated only by Na Yakubu's killing of Na Sumani Zoli. In fact
the pattern in precolonial times, as we have seen, was one of progressive
elimination of collaterals; of the six transitions since 1876, British officials
had dictated perhaps as many as five, with more regard for the peace and
administrative convenience than for custom. To help with the appearance of alternation, the enskinment of Na Darimani in 1900 was omitted from the count, although it reappeared in Andani position papers of
2006 concerning the funerals of deskinned Ya Nas.

After consulting diviners, the kingmakers announced the selection of
the son of the late Na Andani II to be Ya Na under the name Yakubu
Andani.[66] In the course of several subsequent changes of government,
courts reversed and then, in 1986, with J. J. Rawlings's Peoples National
Defence Committee (PNDC, later NDC) in power, reinstated the Ollenu
decision. Na Yakubu Andani once again held the Nam of Yendi; the enskinment of Mahamadu Abudulai was declared by the Supreme Court to
be null and void, although he became at the same time an ex–Ya Na, a
status that had no precedent.[67] Many Abudus refused to accept the settlement; important chiefs refused to acknowledge the new Ya Na, and
some of them were deskinned in consequence. After that, in many villages, including Yendi itself, an Abudu hierarchy shadowed the Andani
hierarchy; adherents of the two sides tended to live apart, to have their

own drummers, warriors, and butchers, and to pray at separate mosques. In 1986 a number of bloody brawls broke out between them.

When the ex–Ya Na Mahamadu died in October 1988, Ya Na Yakubu agreed that he could be buried in the Katin'du but stipulated that his funeral (a separate event that is normally the prologue to the enskinment of a new Ya Na) would not take place in the palace.[68] The question of his funeral revived all the ambiguities of the 1986 "settlement" by the Supreme Court. Despite the apparent agreement of October, Abudus argued that the Court had ruled that Mahamadu, although an ex–Ya Na, was entitled to all the solemnities due to a Ya Na. That meant, according to them, that his funeral would be held in the palace, even though that would require the sitting Ya Na to vacate the place temporarily, which Na Yakubu refused to do. Abudu indignation simmered. After the NPP victory over the NDC in 2000, Abudus openly declared that in return for their electoral support they had been promised the deposition of Na Yakubu. As a matter of practical politics, it is not in the interest of any government to stir up chieftaincy troubles, but lower-level party officials may make such promises, and it is generally expected that voters will be rewarded for their support. On the other hand, as N. J. K. Brukum points out, "No Ghanaian government has ever taken the decisive step of punishing or reprimanding the leaders of any group that starts an aggression," and the government has been unable to develop a mechanism that could resolve such issues.[69]

Mahamadu's son, known as the Bolin Lana (a honorific title), who heads a shadow hierarchy in Yendi although he is not the head of the Abudu house, began, as the Andanis saw it, to act more and more as a rival Ya Na. The Ya Na sponsors the great festivals of Dagbon, which are governed by the Muslim calendar even though some of them are much older than the introduction of Islam. In February 2002 the Bolin Lana apparently aroused the Ya Na's indignation by holding his own celebration of the festival of Eid al-Adha, and still more by reputedly appointing chiefs. A factor in the dispute over festivals is that the two sides adhere to different Muslim orders and look to different authorities to decide the day on which a festival is to take place.

A month later a similar dispute erupted over the Bugum, or Fire Festival, a time of sacrifice to gods and ancestors. "The people hold not only flaming torches but also swords, cutlasses, knives, bows and arrows, and cudgels," writes Ibrahim Mahama. "The mood of the people is warlike.

The atmosphere is heavily charged and disturbed. It appears ominous to any person who has never witnessed the occasion before."[70] Both sides had already been collecting weapons. As sporadic violence continued, the government imposed a curfew and then lifted it. It became a matter of dispute which officials were responsible for this and other errors and what parts were played by the Ya Na and the Bolin Lana. On the third day of the unrest, 27 March 2002, the Gbewaa Palace, together with thirty-six houses, was burned down, and thirty people were killed, including the Ya Na. His body was dismembered and burned; parts were carried around town amid jubilation. Andanis accused the NPP of supporting, if not actually planning, the murder as an election payback. Abudus played the triumphal rhythm "Bangumanga," making it likely that the dismemberment deliberately echoed that of the Gonja king by Na Luro in the seventeenth century.[71]

The report of the government's commission of inquiry, headed by Justice Isaac Newton Wuaku, was published in summary form in December 2002. The proceedings of the inquiry make it plain that there was never any competent police investigation upon which a sound prosecution could have been based. The commission itself met far away from Yendi, in Sunyani. The report blamed both sides for provocative actions and various government agencies for incompetence but exonerated the interior minister and certain others. Andani spokesmen immediately rejected the report because it attributed the killing to the long-standing chieftaincy dispute instead of calling it a deliberate attack by the Abudus. Two men were later tried for murder but acquitted for lack of evidence. The government was criticized for saying little and doing less, but it appointed a committee of Eminent Kings, headed by the Asantehene, to mediate between the parties and to arrange the rituals necessary to any settlement. The first task was to bury the late Ya Na, whose remains had been gathered and put in cold storage; the burial could only take place in the palace, but that had to be rebuilt. Building efforts were hampered by hair-splitting over tradition and by the ability of the Abudus, who form the majority in Yendi, to mobilize youth to cause problems at will.[72]

Na Andani was buried in April 2006 with impressive pomp, and his regent was appointed, with the stipulation by the Eminent Kings that he would not have "power to appoint any chiefs or alienate any lands or other resources belonging to Dagbon State."[73] For the next five years the factional arguments boiled down to the question whether the ex–Ya Na was entitled to a funeral in the palace, thus legitimating not only his status but that of his descendants as sons of a Ya Na. The Andanis demanded that the government find and prosecute Na Yakubu's murderers, while some Abudus argued that his death had taken place in the course of a war, a traditionally legitimate political action. In March 2006 the Eminent Kings announced an agreement, signed by all parties, that came to be known as the "Road Map to Peace." Two months later the Kuga Na, the most senior of the elders of Dagbon, official custodian of traditions, objected that he had been indisposed and thus absent from the meeting; he could not accept one of the map's main provisions, the creation of a temporary committee, chaired by himself and made up of three princes from each of the factions, that was to appoint people to fill skins necessary to the performance of royal funerals but currently vacant. This, he said, was an unconstitutional departure and bore a "cunning resemblance" to the 1948 Selection Committee, creating a parallel authority to the existing Council of Elders.[74] In September he wrote again, providing a list of the locations of long-ago burials and funerals to argue that Dagbon custom forbade that the funeral of Mahamadu be performed in the Gbewaa Palace; pursuing this argument, he was obliged to introduce distinctions between normal and exceptional practice and between tradition, "which can easily be changed," and custom, which can not, although in neither Dagbani nor English is there any difference.[75] Abudus argued that the supposed sacredness of custom did not mean that it had not, could not, or should not be changed. They have had an advantage over the Andanis since 1948 in that their side has a greater number of educated spokesmen, though some of them have long lived in Accra or the United States, but the Andanis are far more numerous.

In 2008 neither faction was willing to give an inch. The Asantehene, evidently tired ("Over the last four years, we have heard repeated interpretations of Dagbon history from various persons"), proposed a Final Peace Agreement, which reiterated much of the Road Map; both parties accused him of bad faith and of exceeding his mandate as a mediator by presuming to tell Dagbamba what to do.[76] Meanwhile both sides threatened violence, development was impeded, some fifty titles were vacant, and chieftaincy itself looked less and less relevant to anything else in Dagbon.

Ghana elected a new government in 2008, the NDC replacing the NPP. Andanis expected that "their" party would punish the killers of Na Yakubu and hasten the enskinment of a new Ya Na, but for a long time nothing happened. The mediation of the Asantehene and the other Eminent Kings was suspended. Before dawn on 10 April 2010 an efficient military operation rounded up thirty men in Yendi, fifteen of whom were later put on trial in Accra for the murder of the Ya Na. Armed police defended the courtroom from Abudu and Andani mobs. One of the fifteen absconded; the other fourteen were acquitted in March 2011 for lack of evidence. In Yendi, Abudus rejoiced; in Tamale, enraged Andani youths burned offices of the NDC, and the city was temporarily placed under curfew. It was more clear than ever that appeals to "historical and traditional fact" were not likely to solve the problem.

Listening to drummers themselves, we have heard that despite the dogma of unchanging truth, there are competing traditions related to political interests; only a political commitment permits choices among them. For events since about 1865 we can see how such commitments inflect the story. The requirements of colonial rule deprived drumming of its traditional function, that of inciting chiefs in battle, and converted it into the semblance of an archive. The tension between these two interpretations continues in fierce debates about the nature of chieftaincy itself, "traditionalists" insisting on its heroic character, while "modernizers" seek to secularize it.

3

Tindanas and Chiefs
Ethnography

The ritual administration of *nam* to create chieftaincy is conducted by tindanas, who are also responsible for the conduct of sacrifices at territorial shrines. One of the arguments of this book is that the chief-tindana couple is fundamental to northern culture and its historical development. The ethnography of Dagbon, largely based on the assumption of cultural difference between invaders and autochthons, builds spurious contrasts between patrilineal and matrilineal succession to office and between the secular and religious functions of officeholders, respectively, chiefs and tindanas. This chapter questions the exclusive religiosity attributed to tindanas, discusses the similarities and differences between them and chiefs, and shows that there is a single, bilateral succession system that responds flexibly to distributions of power. The next chapter reveals certain essential links between chiefs and tindanas and attempts to rewrite the history of Dagbon accordingly.

The foundational myth of Dagbon, the story of Na Nyagse's conquest and the slaughter of the tindanas, was outlined in chapter 1. Since it is, and always has been, well known that the tindanas were not eliminated, the cognitive dissonance that allows general acceptance of the story needs to be explained. In African studies, historians and anthropologists have disagreed about conquests and their aftermath. Conquest stories commonly introduce a division of labor between the conquerors and the conquered, who are relegated to a religious role that includes guardianship of earth shrines and blessing the political role of the conqueror's descendants. This development as it occurred among the Mosse seemed only natural to James George Frazer and apparently also to most historians, not only in the savanna region but elsewhere in Africa. In Central Africa, historians, as well as some anthropologists, have been inclined to recognize as myths only stories involving persons we regard as supernatural and, conversely, as Hayden White puts it in his comments on historiography in general, to accept as historical events those "that lend themselves to the understanding of whatever currently passes for common sense."[1] Invasion stories have been too readily accepted as history rather than myth; Central African examples show, however, that the firstcomer/latecomer opposition is more constant than the stories that purport to account for it and therefore corresponds to a need that goes beyond historical contingencies.[2]

Meyer Fortes described the fundamental cleavage in Tale society as lying between the autochthonous Talis and the immigrant Namoos, who wore cloth in the style of the nearby Mamprusi chiefs, but he declared, "The cleavage is not an artifact of history but the expression of a deep-lying principle of social organization." Some clans held both *tendaan* and *na'am* offices (Talni terms cognate with Dagbani *tindana* and *nam*), and some offices had attributes of both.[3] On the political history of the Mosse, Michel Izard, following Dominique Zahan, writes that the kingdoms were formed by a succession of conquests, or purported conquests, that established them in an evolutionary process such that each wave of newcomers became "indigenous" in due course, after the next invasion.[4] Historians deeply distrust this sort of statement because it seems to deny that history happens, although in fact there is no necessary opposition between structure and process.[5] In later work Izard comments at length on the implausibility of the invasion stories and speculatively constructs more realistic ones that include more of what must have happened in fact. He envisages a much more complex interaction over time between "conquerors" and "autochthons" and embarks on a sustained and sympathetic interrogation of the traditions of the Mosse and their neighbors, including Dagbon, in search of the conditions of invention of *nam* as implied by the stories of Na Gbewaa and his sons.[6]

Time and Space

Instead of thinking of two kinds of people—passive, religious tindanas and their aboriginal followers on the one hand and a superior stock of belligerent, secular, political invaders on the other—we should recognize both as necessary components of a single social system in which locality and descent express the relationship between the spatial extension of society as a productive system (land) and its reproduction from generation to generation (descent). As Michael Jackson put it, "The complementary principles of social organization which are variously called lineage/locality, kinship/residence, ancestors/Earth, descent/territoriality, can be abstractly and heuristically polarized as a distinction between temporal and spatial modes of structuring."[7] Izard likewise says that the distinction between authority and terrain may reflect a history of conquest "but testifies above all to the inescapable divide in the ideological task of representing the relations of men to nature and of men among themselves."[8] Space means coresidence and common dependence on the forces of nature; time is the dimension of social reproduction, in which reference to the past serves as the measure of authority between senior and junior, firstcomer and latecomer, free and slave. People, individually and collectively, always identify themselves, find their place in society, by reference to an ancestral past. The "land" is timeless; its shrines have been there "forever." "The point to be retained," as Matthew Schoffeleers wrote in a study of the Mbona cult in Malawi, "is that African territorial cults constitute an arena in which people claiming to be 'owners of the land' regularly confront others who are considered 'invaders' and that these confrontations may lead to changes in the allocation of ritual positions. A further point to be made is that the term invaders need not always be taken literally, since it may also refer to an elite which rose to power from within a society."[9]

Noting the distinction in many societies of West and Central Africa between ancestor cults and cults of the earth, between "political rituals organized by political leaders of conquering invaders and fertility rituals retained in the control of indigenous priests," Victor Turner pointed out that ancestral and political cults tend to represent crucial power divisions and classificatory distinctions within and among politically discrete groups, while earth and fertility cults represent shared values and "disinterestedness."[10] Among the Talensi, where chieftaincy is not entirely restricted to the Namoos, Fortes says that in the clans that have it, "the most important thing is that every man be able to show his descent from earlier chiefs. For those with tendaanas, the common ritual bond with the Earth is what matters, although in most respects the ancestor cults are similar."[11] As Steven Feierman says of spirit mediums in southeastern Africa, tindanas "inhabit a sphere where the generations do not succeed one another in a linear order, as they do in the world of descent."[12]

The dynamism of northern Ghanaian societies and the historical contingency of their form must be recognized. All over the north the cliché that describes the relationship between latecomers and their supposed predecessors is that chiefs are chiefs over people, whereas tindanas are chiefs over land. The distinction occurs among stateless peoples such as the Konkomba even though both parties may belong to the same clan. The roles of chief and tindana and their relationship exist as models generally, but there is considerable variation in the dual system, from an extreme in parts of the Upper West in which political leadership is reduced to lineage heads, the tindana and an occasional opportunistic big man, to its opposite in Gurma (Burkina Faso), where the tindana is barely recognizable; among the Mosse, the two dimensions are represented by two deities, a married couple, just as in Dagbon the chief is often said to have married the tindana's daughter. The actual functions of tindanas and chiefs vary accordingly.[13] The introduction of a new source of power, such as horses or district commissioners, or a new threat, such as the Zabarima freebooters, might shift the relationship in the direction of hierarchy.[14] People resistant to authority, on the other hand, could, and in the north often did, invoke the taboos of the local shrine to keep chiefs at bay.[15]

Tindanas in Dagbon

In much of the modern literature on northern Ghana and in the discourse of northern intellectuals, the dichotomy introduced by early-twentieth-century anthropology between religious tindanas and political chiefs is ingrained. It carries with it the political implication that tindanas should be excluded from public affairs, especially the administration of land (see chapters 5 and 6). In colonial policy it was axiomatic that progress moved ineluctably from the religious to the secular. R. S. Rattray insisted on his distinction between "spiritual" priest-kings and administrative, territorial chiefs, whose level of irrationality reached no higher than superstition. The inquiries of officials such as Blair into the practices of tindanas went no further than to ascertain that they were matrilineal, and their need to see the chiefs as a secular bureaucracy in the making, to be incorporated in the colonial government, prevented them from recognizing the metaphysical nature of *nam* as an essential component of chieftaincy.

Despite the official story that the tindanas in Dagbon were eliminated, the existence of independent tindanas has always been known. In 1908 a British report on laws and customs mentioned the shrine of Kpala at Galiwe and those at Yong Duni, Taha, and Kakpar'yili in Tamale, all of which still claim to be independent.[16] In 1958 the State Council, presided over by Ya Na Abudulai, appended to a document drawing a line between the rights of chiefs and those of tindanas (as understood in Yendi) a list of some prominent tindanas, including the Tamale Bugulana, the Dakpema, and the Kakpar'yili, Tutingli, Taha, and Yong Duni tindanas (all in Tamale); Kpung Tamale and Yiwogu in Savelugu; the Tampion tindana; and the Gun tindana in Kumbungu. Many of these places can be located on maps 3 and 4; the only thing remarkable about the State Council's list is the number of well-known shrines it omits. A list compiled in 2010 in connection with certain disputes showed twenty-four of them, not including the major dynastic shrines Yogu, Bagale, Yiwogu, and Ga.

Several Dagbani words are variously and inconsistently applied to persons responsible for "shrines" (*buɣa*, s. *buɣuli*, hereafter *buguli*). The most basic term is *buɣulana*, pl. *buɣulanima*, "shrine owner" (hereafter *bugulana*, pl. *bugulanas*). A bugulana may be called or may call himself a *tindana*, but that term usually refers to an independent authority who is,

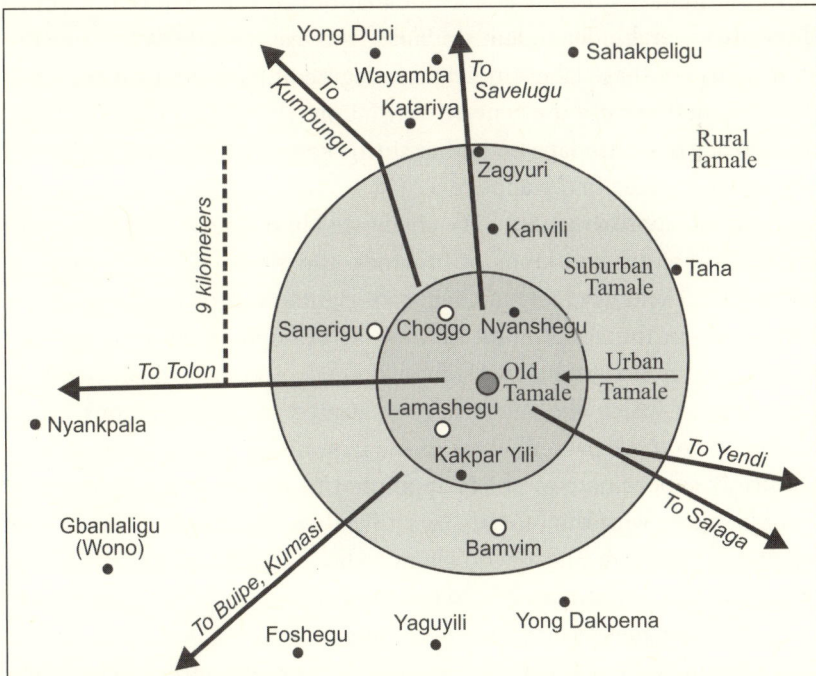

Map 3 Chieftaincies and villages in Tamale

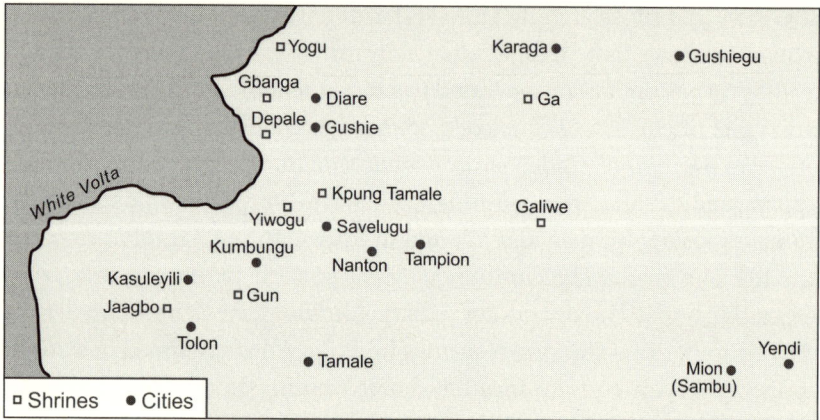

Map 4 Towns and shrines in central Dagbon

as such, a "chief," though he is not subordinate, as other chiefs are, to the overlord of Dagbon, the Ya Na resident at Yendi. A tindana may be regarded as senior to one or more bugulanas and even to chiefs and other tindanas. A *dakpema* is, literally, a "market elder," one who collects tithes from the market on behalf of a tindana, but in the vicinity of Tamale there are several independent tindanas who use the title Dakpema. The shifting use of these labels indicates a degree of local political competition; I sometimes use the generic translation "shrine keeper." An outline of the place of the tindana and other shrine keepers in the ritual practices of Dagbon is given in the appendix.

As a first approximation, to be challenged in the next chapter, we may say that there are two kinds of tindanas, those who see themselves as independent and as chiefs in their own right and those subordinate to Yendi.[17] From the Yendi point of view, as exemplified by Ibrahim Mahama, Rattray was right: in Dagbon there is a kind of dual mandate, according to which the rulers have delegated certain functions called "spiritual" to the representatives of the conquered. Shrine keepers who are firmly subordinate to chiefs appointed from Yendi, as at Depale or Gbulun, agree with the official story that their distant predecessor was killed and replaced. Those who claim to be independent assert that Na Nyagse's magical powers were no match for those of their ancient predecessors, whom he was unable to overcome.

Tampion is the one place where almost everyone agrees the tindana was spared by Na Nyagse. A small grove there is said not to be a shrine but is remembered as the place where the tindanas hid on the approach of the chief; unable to find them, he declared that he had come in peace, so they sent an elder to help him dismount. (This story of peaceful agreement is perhaps unique in Dagbon but foundational in Nanun and Mamprugu, as we shall see.) The tindanas are collectively powerful in the town, although it is the seat of a prince, the Tampion Lana.

In Galiwe, at the shrine Kpala, according to tradition, Na Nyagse approached and threatened the tindana but was warned of supernatural retribution; he was told that if he did no harm, the shrine would support and protect him and subsequent Ya Nas. In Tamale the local inhabitants, with the exception of chiefs and their praise-singers, insist that the area was never under the control of Yendi until the British parachuted in a royal representative, the Gulkpe'Na, in 1930 and that no tindana was killed. Na Nyagse, they say, came as far as Yong Duni and sent a message to the tindana, the Dun'Na, saying that he would come to kill him in the morning, but the Dun'Na sent him so threatening a nocturnal experience that he "disappeared into the ground." The shrine in the bush, called Gbewaa, marks the place, though it is not his grave ("nobody knows where that is"). In these accounts, Dagbon appears not as a single political unit but as a mosaic of chieftaincies, some of them subservient to Yendi, others independent. This is exactly the structure of the Mosse kingdom of Dun'Na, in which every chiefdom has its tindana and but there are also independent tindanas.[18] In his opposition to the chiefs, Eyre-Smith was the only colonial official to recognize that "the invaders having respected the Tengani areas, the Dagomba and Mamprusi kingdoms are therefore Federal States."[19] Confronted with such stories, drummers and royal princes say that the tindanas are in denial.

Several tindanas claim a special, cooperative relationship with the Ya Na, Na Nyagse's modern successor as king of Dagbon, resulting from such an early encounter. At Gbanga, not far from the original capital of Dagbon at Yogu, Yendi tradition says that Na Nyagse killed off the Gbanga tindana, called *yuɣimpini koligu*, "hedgehog's diviner bag," but the present holder of the office says that Na Nyagse found the tindana too powerful and was forced to withdraw. This tindana says that he is paired with the Yogu tindana, the custodian of Na Nyagse's grave; they attend each other's rituals and must appear together at certain occasions in Yendi, the modern capital.[20] The Tamale Guma Na at Kakpar'yili, a man said to be the Ya Na's "wife," must go to Yendi to cook for him at his enskinment; "nobody sits closer." For his services the Ya Na will present him with a hat, a walking stick, the skin of a "tiger," a horsetail, and sandals with red rosettes.

Besides these tindanas, there is a class of officially acknowledged "fetish priests," the Yani, or Yogu, Kpamba, whose lines are said to antedate Na Nyagse and who have special rights in connection with the cycle of royal burials, funerals, and succession. The Yogu Kpamba do not appear as such in the 1930 constitution, though some are listed as "divisional chiefs" or as "members of the Ya Na's judicial council." The senior member of this class is the Kuga Na, the highest nonroyal official, who acts when necessary as an interim Ya Na. As kingmaker he acts in concert with Kpatia Na, Tugurinam, and Gomli, whose offices are hereditary and not controlled by the Ya Na (see chapter 4). Most of the Yogu Kpamba have become secular political leaders over a long period of time.

Some say that the Ya Na must never encounter a tindana after the performance of that tindana's special function. In other places the chief is obliged to avoid the local tindana to some degree. The Nyankpala chief avoids the Wono tindana; the Kumbun'Na avoids the Gun Na, although he and two other chiefs supervise the divination that selects the successor. In Tamale in 1930 it was popularly believed that the first Gulkpe'Na appointed to represent Yendi had died after violating a taboo against meeting the Dakpema, but the Ya Na, eager to have his man in Tamale, said it was time to move on from old beliefs. In 1939 a district commissioner persuaded the chief of Tampion to accompany him on a visit to the Tampion tindana; he reported that the chief was very uneasy about it and that he and the tindana were not in the habit of sitting down together but merely exchanged periodic salutations. Tindanas also, or some of them, were traditionally obliged to avoid one another. Avoidance skirts the question of ranking between similars; it can be seen as finessing the difference between Yendi dogma and the reality that many tindanas are independent, but it also responds to the belief that both parties control dangerous powers. As independent leaders, tindanas are "also chiefs," and in modern times, as "owners of the land" they increasingly claim the same rights to sell land as chiefs now do (see chapter 5). In 1997 members of the new Association of Tindambas of Bolgatanga in the Upper East sent their representatives to a meeting to press for their land rights.[21]

In Dagbon, the "elimination" of the tindanas is a function both of the secrecy that attaches to *nam* and of the drive by chiefs to strengthen their control over land, a drive supported, consciously or not, by colonial opinions concerning superstition. Since 1954 national political parties have offered new political opportunities and profoundly altered the nature of chiefship. In this and other chapters I shall try to reveal the mechanisms by which the pursuit of such opportunities shapes social structure.

Shrines

Earth shrines are general, clearly ancient cultural features of the West African savanna. The Dagbani term *buguli* is cognate with the Bamana word *boli* and likewise designates a broad range of portable and even pocket-sized devices, as well as *buyuduyri,* fixed shrines marked, for example, by clay pots. Jean Bazin offers a provocative interpretation of *boli.* A shrine, he says (citing Heidegger), is what it is, a thing in itself, one that acquires its aura of apparent power by its singularity and its history of contingent events; it is the product of individuation, not representation. An "Earth shrine" in Dagbon is a place, distinguished from other places by some unusual feature—a particularly dense patch of forest, a spring, an unexpected mound of earth. Instead of a division of the world into material and immaterial things (a shrine, as opposed to a deity or spirit), which the Bamana do not recognize, Bazin suggests that we think of a scale of entities, both material and immaterial, from the unique to the commonplace. The more unusual an entity, the more it stands out, attracting attention and speculation as to what special power makes it so. Stories gather around it or him or her, successful petitions and remarkable experiences are reported, pilgrims and tourists arrive, contact is sought, offerings and praises submitted, souvenirs collected. The fame of singularity organizes the space around it; the most singular entities are divine.[22] Bazin's argument was anticipated by Peter Brown: "This cult [of relics] gloried in particularity. *Hic locus est:* 'Here is the place', or simply *hic,* is a refrain that runs through the inscriptions on the early martyrs' shrines of North Africa. The holy was available in one place, and in each such place it was accessible to one group in a manner in which it could not be accessible to anyone situated elsewhere."[23]

This is a universal phenomenon, exemplified by historic battlefields, Abraham Lincoln's birthplace, Devil's Tower in Wyoming, an anniversary, the artist Carl André's *Equivalent VII,* or the contents of a diviner's bag full of unusual objects (heavy iron artifacts from long ago, an iron rattle, an old bracelet, West African coins of George VI, and a cluster of stones bearing signs of past sacrifice). Bazin strongly opposes other ethnographers of the Bamana who assume that sacrifice to a *boli* is an act of worship at the altar of a god. One can always find an informant accustomed to European questions who will confirm such assumptions, but in ritual practice no one mentions a god. But what exactly is going on when blood is sprinkled on the shrine? Is the offering made to the thing itself? Do the adepts mistake an object for a god?[24]

That a shrine has a name does not mean that it refers to a fully formed personality, a god independent of the place; Bazin writes that this is "a religion of presence, not mediation." Describing northern gods in southern Ghanaian Vodu, Steven Friedson writes, "*Gorovoduwo* do not re-present, nor are they symbolic of, something else. Fetishes are there, in the world, in particular places and locations."[25] As Brown puts it, "*Praesentia,* the physical presence of the holy . . . in the midst of a particular community."[26] Michael Singleton cites the example of Smallpox, which in parts of both East and West Africa is addressed, not as something like a human being, but as "someone with whom one could talk things over . . . the aim of interlocution is interaction and not disquisition." African "religions" are about solving problems rather than about spirituality or worship.[27] A territorial shrine in Dagbon is a special place where people, collectively and individually, may address the dead of that place. "It does not matter, in ascribing 'social agent' status, what a thing (or a person) 'is' in itself; what matters is where it stands in a network of social relations."[28]

A fixed shrine associated with a local community is in the charge of a *tindana,* a term usually translated by scholars as "Earth priest" or, in colonial English used in Dagbon today, "fetish priest." The word *fetish* belongs to a particular context in the past history of European misunderstanding of Africa, and in the present context it is best abandoned. As in colonial times, it is used all over Ghana to described any kind of pagan ritual or its practitioner. *Earth priest* is not much better; the expression used in Burkina Faso, *chef de terre,* is a more nearly literal translation. *Tindana* may be literally translated as "owner of a *tiŋa,*" where *owner* means a person linked to, possessing, or in charge of something. *Tiŋa* is the terrain occupied by a human community as its place of residence and source of livelihood. As such it includes the soil itself and what science calls the forces of nature. *Territorial cult* is preferable to *earth cult,* since such cults, as Schoffeleers puts it, "are centrally concerned with the political life of a specific land area and since their constituency is a group identified by their common occupation of and rights in that land area."[29]

The responsibilities of a tindana include the performance of sacrifices at shrines located within his domain, normally a principal shrine and a number of subsidiaries. The tindana, who may also be called the bugulana, "owner" of a shrine, supervises while others sacrifice. *Shrine*, like *priest*, is not quite the right word. A buguli is a privileged place of access to the collective dead. To have such access one must know the name of the buguli, but it is not otherwise personified, and there is no history of its origin; supposedly it has been there forever. Minor local shrines, called *tiŋbani* (a word that also means "tract of land"), of interest only to a few people who remember them, may have no keeper other than a family elder. There is no personified and separate earth god, although *god* is used by Dagbamba when referring to a shrine in English. For the Talensi, "the Earth is impersonal, but 'alive'—that is, a controlling agency in the lives of men."[30] Some shrine keepers say that the name is secret and that merely to mention it is to invoke the shrine, which then expects a gift; others freely tell the name, and some shrine names are so well known that the Ghana Tourist Board broadcasts them.

Sacrifices

"Prayers" and "sacrifices" are offered to shrines. In Dagbani, *jem* means "to give presents to a superior person; to worship"; it describes gifts either to a shrine or to an elder whom one wishes to put in a good mood. *Jema* means "worship, humble service."[31] The sense of the word closely corresponds to the medieval meaning of *worship* in English, "to honor with gifts or respect." In that sense the word has been obsolete since about 1600; its modern meaning is "to revere as a supernatural being or power." Its semantic evolution tracks the progressive differentiation of the religious from the secular in the course of the Enlightenment. By the end of the seventeenth century the idea that there are two kinds of truth, religious and scientific, was well established in Europe, although the conflict engendered by the distinction continues to this day. In our present way of thinking, living elders are honored, but dead ones are worshiped, a distinction we would not have needed to make in the sixteenth century. Moreover, we now distinguish, ideologically though not always in practice, between honored persons, such as gods and kings, and honored things, such as monuments, flags, relics, and works of art.

The distinction between the natural and the supernatural is not African. The usual logic of sacrifice to shrines or ancestors is that of the gift, to please and persuade "the grandfathers" to provide some desired outcome, although nothing compels an elder or a shrine to do so.[32] Address to a shrine has two phases: *puli*, "promise" (also "to gamble"), when you ask for help, and *mali*, "performance," when you make the promised gift if your wish is granted. When the Foshegu village football team won an important match in June 2010, its supporters (Muslims or Presbyterians all) had to go to the village shrine to thank it. The annual festival to renew or "wash" a territorial shrine is *buguli malibu*, "shrine business." The verb *payi* used in this connection means "to wash; to thank; to praise."

Igor Kopytoff long ago and, more recently, Michael Singleton, a missionary anthropologist with extensive experience of Africa, agree in assimilating ancestor "sacrifices" to gifts made to living elders.[33] The older one is, the more numerous one's children and grandchildren, the more useful one has been for the common good, and the more important one has become as a point of reference for future generations, establishing identity and social rights and obligations. Elders are formidable figures, to be addressed with appropriate obeisance; offering beer, palm wine, or a chicken to a deceased elder is no more religious than offering it to a living one. A. W. Cardinall, more understanding of northern culture than perhaps any of his contemporaries, wrote: "Sacrifice, or rather food-giving to the dead."[34] The things given are foodstuffs, including domestic animals. The dead are immediate, all around, everywhere; their bodies are buried in the family compound, and the map of compounds in the village shows where they lived and how they are related. Webb Keane, putting forward an approach to religion that moves away from belief to focus on ritual language, suggests that it is language recognized by practitioners as unusual, which thus serves to frame "a qualitative difference between ordinary experience and entities or modes of agency that are situated across some sort of ontological divide." He admits that the line separating ancestors from elders may be quite blurred.[35] In fact, in Dagbon, not the vocabulary but the tone of address to the dead is different from ordinary speech but specifically similar to that of address to elders when making a request: voice very quiet, eyes lowered, attitude deferential. Only in praise-singing is the vocabulary markedly different.

In Dagbon, however, we also find a kind of sacrifice that conforms to classical anthropological models. What I shall call "sacrifice proper" occurs mostly in connection with the interests of chiefs. It is always bloody, and it is explicitly piacular and prophylactic, intended not to request a favor but to ward off a possible punitive event occasioned by some offense to the royal ancestors and their acolytes, the great drummers of the past. It takes place at a palace, for example, that of any chief important enough for a drummer's historical recitation *sambanluŋa* to be performed. The sacrifice is straightforwardly a killing, substituting for the drummer's own death; it does not take place at a shrine or altar, nor does it make use of blood to feed or strengthen anybody except fellow drummers, who get to eat the animal. The chief provides a ram, with which the principal singer identifies by holding its tail while it is killed; he may not eat any of the meat, which is shared by the other drummers present, and he must make the personal sacrifice of a white chicken before reentering his own compound. Lesser sacrifices are required to avert the wrath of the royal dead when shorter but still dangerous stories are to be told. At the Gbewaa Palace in Yendi, during Somo Damba, the first phase of the annual festival, the Ya Na, representing the kingdom, circumambulates a white bull three times; before each circuit, malams squatting around the animal recite Qur'anic prayers. After the third time, the king holds the tail while the animal's throat is cut. The bloody knife is handed to him so that he and other dignitaries may anoint their foreheads with it.

Nancy Jay has convincingly shown the association of animal sacrifice with male hierarchies, including both patrilineal descent groups and the priesthood of the Catholic Church. Sacrificing, she says, "can identify, and maintain through time, not only social structures whose continuity flows through fathers and sons but also other forms of male to male succession that transcend dependence on child-bearing women." Since it denies and substitutes for the role of women in reproducing social order, it should be absent or rare in societies with matrilineal descent. Jay remarks on its absence in several Central African matrilineal societies and shows that in matrilineal Asante sacrifice occurs only in connection with patrilateral relations (*ntoro, sunsum*) and succession to royal stools, not in connection with matrilineal descent groups.[36]

As we have already seen, chieftaincy in Dagbon is an almost entirely male hierarchy and is almost obsessively bound up with continuity over time. It is also an organization of competitive violence, as we learn not only from the praise-names of chiefs but from the frequency of actual violence in succession disputes. Sacrifice displaces the potential violence of chieftaincy away from individuals onto animals, although it also, as at Damba, may express the common interests of chiefs and the kingdom.

Insistence on the purely religious functions of tindanas, as opposed to the political and secular functions of chiefs, derives in part from the evolutionary assumptions of anthropology and in part from the modern claim of chiefs, especially the higher chiefs, to exclusive control over land. In reality, chiefs not only have religious functions comparable to those of tindanas but are themselves dependent on tindanas for the reproduction of the essential power of chieftaincy, *nam* (see chapter 4). Chiefs are also responsible for shrines. Traditional chieftaincy cannot be understood if its religious aspects are ignored, although in modern times they are less recognized and less salient. The missionary anthropologist J. P. Kirby, with long experience of Ghana, writes that when he first met the Ya Na in 1975, he asked him, because of his long robes, whether he was a Muslim. The whole court laughed, and the king said that no Dagomba chief could ever be a Muslim, because of the sacrifices he must make to the various shrines. Nowadays, the chiefs say they are Muslim and always have been, and there is—or was until it burned in the violence of 2002—a mosque behind the Ya Na's Gbewaa Palace, but the sacrifices continue.[37] Every year the Ya Na is expected to go amid a huge crowd to Yenndiri, which is in effect the territorial shrine for the whole of Dagbon, there to sacrifice a red cow and a black cow. If the Ya Na delays in doing this, certain birds fly about in Yendi, crying in apparent distress.

In the past, at the death of a Ya Na the ground was said to have "collapsed," but the Dagbani term seems to refer to the state rather than to the weather or the crops, for which tindanas have greater responsibility. (In Mamprugu, however, the Nayiri is expected to perform rain rituals.) The Ya Na is said to be a lion, his gaze so formidable that he does not look people directly in the eye, though in fact the late Ya Na Yakubu did so. Like all senior chiefs, he is addressed as Bimbiegu, "a bad thing," meaning that he is imbued with fearsome force, both physical and metaphysical, and he is hedged about with restrictions. In all this the Ya Na embodies, more intensely than any other figure, the mystery and danger of power. All chiefs, and tindanas too, are dangerous, possessors of *tim* (magical power, medicines) and *nam*, chieftaincy itself.[38]

Succession Rules for Tindanas

The principal difference between chiefs and tindanas is that whereas chieftaincy is a matter of hierarchy, competition, and potential violence, shrines are egalitarian ("for everybody"), and that nobody wants the tindana position, let alone competes for it. The sign of the tindana's office is a horsetail, which is said to go of its own accord to the successor, who has no choice but to accept it, "even if he were living in the United States." Among Talensi, elders compete for *nam*, paying heavily for it, but tindanas succeed by right of seniority or are chosen by divination.[39] In neighboring Burkina Faso candidates for succession do not normally compete for the office, which is regarded as "time-consuming, not very profitable and spiritually dangerous"; if one is chosen, however, he must accept. The "priest kings" of the Diola in Senegambia were likewise seized to be the guardians of shrines, but the spirit-imposed restrictions were so severe that only slaves were chosen or captured for the position.[40]

The egalitarianism of shrine communities is a function of succession rules, not of moral or aesthetic choice. Whereas in principle chieftaincy is a matter of masculine hierarchy, the office of tindana builds on lateral linkages through women. Succession practices for tindanas and chiefs form a continuum between extreme lateral diffusion of power through women and a potentially extreme concentration of masculine power in the Nam of Yendi. Since 1948 the Abudu faction has been pushing for what amounts to a rule of primogeniture, with the Andanis not far behind in this regard. The continuum is exemplified in what follows by the rules governing the succession of tindanas at Katariga, Yong Duni, Wono, and Gun, with others that are similar to each of them.

Discussing succession systems in English, Dagbamba use the word *gate* (*dunoli*) in three different senses besides the literal meaning, "entrance." The three royal titles, or *skins*, of Karaga, Mion, and Savelugu, whose incumbents may compete for Yendi, are *gate skins* to Yendi. The Abudu and Andani branches of the royal family, each eager to have one of its members become Ya Na, are also gates. In gates (lineages) of this kind, it is usually only the senior member who has a chance to take the title, but all members expect to benefit from the distribution of subsidiary titles and other benefits. Lastly, *gate* can mean a line of individuals who expect to succeed in turn to a title; this is often the rule for tindana titles, as we shall see.

Katariga: Women Only

Colonial authorities' assumption that they were dealing with two different cultural strata was based on a reification of patrilineality (son succeeds father) and matrilineality (nephew succeeds his mother's brother)
as contrasted social forms and markers of different evolutionary stages.
Rattray's opinion that the indigenous inhabitants of Dagbon were matrilineal was based not on evidence but on his idea that the invasion of
Na Nyagse interrupted what would have been the natural evolution of a
peaceful, kin-based social order to something like that of the matrilineal
Asante, whose "wonderful decentralization" he admired. In Dagbon, he
believed, the primitive priest-kings had mostly been killed off in favor of
a territorial hierarchy. Local intellectuals, aware that tindanas still exist,
insist that succession to the position is always, or mostly, matrilineal. As
an example they cite the tindana of Katariga, in a northern suburb of Tamale, who is always female (*tindanpaɣa*). She, however, explains that the
three gates are in fact three lines of women, each the eldest daughter of
an eldest daughter who was herself *tindanpaɣa*. The division into three
lines is not explained, although all three are supposedly descended from
the original tindana, whose identity is lost in the depth of time.

In effect, the three lines constitute a corporate group whose members
jointly own the office. The members are all oldest daughters of previous tindanas, except that sometimes a younger daughter may replace a
deceased sister. The succession moves in strict rotation from one line to
the next, which means that an incumbent is never succeeded by her own
daughter and no "mother's brother" enters the picture, as in matrilineal
systems. The three lines are not families, and no other relative has any
direct interest in the office, except that the tindana's sons may become
elders in her court. The successor has always been married off by her
father in the ordinary way, but when the time comes for her to succeed,
she must be a widow; it is uncertain whether, should she be still married,
the succession causes the death of her husband in some mysterious way
or she just leaves him.

The social effect of the arrangement is that the group of women as a
whole, the owners of the shrine, is linked by marriage to many, perhaps
all, of the families in the neighborhood that the shrine serves. In fact,
it is said that at the time of the annual renewal of the shrine, although
anybody may attend, those mostly likely to do so, besides male residents

of the community, are men who have married women from it. Detailed research might show how widely the marital alliances extend, but in any case one should not assume that the cluster of families linked to the shrine through women is thereby stabilized or functionally integrated.

An arrangement similar to the one at Katariga is found also at Depale, except that the chief, the Depale Lana, is firmly in control of the office of tindana and of the tradition relating to it. The chief appoints the tindana, who is always a woman, chosen from one of three gates in turn, each a line of daughters of women who have also been tindanas. Depale is close to Yenn'dabari, often cited as the place where Na Nyagse settled. On the occasion of our visit in July 2009 the chief summoned his spokesman (*wulana*), as an authority on history, to confirm the story that Na Nyagse killed the Depale tindana and replaced him (her?). According to Ibrahim Mahama, on the other hand, the Depale chief is one of the "original Kpamba," enskinned by the Kuga Na, whose position therefore dates from before the time of Na Nyagse or was at least contemporary with it.[41]

Yong Duni: The Pakpon Rule

In the most common system, the one specifically mislabeled "matrilineal" by inquiring British officials, a tindana is succeeded by the eldest son of the daughter who played the role of *pakpoŋ* (hereafter *pakpon*) at the funeral of a previous tindana, her father; normally the pakpon is a man's oldest daughter. Commissioner Blair, whose knowledge of the Dagbani language and culture was exceptional, wrote more than once that a tindana was always succeeded by the son of his *youngest sister*. This would seem to invert the normal insistence on the priority of the elder in all social relations.[42] Not having found a single example of such a rule, I have to conclude that he was mistaken, perhaps because of a linguistic error: though a woman calls her older sister *bieli* and the younger sister *tuzo*, a man calls both older and younger sisters *tuzo paga*.

Figure 5 shows that a tindana (1), like any other father, marries his daughter to a man whose son, the tindana's uterine grandson (4), will succeed him after the succession has passed to two other tindanas. A succeeding grandson stands in the relationship of *ma yili bia*, "mother's house child," to his grandfather's family, but he has full membership in his father's family; whatever power, prestige, and material reward attaches to the office of tindana will indirectly benefit that family. It follows that, as at Katariga, the shrine is linked to other families through women as wives and mothers and that power associated with it is constantly diffused rather than concentrated. This succession rule is an application of the rule (called *zuɣulem,* "adoption") in the hereditary trades that a woman, unable herself to be a butcher, barber, or smith, should return her oldest son to take her place. The Katariga rule differs only in that men are eliminated altogether from the office itself, to which they are "unnecessary." As a social form, a shrine is an unbounded network, not a hierarchy.

Although the norm is for the successor to be the oldest son of the oldest daughter, other factors may influence the succession. The oldest surviving daughter plays the essential role of pakpon at her father's funeral, but she and her partner on this occasion, the *gboŋlana* (the oldest son), should be the children of different mothers. Divination is often the medium through which choices are made as necessary. The number of gates (lines) depends on how many tindanas are remembered because they have grandsons qualified or eager to succeed. The Tamale Bugulana knows the names of his own grandfather and four of that grandfather's successors (see chapter 5); he also knows that of his own grandfather's grandfather, but he does not know the name of other bugulanas of that generation.

The pakpon rule obtains also for the Dun'Na at Yong Duni and the Foshegu tindan'Kpeogu. The tindana at Gbanga says that any uterine grandson of a tindana will do, not just the oldest, and that the grandfather probably had several wives. He does not know how many gates there are. No woman may be tindana at Gbanga, but no man wants the job, not because of any ritual restrictions but because as chief of the village the tindana is expected to deal with all problems and calamities. He must consult diviners about the sources of the problems and pay for the necessary sacrifices himself, nobody in the village being willing to help.

The shrine of the Nzogu Na is situated not far from the palace of the Ga Na, even though the tindana is associated with another chief, the Galiwe Na, in the sense that while that chief does not choose the successor and is merely informed, he must visit this shrine during his induction. According to tradition, the original tindana's wife gave birth to twins, a boy and a girl, and Na Nyagse married the girl, which is why he spared this tindana. The shrine is where it is because this tindana, we are told, was also a warrior, who moved about as such but settled here "to be near his grandfather the Ga Na." The story raises the possibility of

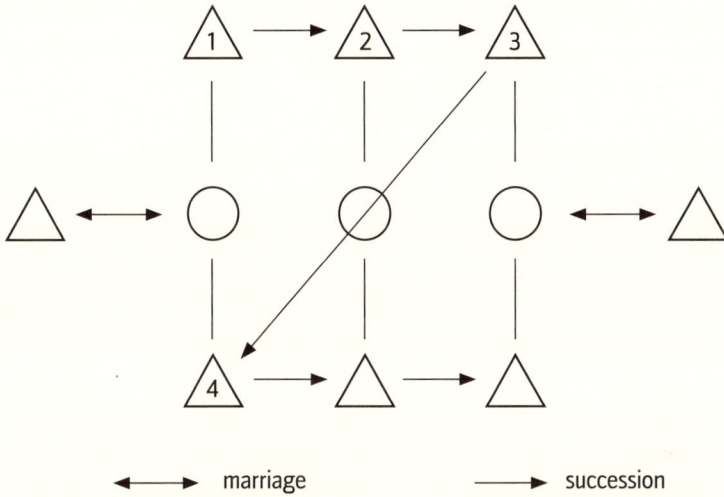

Fig. 5 Pakpon succession. A title passes from its holder (1) to his successors in the second and third gates before it reaches the son (4) of the original holder's oldest daughter, his pakpon.

situating a shrine in history, a possibility pursued in the next chapter; it is also paradoxical in presenting an "Earth priest" who is both military and mobile. In Nanun, tindanas are "also warriors," one of a number of signs of a common heritage.[43]

The Nzogu succession follows the grandson rule, with three gates in a cycle, each tindana normally being the oldest son of the pakpon of a previous tindana, but the actual designation is by a form of divination in which, there being no tail, the corpse of the late tindana is carried about until it indicates the successor. This is a variation on the custom, widespread in Africa, of carrying a body until it points, as a divination device, to the witch responsible for the death. The office was vacant at the time of my visit in 2010; the designated successor preferred to stay in Yendi rather than take the job, for which he might well have to provide his own sacrificial animals unless the chief helped him out. This is not a high-income shrine, and if it felt neglected in the matter of sacrificial gifts, it might do the keeper harm. While we were discussing the succession in the presence of the Ga Na, the late tindana's brother, who had been invited to participate, became increasingly agitated and walked out. He was afraid that the shrine, in an enclosure of sticks near the abandoned house, having no keeper to pacify it, might be annoyed by this talk and punish him. Because the office had moved on to the next gate, he said that it was for others to talk about it.

Wono: Alternation

The succession rule for the office of Wono tindana in the village of Gbu-lahagu, about ten miles southwest of the center of Tamale, is sufficiently complex that it took us two visits to understand it. The present tindana is a woman; as usual in formal situations, a man speaks for her, although she nods and laughs with us. The man is the bugulana of the shrine in the nearby village of Gwalenga. His situation is simple: there are only two gates, one a line of men, the other of women. The tail passes from one line to the other and thus from a man to a woman and back to a man. Wono is the important shrine, and the rank of the tindana is clearly superior, but he functions as her spokesman and performs her sacrifices for her; women do not sacrifice. At his annual festival, which takes place on the same day as hers, she attends, but he performs his own sacrifices.

Succession to Wono alternates between a man and a woman and also circulates among three gates, named after their "grandfathers": Sugre, Yakubu, and Kusahe. Although the incumbent is the daughter of a man in Kusahe, her right of succession is derived from her mother, who was a tindana before her. At her death the tail will go to the oldest man in Sugre whose father was a tindana before him. At his death in turn, the tail will go to the oldest woman in Yakubu whose mother was a tindana before her. When the tail gets back to Kusahe, the holder will be a man. It is said that the gate "opens" to him or her who is to come and close it. These gates are thus cognatic families that reckon filiation with reference to past incumbencies and, as the elders put it, "spread out" (*daŋ yeligira*) through coopted women. It would be very interesting to know the actual genealogy and affinal relations involved. The gates, as families, are evidently large enough that in-marriage is permissible.

This system differs from the pakpon rule in that the three gates are permanent and the diffusion of power through women occurs only in alternate incumbencies. When a woman becomes Wono tindana, she is coopted into her grandfather's family; if she is not already a widow, she must divorce her husband, who will have to find another wife. Because of the "difficulties," which include the expense of the annual shrine renewal and the requirement that the tindana stay inside her or his house after dark, nobody wants the job. The Wono tindana says that in her capacity as tindana she owns all the land between the land of the chief in nearby Nyankpala and that of the next shrine north, Sanga in Sagnarigu. Her elders say that the tail means that the tindanas were here before the arrival of the chiefs, that they owned the land and rode horses; they deny any visit by Na Nyagse.

Gun: Men Only

The other most common system is "patrilineal," in that there are (usually) three gates, ordinary families among whom the tail circulates regularly; there is variation as to whether it goes to the oldest son, divination is employed to choose the candidate, or the elders themselves choose. Under this rule, there are no prescribed links to other families through women, and power is not systematically diffused. In Gun, near Kumbungu, a diviner is consulted when a tindana dies. (The special grave vault located in a grove, in which the bodies of some tindanas, including the Gun tindana, are placed, is called *guŋ* pl. *guma*, hereafter *gun*, or *siliga*.) The three gates, taking the tail in rotation, are named after the "grandfather" of each: Gun Na Damba, the senior house; Gun Na Dakwogu; and Gun Na Sibrie, the incumbent's. The gate is known, but the designee may be a young man, as the present incumbent was; in fact he was not only young but unmarried ("but now he has two wives and a cell phone"). The elders say that they always wait until the successor-to-be is away from the village, perhaps working at a distant farm. If necessary, he will receive a false invitation to an event in another village; the elders will take the tail there, equipping themselves with bicycles for a quick getaway. No one wants the tail, because the tindana is severely restricted. He may not eat the first fruits of millet, yams, *dawadawa* (locust bean, *Parkia biglobosa*), and certain other crops lest he die, and he may never leave the village—for example, to go to market or to a wedding elsewhere—though he may farm within the village territory.

In a nearby village, a female tindana is said to be the "wife" of the Gun Na. In 2010 she was very old but still lively. She sits on a skin and has a very ordinary stick with no hook for the tail, a large new one that she waves about. It goes to the next of four gates, Nabila, Ashetu, Fatima, and Lahabila, all named after women. This system is therefore like that at Katariga, though with four lines of women rather than three; the successor is not necessarily the oldest daughter. When a death occurs, chiefs of the neighboring villages, including Gun Na, Gingaan'Na, and Napatua Na, inform the Kumbun'Na, an important nonroyal chief, and gather to consult a diviner, who selects the successor from the next gate. The tindana has an avoidance relationship with Kumbun'Na. Her establishment is a classic: her compound sits apart from a small village and at the edge of the remains of a heavy forest with huge baobabs. Under them are mounds that look like the remains of house sites; her *guŋ*, closed by a flat stone; and the shrine, an enclosure of sticks.

At Kpala, in Galiwe, there are three gates, each named for a past holder of the office: Luro, Yidantogma, and Sayibu. Because the successor is always the oldest son of the oldest son in the succeeding gate, he is known beforehand and is called Yikurigu (from *kurigu*, "iron"). The tindana himself wears anklets of iron links. The dogma is that the he does not die; his anklets are transferred to Yikurigu, who thereby becomes tindana, and it is said that Yikurigu has died. There is also a tail, which the new tindana "finds" in his house; the next day, he goes to the house of his predecessor to be invested. Investiture requires that he also go to Yendi, where the Ya Na gives him his red hat and a cloth.

The Kpala tindana died three months before our visit in 2009, but the successor had not yet been installed; his people were waiting for the harvest to be gathered so that there would be plenty of food. He has a double set of *timpana*, "talking drums," introduced to Dagbon from Asante in the eighteenth century. Normally a double set is the privilege of the Ya Na alone; those belonging to the Kpala tindana are said to recognize Kpala's high status and special relationship to the Ya Na. The Kpala shrine is not in Galiwe itself but in a smaller village, also called Kpala, although at the chief's palace in Galiwe there is a subsidiary shrine, Kpalibila, "little Kpala." So powerful is the Kpala tindana that long ago the chief of the village, the Kpala Na, was afraid of him and ran away to found his own village, Kpalipalla, "new Kpala." Besides Kpala itself, there are several small subsidiary shrines and two lesser tindanas, the Jevili tindana (a man), and a woman called Nangwogo tindana. She also wears anklets of iron links; she is a young woman and not a widow, but she had to leave her husband to take the job.

The well-known shrine Jaagbo in Tolon, which attracts people from a wide area, has an appropriately elaborate organization. There are four gates, each domiciled in a different village: Jagboyili, Tindan, Chirifoyili, Yogo. The tail does not necessarily go to the oldest man in the next gate.

Fig. 6 The Jevili tindana.
(Photo by the author)

When the tindana dies, oracles are consulted, and a family in the village of Kpaligun, which has custody of the ritual items, takes the tail, throws it in the doorway of the successor, and runs away to avoid hostility. In the fourth village, Yogo, there is a female tindana, who is succeeded by her daughter, not necessarily the oldest. This, then, is a single female line; there are no other gates. On taking office she leaves wherever she is living and returns to Yogo. She has a shrine of her own but functions at Jaagbo as assistant tindana, holding the water for the leading elder to pour the libation. The relatively great importance of this shrine may be due to its location in a frontier area that was never clearly Dagbon or Gonja until modern times.

Although there is little or no hierarchy, two or more keepers may be associated in a sort of collegial relationship with a central shrine, as at Tampion, the Kpala shrine in Galiwe, or the Gorugu group in Tamale. Tindanas in a given district may recognize one of their number as *primus inter pares,* but accounts may differ as to who installs whom, who the senior is, and who is regarded as among the number. In 2009 the tindana position at Gumani, on the northern border of Tamale, approaching Nanton, seemed to be collapsing. There was, or should be, both a woman (*tindanpaya*) and a man (*tindando*) operating as a couple and as a subdivision of the Taha shrine, but they had quarreled and the man had abandoned the tail and gone to live elsewhere. The woman said that she was not called *tindanpaya,* but *daŋkali* (from *daŋ,* "family," and *kali,* "custom" or "ritual"). Outside her compound are two hillocks, his-and-her burying places.

Two tindanas in Tamale, the Dakpema and the Guma Na of Kakpar'yili, are said to be like two halves of a calabash, investing one another. They and the Dun'Na are exceptional in that they have subordinate chiefs as well as lower-ranking tindanas; this irregularity is related to exceptional concentrations of wealth and power in Tamale. In Yaguyili, in southern Tamale, the shrine keeper is variously called *bugulana, tindana,* and *dakpema.* He calls himself Gorugu tindana, which he says means that he is the tindana for Bamvim, where the skin is that of the Bamvim Lana, a royal chief. He is the senior member of a group of four tindanas: himself, the Yentu tindana, the Foshegu tindan'Kpeogu, and the Jaʒi tindana (Kpeogu and Jaʒi are the names of the respective shrines). If one of them dies, the tail comes to the Gorugu tindana, who sends it to the elders of the next gate to hold it. They decide among themselves who is to have the tail; then, accompanied by some young and active men, they cast the tail on the elect and run away. The Gorugu tindana does not want the job, because of the danger: it is said that this tindana always dies young because of some inevitable fault in the performance of the rituals or some other offense to the dead. The only restriction is that he, like some others, must be at home after nightfall so that the dead may communicate with him. There is no avoidance relationship between him and the Bamvim Lana, though they should not sit long together. The tindana may dispose of land as he pleases, informing the chief afterwards, but the chief has no say in the matter nor any authority over him, or so the Gorugu tindana says.

The degree of autonomy of tindanas is as variable as the succession rules, the ritual restrictions on the officeholder, and other details of tindana practice. Where the shrine keeper is firmly under the control of a chief, he or she is simply one of the chief's elders, appointed by him after some degree of consultation with the elders of the next gate. In Tamale, the Choggo bugulana is subordinate to, and one of the elders of, the chief of Choggo. There are three gates, said to be descended from wives of the same man and located, respectively, in the villages of Nyanshegu, Gumbihini, and Choggo. The succession is decided not by divination but by consensus, supervised by the Choggo Na's senior elder, the Nyanshe Na, who tells the chief the outcome. Although this is a politically dependent shrine, the elders know no story of Na Nyagse having killed off their grandfather, and the shrine is said to have been there "forever"; maybe it has. The chieftaincy itself dates from no earlier than the mid-eighteenth century, but the villages may be much older than that. The shrine serves all of the Choggo Na's domain, although each village also has its own subsidiary shrine.

It is possible, but unlikely, that succession rules and other practices are all derived from a uniform pattern that once existed; there would have been no authority to enforce it. It is clear that in what Dagbamba call "modernity" many customs have been abandoned; there are indications that modern political competition has modified succession rules in

Fig. 7 Choggo Na: chief with caparisoned horse and attendants. (Photo by the author)

some instances toward a more dynastic, or chiefly, form, and there are some signs that in the past more women could hold the office. In Tamale, it is said that the Tutingli tail might go to a woman but that if it did, she would have to pass it to her brother; she, however, is entitled to be buried in the special tindana mausoleum, the *siliga*. This may be a masculine takeover in a situation of greatly increased political competition; some traditional stories suggest that the Kakpar'Guma Na was originally a woman. At Katariga, in northern Tamale, however, the shrine is firmly in the hands of women. Nevertheless, evolution does not account for the fact that independent tindanas are "also chiefs"; in modern times, in relation to control over land, their right to this status is highly controversial, as we shall see in chapter 5. In Taha the shrine elders say, pointing to make themselves clear, that although the chief of Taha, the Taha Na, owns—could give to others—land "on this side," the tindana owns land on the other side, where the shrine is.

Succession Rules for Chiefs

The succession rules for chieftaincy are complex, not so much rules as products of historical developments and political realities. The hierarchy of chiefs subordinate to Yendi has several levels. The skins of Yendi, Karaga, Savelugu, Mion, and more than a hundred others are reserved to royals (*nabihi*), sons and grandsons of Ya Nas and the sons of princes and princesses. Some families that were once royal and had access to Yendi but lost it or refused it have certain skins reserved to them. A small class of families, those of the Yogu Kpamba, "Original Elders," own their own titles; they are enskinned not by the Ya Na but by the Kuga Na, the senior Yogu Kpamba. Others, such as Sunson Na, enskinned by the Ya Na, are regarded as royal because they date from the beginning, though they are not eligible for Yendi. Titleholders enskinned in the Katin'du exercise a variety of functions in the complex affairs of Dagbon. The lists of titleholders given to me do not agree but include the following: Bagale Na, Kuga Na, Zohe Na, Gushie'Na, Ga Na, Gulkpe'Na (court elders and ritual functionaries); Tolon Na, Zandu'Na (military); Yelzoli Lana, Sunson Na (royals not in the line of succession to Yendi); Gundo Na (female royal); Namo Na (chief drummer).

By far the largest class of chiefly titles are allocated to commoners directly enskinned by the Ya Na and to those enskinned by lesser authorities. *Commoner* is, however, a relative term, since the holders of these titles are often royal grandsons, sons of princesses. People called "chief," *na*, include the headmen and elders of villages, each of which has its own hierarchy. They may include the headmen of occupational specialties attached to chieftaincies, such as smiths, drummers, warriors, Islamic malams, butchers, and barbers. With the exception of a number of the higher titles, both royal and commoner, enskinments are similar and relatively simple, although rejoicing and partying accompanies them.[44]

Candidates for a chiefly title must belong to the appropriate estate and must "contest" for it by visiting the authority who controls the enskinment and by distributing honorific gifts (*kola*) to him, his elders and wives, the people of the community, and influential mediators. A candidate for a minor royal title explained that he went to a particular chief, asking him to be his sponsor or front man in dealings with Yendi, but concluded that this man was playing a double game and was not really committed to the cause, so he chose another chief, with whom he went "at night" to Yendi. The point of going "at night" (meaning "informally" but also literally at night) is to keep the visit secret not only from rivals but from the Ya Na's elders, with whom one has to negotiate and who represent multiple other interests. It is universally said that to increase their competitive chances, candidates may spend considerable sums on sacrifices at shrines, on divination and on the services of Islamic experts who provide prayers and talismans, and on presents to the Ya Na's wives. Because it is important to be known, a candidate has a better chance if his father or grandfather once held the title in question or if his mother had been a local woman; this political reality often creates apparent "career paths" from one part of Dagbon to another. In principle, the Ya Na can appoint whom he likes, but local precedents and public opinion of the nominee are important; the people may refuse to allow him to occupy the palace if they do not like him, and violent confrontations may ensue. There is, however, no formal mechanism for soliciting popular input.

The ordinary Dagbani family is not really patrilineal; instead, it is a bilateral kindred with a patrifilial bias, descending from a distinguished great-grandfather or other ascendant. The literature on Dagbon often includes incorrect statements that the specialized occupations are inherited in the female line, misrepresenting the rule that a woman from a drummer family should return one of her sons to be trained by an uncle, whom he will then treat as his "father." Even without such a rule, there is a strong tendency to lodge children in the household of their mother's family or of another family with higher social status. Only in the highest ranks of the aristocracy does the family approximate to the form of a patrilineal descent group, because in situations of intense competition members attached through women tend to be excluded. The royal family is not exogamous, but in the past its princes deliberately built alliances by taking most of their many wives from commoner families, including those of tindanas. Though partially excluded, uterine descendants are loyal supporters; in return, besides sharing in the triumphs of their "grandfathers," they expect to be rewarded with titles appropriate to their own estate. It is therefore a mistake to think of Dagbon as built on a political hierarchy rather than on kinship; on the contrary, networks of family ties make hierarchy possible (see chapter 5).

When it is the turn of a particular gate to fill an office that the family owns, the candidate with the best claim is the oldest son of the previous holder in that gate. Primogeniture tends to create a gate within the gate; the junior line has a preferential right to a lesser title, but younger sons of younger sons are likely to hive off altogether.

The Appearances of Office

The universal sign of the authority of any chief is a staff, traditionally loaded with amulets, without which he or she should not appear in public (nowadays any walking stick will do). Chiefs also wear headgear with more amulets, bound in leather. These are not so much protection against occult forces, like those worn under their clothes by drummers and many others, as they are conspicuous advertisements of power already attained. The sign of a shrine owner, independent or subordinate, is a horsetail, often attached by a hook to a staff. Scholars have explained that the tail is a reminder of resistance to horse-riding conquerors on the part of indigenous people and their leaders, the tindanas.[45] In Dagbon, however, there are no traditions of armed resistance; tindanas either were overwhelmed by Na Nyagse or were able to repel him by superior metaphysical power. (Only in Tampion was there a peaceful agreement.) The elders of the Jaagbo shrine say that they have never heard even that Na Nyagse came their way. They, as well as others, say that they have no idea what the tail signifies. Several tindanas are entitled to receive a tail from the Ya Na himself. Tails in general are thought to be powerful; in one version of the story of Na Luro's fight with Kalosidajia he is said to have pulled a tail from his pocket to deflect from himself an arrow that then killed seven of his warriors. Cardinall found that among the state-less peoples of what is now the Upper East the horsetail was the sign of a big man.[46] In Tamale I have been told that the tail one is allowed to see at rituals, or as part of the costume a tindana assumes for photographs, is not the "real" and powerful one, which is kept hidden. Elsewhere, tin-danas and their elders denied that there was any other tail than the one on view, which was treated with no special respect. A few who say they are tindanas nevertheless carry no tail.

The horsetail is associated with a staff or walking stick, which is also the essential sign of any chief (including women), although the tindana version does not usually carry amulets. The Tamale Bugulana's staff is of iron, with a point and a hook, from which the tail hangs. I was told that a female tindana's staff had to be of wood, as at Katariga, but away from Tamale I found that most staffs were of wood, no matter what the sex of the holder. In Jaagbo the staff is of wood, with a carved human head at the top and a place to hold it by, and unusual in having amulets below that. The Jevili tindana's bamboo staff has no hook; he carries the tail looped over his wrist. At the Wono shrine, in Gbulahagu, both tindanas, the woman and the man, carry a wooden stick, but with an iron point and an iron hook for the tail. In Gun, the iron staff is headed by a brass figure said to represent a Gonja woman; the elders said they would be happy to tell me about it if I had the time and were willing to provide a chicken to inform the shrine that I was a member of the community.

The rest of a tindana's costume resembles that of any chief. It includes sandals with red rosettes and a red hat appropriate to a chief who has "reached his limit," that is, may not advance any further in his particu-lar hierarchy; since tindanas do not belong to a hierarchy and cannot be promoted, they have all reached their limit. The Tutingli shrine keeper asserted that he was of such importance that, like a high-ranking chief, he was entitled to use a parade umbrella, but he was bragging. The red hat is not related to the red fez worn by some northern chiefs recognized by the colonial government; it does not look like a fez, and it is worn only by those chiefs or tindanas who have reached their limit.

The actual investiture of a tindana appears to be simple. (Mahama in-sists that only chiefs are "enskinned," but people often refer to a tindana's investiture as enskinment.) At Depale the chief is firmly in charge of the event, whose timing does not depend on the season. He provides fowls for sacrifice and gives a cowskin and a cushion to the tindana, a woman

Fig. 8 The Tamale Bugulana. (Photo by the author)

chosen by a diviner from the next gate. She will also receive a sheepskin, which she can wear and may carry to sit on, but not a wildcat skin, which is reserved to men. The elders tell the new tindana what the grandfathers (*yabnima*) told them. The Yiwogu tindana, keeper of a dynastic shrine, is enskinned by a representative of the Yo Na (Savelugu), but the Ya Na is supposed to send the regalia: a gown, trousers in the striped cloth called "guinea fowl feather," a tall red cap, and a horsetail whisk. In 2001 the incumbent tindana said that when he had gone to Yendi with his elders to ask for these things, the Yendi elders had brushed him off with a small sum of money, so that all he had to show me was the handle of an old whisk, with no hair left. The Ya Na and a few other high-ranking chiefs once sat on lion skins; tindanas and other male shrine keepers may sit on "tiger" (wildcat) skins, as well as on cowskins, as all chiefs do.

A tindana's court, assembled in his or her entrance hall, or *zoŋ*, resembles that of any chief, with the exception that a female tindana, as at

Katariga, does not preside in her own court but sits to one side while the men do the talking. It is said, nevertheless, that her elders are afraid of her powers. The elders are the usual, that is, a Wulana and as many other titleholders as possible, depending on the importance and ambition of the tindana, possibly including (despite the professed peaceful nature of shrines and tindanas) a *kambon'na,* or chief warrior, who, being of Asante origin and thus a "foreigner," sits on a chair, and, in Tamale at least, a malam to offer Muslim prayers. A peculiarity of the Katariga skin is that except for the Kambon'Na, everyone in the entrance hall sits directly on the floor, not on a mat or a skin. At Yong Duni the court includes the Wulana, the Kambon'Na, a drummer, the chief butcher, the chief blacksmith, and a malam, although the elders are well known to be pagans and unashamed drinkers. The Choggo Bugulana is a devout Muslim, and his malam recites prayers before the annual renewal of his shrine.

The organization of the reception hall is always the same: The entrance should face south, because that is the direction of progress. On the west side is space for one or more horses, if the chief has them, and the young men who look after them. A tindana is not expected to have a horse, but the Sang'Na in Sanerigu, who describes himself as a tindana and a chief, has one. The Taha tindana told me that at the time of his annual festival he would ride a horse if he had one, and the Jakpahi tindana does ride one when he takes the new Gbulun Na to his palace (see chapter 4). In the modernized entrance halls of well-to-do chiefs, a special gallery is provided for the horse, with a window into the chamber "because the horse likes to know what is going on." If the chief happens to have traveled, one can still call upon him at his palace, "because his horse is there." All official functions take place in the entrance hall, except when a large gathering requires the use of the pavilion opposite the entrance. Beside the entrance is another, small one for everyday use, especially by women.

Inside, the chief sits on a platform facing the entrance. In front of him are his household elders: the Wulana, the Kpanalana, and others. Subchiefs sit on the floor on the chief's left, except for the Kambon'Na. To the chief's right, another doorway opens into the compound, from which a young woman, the *komlana* (lit. "owner of water"), may be summoned to offer a calabash of water to visitors. Visitors present *kola*—both kola nut and cash "on top"—to the Wulana and explain their business; the chief distributes kola nut to them and to his elders. The proceedings are formal but leave room for humor and for honorific variations on the routine. Elders always skim off part of what is given to them to present to the chief, often making a joke of it: "I was on my way to the palace when a gust of wind blew away some of the money." Elders are often literally elderly retired farmers for whom skimming is their "farm." The elders at Yendi are notorious for their greed and for their ingenuity in discovering "traditional" pretexts for extracting money.

Talensi tindanas were forbidden to wear cloth, which was associated with the "immigrant," horse-riding Namoos; nowadays they wear clothes, but with skins over them. Tindanas in Dagbon are said to be guardians of tradition, but the principal sign of this supposed responsibility is the practice of closing the entrance hall not with a wooden door but with a mat made of canes or bundles of reeds. The doorway itself should be oval in shape, as all doors were before carpentry was introduced in the twentieth century. In practice there may or may not be a cane door, and comments on the matter were inconsistent. Some said that the door had to be of cane so that the tail, in its rush to find its next owner after the death of his predecessor, would not be impeded. Others shrugged and excused their wooden door by saying that modernity was overcoming tradition. The Dun'Na at Yong Duni said that because he was the senior tindana in Tamale, he could do as he pleased. At Gumani, the shrine owner's compound had only one cane mat, which blocked an opening in the wall through which her body would be carried to the burial place on a nearby hillock. Besides the cane door, if any, I have been told that tradition requires natural stones, not cement blocks, at the place of sacrifice. There is no tradition of tindanas' being forbidden to wear cloth.

Traditionally, a man is buried in his compound, although in urban areas nowadays legal burial takes place only in the cemetery. A chief's compound is appropriately larger and more complex than an ordinary compound; houses for his wives and perhaps certain officials are located on the west side, while on the east are rooms that shelter the graves of previous chiefs. A tindana may have a special grave, *siliga*, consisting of a deep hole with hollow places like shelves, in which successive corpses are placed. The grave may have a hemispherical top, or "head," above the surface, or it may be closed with simply a large flat stone. The Katariga tindana is buried in her compound, "because she is also a chief." The Kpala tindana at Galiwe has a special burial place but no *siliga*. Gravedigging is done by certain families called *kasiyiriba*, but the burial of tindanas is handled by specialists called *siliga kasiyiriba*. The Reverend A. H. Candler, in a long memoir on Tamale tradition based on what he was told in 1930 by J. S. Kaleem, a son of Dakpema Nsungna, wrote that these gravediggers underwent rigorous training that included drinking a potion of disgusting materials, after which those who survived were thought to be immune to disease. After a burial they were considered to be unclean for a hundred days.[47] Kaleem's son Henry told me, after the death of Dakpema Richard Alhassan in 2008, that traditionally each of the local tindanas would send someone to be initiated but that no new vault undertakers had been initiated since the previous Dakpema's death. At the burial of a Dakpema, after the vault is closed, the funeral calabash, *kulŋmana*, containing three stones from the grave (four in the case of a woman) and the cloth that covered the body, is placed on the head of a young woman, where it proceeds to dance by itself, to lead her to the pavilion where sit the assembled chiefs and dignitaries and to indicate which of them is to conduct the funeral. In 2009 it selected Choggo Na.

Shrines Territorial and Dynastic

In Dagbon there are three kinds of shrines—territorial, dynastic, and household, as well as "medicines," which are also called shrines—and two

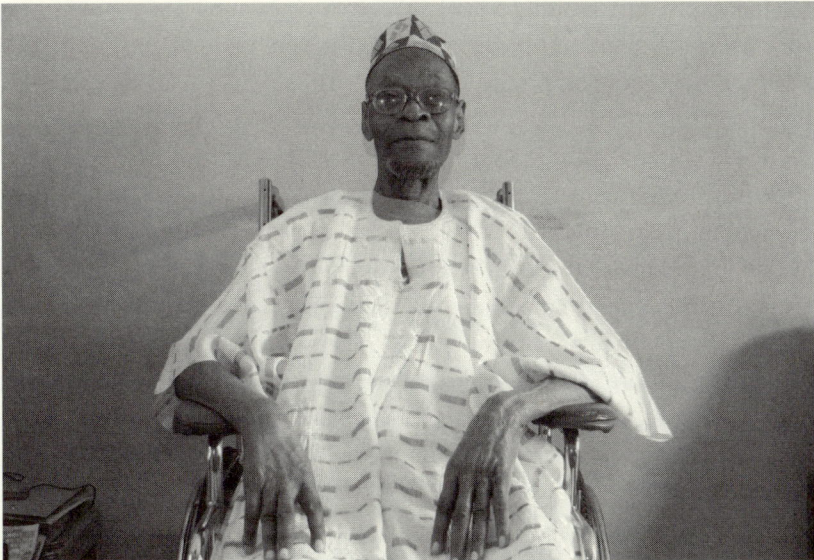

Fig. 9 The late Dakpema Richard Alhassan. (Photo by Lindsay Cameron)

kinds of sacrifice—gifts offered at shrines and sacrifice proper, which is expiatory, performed on behalf of chiefs and drummers (see the appendix). Both territorial and dynastic shrines are kept by tindanas. Territorial shrines are permanently located at a particular place, although they may be appealed to by anybody; dynastic shrines are dedicated to the spirits of past kings, through whom *nam,* the power of chieftaincy, is handed down.

Through the shrines they supervise, tindanas are expected to ensure collective economic well-being by appealing for rain and fending off pestilence. The tindana must be approached by anyone who wishes to make an offering at a shrine. Tindanas are associated with the weather, markets, and the first fruits of the agricultural (rainy) season. To make first fruits safe for the Ya Na and his elders to eat, the Kpala tindana goes to Yendi, where he offers the Ya Na and his assembled elders a mixture of millet flour and honey to taste. In return, the Ya Na gives him a cloth and a hoe blade. At his installation a tindana is carried to the market on men's shoulders; in Tamale, his or her followers will raid any stall that has not been shuttered for the occasion. Tindanas are entitled, traditionally at least, to market dues, collected by an appointed *dakpema.*

Normally a territorial shrine complex includes a major shrine in the bush, considered to be male; sometimes it is situated on a small hill, often in a grove surrounding a baobab tree. Shrines are often situated near springs or streams. A subsidiary shrine, female, is usually located at or near the tindana's compound, which in rural areas is usually at a short distance from the village. Shrines have associated animals, called "totemic" in colonial ethnography. These animals, which are remarkable in some way, often because they are dangerous, include elephants, crocodiles, pythons, monitor lizards, lions, and swarms of bees. Most of these are no longer physically present. At Tampion the two shrines, male and female, control the market and will not allow it to be swept or the trash burned except once a year; they send bees to attack anyone who tries to collect taxes there. They also dislike electricity, "which is why the street lighting doesn't work." The annual festival alternates between the male and female shrines, the latter being more "pacific." The male shrine, located in the bush, so I was told, is Ngandabuguli, "Very Big Shrine," but Cardinall was told its name was Wunwon. The stockaded shrine of the female, Zinyebo, is in the village. Its entrance is deliberately very low, obliging one to stoop to enter after removing hat and shoes. Zinyebo's familiar animal is a monitor lizard. Neither shrine is in a grove; a nearby grove, possibly an old house site, toward which the tindanas' doors face, or seem to, is only of historical interest: when Na Nyagse arrived with his warriors, the tindanas hid in it, and he could not find them, so he declared that he had come in peace. The male and female shrines have a male and a female tindana, respectively, "so no discrimination." In fact, men perform the sacrifices at both shrines, and the woman is allowed to provide only water.

In Choggo the guardian is a *gboŋli* (wildcat). The Bugulana, while officiating at the shrine, sits on a wildcat skin. He tells the story of a certain old woman who was captured and taken to Ouagadougou, where she constantly prayed for the shrine to deliver her; eventually a "tiger" appeared and led her to safety. When he himself was a small child, a young woman gathering wood in the forest where the shrine is located found a cub, which she took home, thinking of it as a cat, but she was told that it was no cat and to take it back; since then no tigers have been seen. At Tanyam, in Savelugu, a now desiccated swamp, there used to be turtles, which were forbidden as food; it was said that the meat would remain raw no matter how long it was cooked. Of the dozen or so shrines supervised by the Tamale Dakpema, Nyab'gurugbaya, "Grandfather Gurugbaya," is regarded as the special guardian of Tamale and is the subject of a popular song. It is said to be the home of a gigantic serpent that emerges from time to time to circle the city. The British built a bungalow near the shrine but found that it was "haunted"; nobody spends the night there. The shrine's "totemic" animals are crocodiles, pythons, lions, and monitor lizards. "They hold it together," and no local person would eat of them should the opportunity arise.

There are innumerable small shrines everywhere. Many have fallen into disuse, although it is said that no one could build on those sites. I suspect that some shrines are the sites of ancient homesteads, but people deny this possibility; shrines were given by God and have been there forever. Individuals may invoke shrines at any time, on the advice of a diviner and with authorization from the keeper, if there is one. A few shrines have no invested keeper but are tended by elders who offer sacrifices as necessary. One such is Tindangun (tindana's grave?), located south of Diare, which is looked after by the Ditilampelana and his brothers, a family appointed to this function by a former chief. The title has no meaning, and the holder has no horsetail, no red hat, and no cane door, nor is there a "female" shrine in the village to complement the one in the bush. The shrine, on the top of a large hillock in the midst of an extensive grove, is marked by a number of lateritic stones, on which at the time of my visit white chicken feathers remained from a recent sacrifice to pray for rain. The hillock is home to a family of aardvarks, which feed in nearby anthills. According to Goody, artificial mounds some thirty feet in diameter and fifteen feet high, such as this one, are scattered all over central Gonja and Dagomba. They may have been dwelling mounds built for defense.[48]

Whereas local shrines are explicitly nonhierarchical, "for everybody," and oriented toward the collective dead of the community, dynastic shrines are places where princes send sacrifices to seek the favors of their forebears, even though royals may not themselves visit them lest they be invited to join the dead. The king must cause sacrifices to be offered to the royal ancestors at these shrines from time to time, especially at his installation. It is said that on these occasions sounds of festivity can be heard, emanating from the village of the dead. Princes eager for political advancement may also present personal sacrifices. These also are basically gifts in return for favors or in expectation of them, but at the same time they celebrate the exclusive claims of a dominant group that trace their rights to an original conquest.

The most important dynastic shrine is at Bagale, a body of water northwest of Yendi where it is said that the souls of all past Ya Nas, beginning with Na Sitobu, dwell in a special house. The shrine keeper is the Bagale Na, one of the Yogu Kpamba, Original Elders. "The Bagele Na is respected more than any Dagomba Chief. He is called Yaba (Ancestor [grandfather]) by reason of his being attendant on the tomb of Sitibo. A Na bihi [sic; royal prince] must never go to Bagele, nor may a Chief of Bagele ever see the Na of Yendi."[49]

On the other hand, the graves of Sitobu and Nyagse are said to be at Yiwogu and Yogu, respectively, according to the keepers of those shrines. Traditions tell us that this or that prince "died" in more than one place and may have "disappeared" at yet another; evidently they are not to be taken literally. When I visited Yiwogu in 2001, the progress of the conversation was interesting in its own right. The elders alleged that Na Nyagse had lived at Yiwogu first, before going to Yogu and building Yenn'dabari. And why would he have done that? Well, no one knows where his father, Sitobu, was buried. Or perhaps people do know but are afraid to reveal the secret. Conversation drifted toward the possibility that these elders did know the location of the grave of "the one we were talking about" and eventually the admission that he is buried *here*. This, they revealed, is the original capital, and its chief, the Yiwogu Na, is the Ya Na's tindana. That is why after his enskinment the Ya Na must send for sacrifices to be performed here (as he may also do on other occasions and to other places).

The shrine is in three parts:

1. Takarfen (lit. "hoof"; no explanation forthcoming), a substantial grove with large trees, including a huge baobab. It is the place where the tindana is enskinned, and it is said to be the original Katin'du, the house in the palace at Yendi where the Ya Na is enskinned nowadays. There are swarms of bees there, which keep quiet and harm no one while the ceremony is in progress. Thereafter the tindana is forbidden to eat honey from this grove, nor does anyone else in the village eat it lest the tindana be indirectly contaminated, but anyone else may do so.

2. Kuntili, the grave of Sitobu. Only princes of Yendi (*nabihi*) may address it, and they must use intermediaries lest the spirits recognize their own and take them away. (Presumably, supplicants are aware, despite all the hedging we were hearing, that this is the grave of Sitobu.) Kuntili is also the name that an almost forgotten tradition assigns to a character it calls "the first Ya Na" (see chapter 4). The grave site is a small cluster of bushes with a termite hill in it. The essential feature is a flat stone with traces of sacrifice (guinea fowl feathers). No words are used in addressing the shrine, only the drum language, "because of Na Nyagse." The drummer who knows the invocation comes from a drummer family in Savelugu; he uses a special drum kept in a lionskin bag. No other drum may be sounded in the vicinity of the shrine, and a chief passing by must proceed in silence (the horse of a certain chief who inadvertently broke the rule died after he arrived home).

3. Buguli Kpahinyaŋ, a large grove of mostly young trees containing a "hearth" of stones with obvious signs of sacrifices. Ordinary people come to appeal to this shrine.

At Yogu (Yenn'Yogu, the Yogu that was the original Yendi) they say that the idea of killing off the tindanas came to Na Nyagse as he was hoeing his field; he left his hoe there, where it still lies, and went off to war. Nobody dares touch the hoe, which is said to stand on end to warn of the impending death of an important chief. (Official tradition says that Na Nyagse only settled in Yogu *after* killing the tindanas.) In the village, kept in the house of whoever happens to be the Yogu Na, the chief, there is a bundle tied with a very modern nylon cord that includes Na Nyagse's spear, knife, and "walking stick," a thin baton. There is also his stool, which is not of the Akan pattern; it is low and flat and has a knob that serves as a handle on either end. The chief takes it with him to Ga when he is enskinned by his superior, the Ga Na, another of the Yogu Kpamba. These things are not handled in any special way and are not kept in a special place. While they are not much to look at, they testify to the presence here of Na Nyagse.[50]

Na Nyagse's grave is at some distance, in a small grove on a knoll, clearly the remains of buildings, under an enormous baobab. Approaching the tomb of their "grandfather," Dagbamba remove their shoes, but others need not. No prince may come here. The tomb consists of a small hut on the verge of ruin, square rather than round, with a badly thatched roof repaired recently but carelessly. In the wall is a crawl hole, the entrance and only opening. The shrine resembles the "miniature homestead" that symbolizes the ancestral home of a Talensi clan.[51] Tradition requires that if the shrine has to be rebuilt, the walls and thatch must be completed in a single day. Only the tindana may enter, presumably to pour a libation, so nobody else knows what, if anything, is inside. The spirits of dead Ya Nas are said to inhabit the shrine and to be active at night; one of the titles of the Ya Na is Yogu Lana, "owner of Yenn'Yogu." Sometimes nearby villagers hear drumming at night, though inquiry reveals that no village among the living has in fact been drumming. Such drumming presages the death of an important chief; the song that is drummed is his praise-name, announcing his arrival among his relatives. When animals sent by the Ya Na or another royal are sacrificed here, the surrounding villages eat well.

Another shrine that royals must avoid is dedicated to Tuvieligu, the original Ga Na. The chief himself, who is one of the Yogu Kpamba, performs the annual renewal, or "washing," together with his own elders. The story of his title is best told in the words of the drum chant as translated by Abdulai Salifu:

King Nyagse fought stealthily
And got to Ga that day;
And when Ga folk heard of him, they all fled,

Leaving behind a headstrong boy to watch over the *ga* (monkey-guava)
    tree.
And when the king descended beneath the tree that day,
And the child ate and threw some dry fruits at the king.
And the king raised his head and looked and saw the child
And ordered that they bring the child down.
And they brought the child down,
And he asked the child, where are your townsfolk?
And he said, My Lord, we always come to eat these fruits,
But today I came and did not see anyone.
And the king got a white robe and robed the child that day.
And a hooded cape and adorned the child that day,
And a staff and gave it to the child that day
And made him Ga chief.
And we say, Ga Tuvieligu chief's father is Sitobu's son Na Nyagse.[52]

The story as the chant tells it, and as the present chief told it to me, did
not mention that the title falls in the class of the *namoyila,* court officials at Yendi who were formerly slaves and eunuchs. The shrine, under
a young baobab, is supposed to be on the spot where the *ga* tree stood.
It is the center of the village of Ga. The ground around it is left clear; no
one builds there. The shrine itself, on a large mound, is a small, round
building made of unplastered mud bricks, thatched; the small doorway is
open. Only those performing sacrifice enter, but it is supposed to contain
the relics of Na Nyagse in the form of amulets and a bow with arrows,
formerly located in a small fenced area nearby that was cleared to make
way for the modern road. The place is thus at least as much a shrine to
Na Nyagse as to his slave chief. Continuing on his invasive progress, the
king went from Ga to Yenn'Yogu, which is why the Ga Na installs the
Yogu Na; thereafter they avoid one another.

The explicit association of dynastic shrines with the history of the
kingdom, their use as sacrificial sites in connection with royal enskinments, and the obligation of royals to avoid them distinguish them from
local shrines. The role of Yiwogu, however, is ambiguous. The elders there
say that it includes the grave of Sitobu and is the place where he conferred kingship upon Na Nyagse, with the grove Takarfen as "the original
Katin'du." This account suggests that chieftaincy was once much more

like the tindana office than it is now, but the site, though well known, seems to go unrecognized by any more official body than the Ghana Tourist Board. Is "the grave of Sitobu" an invention? If so, for whose benefit? Or is this a genuine piece of history abandoned by the official story? In the next chapter the historical importance of Yiwogu is clarified. We shall see that differences between territorial and dynastic shrines, like that between chiefs and tindanas, are more like points on a continuum than a contrast and that, as always, history is contested.

Chiefs and Tindanas
Making *Nam*

4

The data are scanty, the rituals not exactly the same, but the correspondences among rituals undergone by chiefs in Nanun, Mamprugu, Dagbon, and even Taleland are so close that we must assume a common origin and therefore reconsider the history of Dagbon. So far from being the product of alien intrusion, the kingdoms, like the stateless societies, could be regarded as separate developments on different lines from a common cultural base; the stateless, or "egalitarian," societies are those that "refused" to develop hierarchies from the same base.[1] That argument is advanced for Southeast Asia by J. C. Scott, following E. R. Leach, but it was also put forward by Luc de Heusch with respect to the Kuba and Lele peoples of Kasai, in Central Africa. One of these two peoples of similar language and culture, the Kuba, developed a fully fledged "divine kingship," supposedly founded by conquest. The Lele, on the other hand, "neutralized a nascent structure of subordination" by inserting a kingship, similar to the other in many ways, into a system of exchange marriage that resulted in an "egalitarian" social structure. The comparison, as De Heusch says, poses concretely the problem of transition from kinship to kingship, "du clan à l'Etat."[2] Although Central African kingships are distant from northern Ghana in space and culture, certain parallels are highly suggestive.

A chief becomes such by "enskinment." In Dagbani the act is *n'legi na*, "to make someone a chief"; *nam le bu*, "enskinment, making *nam*." In simple versions, for minor skins, the candidate wears a gown, ideally of undyed homespun cotton, which will one day be his shroud, and a tall white cap. He is ceremonially lowered three times onto a cowskin, said to be a sign of wealth. Afterwards the chief is paraded amid rejoicing, preferably on a horse, even though he may not own one or ever mount one again. The installation of major chiefs is considerably more elaborate; it may take place in stages, last for more than a week, and require the participation of ritual experts and tindanas.

In addition, certain chiefs are inducted into their domains with additional ceremonies in which the principal theme is that the chief is dependent upon the authorization of the local tindanas. The form of the induction is that of a rite of passage, a shedding of one identity in order to assume another. It takes place at night, requires passage through a series of villages, bathing, medicines, a change of clothes, and a period of seclusion, and it is directed by shrine keepers and officials, who refer to the chief as their escaped slave. Despite his enskinment as *na*, it is only after undergoing this rite that the chief achieves recognition as such. A similar sequence has been observed in the kingdoms of Nanun and Mamprugu, and there are even suggestions of it among Talensi, who are well known for not having a "kingdom." To have in mind a model of chieftaincy and even to undergo a ritual may not mean much, however, unless appropriate political resources are at hand. Who is and who is not a "chief" ultimately depends not on rituals or definitions but on the distribution of political resources.

Making *Nam*

In Dagbon the most elaborate and powerful rituals of enskinment take place at Yendi in the Katin'du, the section of the royal palace allocated to the third of the Ya Na's wives, Katini, who vacates it for the event. Only some of the highest chiefs, those who have reached their "limit," beginning with the Ya Na himself, are enskinned in the Katin'du; they include most, but not all, of the Original Elders, the Yogu Kpamba: Kuga Na, Bagale Na, Gushie'Na, Gulkpe'Na, Sunson Na, Yelzoli Lana, and Gundo Na.[3] The enskinment of a new Ya Na begins with the burial and then the funeral of his predecessor, followed by the installation of a regent, the *gboŋlana*, lit. "owner of the skin," normally the king's oldest son.[4] Much of the protracted dispute between the Abudu and Andani gates of the royal family after 2002 turned on the principle that the proper performance of these rites was essential to qualify the children of a Ya Na as potential future kings. The regency is a period of intense political activity on the part of the candidates and their supporters. "Traditionally," or in principle, a new Ya Na is selected from among the sons of former Ya Nas, who are occupants of the three gate skins—Karaga, Mion, and Savelugu—by a process of divination supervised by the Kuga Na as leader of a group of four "kingmakers," including Gushie'Na and the court officials Tugurinam and Gomli. Diviners successively suggest several candidates to test the reactions; meanwhile, "bribes are heaped upon the diverse elders in secret by the chiefs or the candidates concerned, who again spend large sums of money on the malams who used to make for them charms and kindred necromantic and magical amulets to be buried on the graves of some notable men, and on the various roads leading into the town."[5] The decision is made known only at the last minute, when the Kuga Na hands the successful candidate grass pulled from the roof of the palace by Gushie'Na on the first day of the funeral. In practice, in precolonial times this procedure was sometimes ignored in whole or in part. Under British rule it began to be challenged by candidates who were not sons but grandsons and by sons who did not hold a gate skin.

The power of chieftaincy, like the tail of tindanas, is said to catch the chief-elect, who is ritually reluctant to receive it, although in fact he has campaigned vigorously for it. The Ya Na–designate "runs away" and has to be caught. He is taken at night to the Katin'du, where he is bathed with medicines and invested with the regalia, all of which are said to have been seized by Kpogonumbo (son of Tohazie, "the Red Hunter," and grandfather of Na Gbewaa) from the tindana of Biun, whom he killed. Most important is Gbolon, a stool, also described as a lump of wood, which makes the candidate definitively Gbewaa, Bimbiegu ("a bad thing"), and Ya Na; the new king may see this object, kept by Kpati'Na, only once. A cow is killed, the meat roasted, and parts of it fed to the new Ya Na. All this takes place at night. Various officials advise the new king on how to conduct himself; he is not allowed to sleep.

At dawn there is more bathing and medication. The Ya Na is offered a donkey, or *buŋa,* and pretends to ride it but mounts a horse instead and sets off for Zohe Na's palace, where he remains in seclusion for a week; while there he must marry new wives. Gundo Na, the highest-ranking female chief, announces that the Nayiri of Mamprugu has sent her a slave but that she, being unable to keep him, has sent him to Zohe Na, where he is to be locked up for seven days (Zohe Na is Kuga Na's principal deputy). At the beginning of the week and again at the end, the Gulkpe'Na and his assistants, Mba Buŋa, and Choo Na, shouting "Palo! Palo!" and throwing stones to clear the way, "bring the spirits," that is, the spirits of past Ya Nas, who reside at Gulkpeogu, the Gulkpe'Na's village, near Yendi, in a house called Kpema Du, which translates as "Elder's room." At dawn on a

Friday the Na escapes from Zohe Na's compound and runs away to that of Mba Buɲa, where he changes his clothes, leaving his old ones. He then runs once more, to the house of a court official, Mba Dugu, pursued by the Zohe Na, who asks, "Where is my slave?" Mba Buɲa replies, "I have not seen him, but I found these things in my house." Eventually the Na gives Mba Dugu thirty-three thousand cowries for Zohe and Mba Buɲa as a reward for housing him for seven days. Prayers, feasting, and dancing follow.[6]

A similar but less elaborate procedure is followed, according to the account I was given in 2010, at the induction of the Kumbun'Na, holder of one of the oldest and most important commoner titles, traditionally the commander of bowmen in the Ya Na's army. I distinguish between enskinment, which may take place in Yendi, and induction, the process by which, on his way from Yendi through Savelugu and the village of Langa, the chief is led to his seat in Kumbungu by way of Kukparigu, where the Kukpar'Na is the keeper of the shrine Salim.[7] Although a shrine keeper, the Kukpar'Na is not called either *tindana* or *bugulana*. He wears a red hat but does not carry a horsetail, although there is also a female tindana who does. At the time of our visit the office was vacant.

According to local tradition, there was a Kukpar'Na before there was a Kumbun'Na and, contrary to official tradition, Na Nyagse did not pass by Kukparigu. This official, like the Kuga Na in Yendi, existed prior to the chieftaincy over which he presides and is independent of it. Once upon a time, according to local tradition, Kukparigu was quite separate and independent. Kumbungu, then a small village, was at some distance, but women from there would fetch water from the Kukparigu spring. Sometimes Kukparigu women would help them. The Kumbun'Na took a fancy to one of them and married her, and that was the origin of a rule whereby the Kukpar'Na gives a wife to each new Kumbun'Na.

On arriving at Kukparigu from Langa, the new Kumbun'Na is challenged: "Who are you?" Among the customary observances is the rule that if he arrives on a horse or in a car, he will be heavily fined, so he must dismount and arrive on foot like a poor man. He enters the entrance hall of the Kukpar'Na and sits on the horse side, as a nobody or a stranger would have to do. Informed of the arrival of a stranger, the chief sends a *komlana,* the wife-to-be, with water for the guest and provides a ram.

At night the Kumbun'Na removes all his clothes, presumably donning others, and leaves. He sends a cow to the Kambon'Na, or chief warrior, in Kumbungu, where it is killed and immediately cut to pieces by anyone who has a knife in hand. There is a parallel here with the funeral (not the enskinment) of a Ya Na, when the royal corpse is walked over the body of a cow, which is immediately killed. "The meat is everybody's property," writes Ibrahim Mahama. "Any one of the King's subjects who wants the meat can cut part thereof."[8] The Kumbungu Wulana, the chief's spokesperson or linguist, providing himself with a rope, asks, "Where is my slave?" The Kukpar'Na hands over the new Na, but only in exchange for a sum of money described as "thirty three," perhaps thirty-three cowries, and an agreement that in future the Kukpar'Na's people will not be subject to fines, penalties, or market taxes. The new chief spends the night in a house other than his eventual palace. The details are not at all clear; we are assured that we would have to be present and see for ourselves. Unfortunately, since the murder of the Ya Na in 2002 there have been no major enskinments.

There are three gates who succeed regularly to the Kukparigu title, but diviners choose the actual successor, who is not reluctant to accept. Their choice is referred to the Kumbun'Na, who has veto power and is obliged to provide all the materials in the form of food, sacrifices, and insignia required for the installation of a Kukpar'Na, but only once in his tenure. If a second Kukpar'Na dies while he is still Kumbun'Na, the position remains vacant until there is a new Kumbun'Na, although the Kumbungu regent may install a Kukpar'Na to be ready for an incoming Kumbun'Na. At the time of our visit in 2010 the divination process was ongoing. Our informant, the oldest son of the late chief, his regent, carries out any ritual at Salim that the Kumbun'Na or anyone else might require. The female tindana was dead, and there seemed to be no pressure for a new one. After the installation of a new Kukpar'Na, the Kumbun'Na may not visit Kukparigu, though the Kukpar'Na may go to the palace at Kumbungu.

Although he is responsible for a major shrine, the Kukpar'Na is one of the Kumbun'Na's elders and is not called a tindana, yet his role in the induction of the Kumbun'Na resembles in many respects not only that of Zohe Na in the enskinment of a Ya Na but also that of the Dun'Na at Yong Duni, north of Tamale, with respect to the Gulkpe'Na. Not only is Dun'Na unequivocally a tindana but he is recognized as the senior tindana in the area. The position of the Gulkpe'Na in Tamale has been controversial since 1930. The nature and origin of his office are discussed in chapter 5. Meanwhile it is enough to note that any Gulkpe'Na newly enskinned in Yendi must pass from Nanton, a major chieftaincy northeast of Tamale, through the small villages of Sahanaayili to Sahakpeligu, where he spends the night (see map 3 on p. 73). He provides white animals for the elders of Sahakpeligu to send to Fazihini for sacrifice at the shrine Tulebi. In the morning they pass the new chief on to the elders of Wayamba, who ritually bar the way. He has with him a basket and a cutlass and says he wants to cultivate the soil; they refuse (this is said to be funny, a piece of theater). At the boundary between Gulkpeogu territory and that of Nanton, the Wayem'Na and the aspirant make a sacrifice of a white chicken and maize flour. At this point the drummers play the rhythm "ʒiem," which is associated with tindanas; "that is why some people say the Gulkpe'Na is a tindana." The drummer Ibrahim Abdulai told J. M. Chernoff, "Zhem was used in installing the first Ya-Naa . . . and it has come down to all chiefs who are being installed, especially the powerful ones."[9]

Bypassing Wayamba entirely, the ritual progress moves on to Yong Duni, where sacrifices are performed, there is a big feast, and the Gulkpe'Na is put in a house. In the middle of the night the chief puts on new clothes and disappears on his way to his palace at Zagyuri, leaving by a special doorway that has a mat as closure. Finding him gone, the elders follow him with a rope, saying, "The slave has escaped." The tindana at Katariga says he banged on the door with his staff as he passed but did not stop; her elders join in the pursuit. At Zagyuri the pursuant elders are compensated, and more feasting takes place. My informants agreed that I would have to witness all this to understand it; moreover, it had been thirty-six years since a Gulkpe'Na had been enskinned.

Even more important for the Kumbungu skin than Kukparigu is the village of Mbanaayili, where the Mba Na keeps the grave of Bimbiem, a son of Na Nyagse installed as the first Kumbun'Na. Mbanaayili traditionally provides the Kumbun'Na with poisoned arrows and a squadron of aggressive bees to fly overhead when he goes to war. The present Kumbun'Na has forbidden research in Mbanaayili; he may never go there himself "because of Bimbiem." Although this skin is held by commoners, there is a parallel with the avoidance by royals of royal shrines; Mba Na keeps the grave of Bimbiem, just as another Mba Na in Yendi guards the grave of the most recently deceased king. When a Kumbun'Na dies, Mba Na and his people go to Kumbungu and play "ʒiem." It appears, therefore, that the two shrine keepers, Kukpar'Na and Mba Na, ritually manage the beginning and the end, respectively, of the incumbency of a Kumbun'Na.

For the induction of a new chief of Gbulun, a village near Kumbungu, the principal officiant is the Jakpah'Na, tindana of a different village and guardian, like the Mba Na, of a royal grave, that of Lukpaa, the youngest son of Na Nyagse and the first Gbulun Lana. A new Gbulun Lana arrives with his farming tools, is taken to the grave of Lukpaa, spends the night in Jakpahi, but changes his clothes and "disappears." In the morning the Jakpah'Na, wearing his red hat and riding a horse, pursues his fugitive "slave" to Gbulun and installs him in the palace. The two must never meet again. This ritual complex is clearly under the control of the Kumbun'Na.

At Savelugu a new Yo Na, enskinned in Yendi, likewise moves through a series of villages, spending Thursday night at Chaghayili, where he leaves all his clothing and disappears. The information available suggests that in this instance the chiefs, occupants of a gate skin to Yendi, have appropriated and "secularized" much of the tindana function, which is carried out by a collection of the Yo Na's elders and other elders, only one of whom is called a tindana. The chief of Kpaliyoghu, though he seems to preside over the mortuary proceedings much as a Mba Na does elsewhere, though the Yo Na calls him "my father" (*mba*), and though he supervises three shrines and wears a red hat, is not a tindana. He is a chief enskinned by his "son" the Yo Na, with whom he has no avoidance rule, although the Yo Na does avoid the village of Kpaliyoghu lest he set eyes on two of the Kpaliyo'Na's elders, one of them a tindana, who are active in the mortuary ritual. The deceased Yo Na is buried in the palace, but the skin on which his body lies and the cloth in which it is wrapped are dragged by these officials to Kpaliyoghu, seemingly as a substitute for burying the body itself there. The name Kpaliyoghu, "Left behind in the bush," itself suggests a shrine and is in fact the name of the shrine at Katariga.

In the induction phase, after the new Yo Na disappears, to be tracked down at Gushienaayili in the morning by the Chaghi'Na's elders, looking for their slave. Meanwhile, a mock Yo Na parades around town with his entourage, arriving at Gushie'Na's palace, from which eventually the real Yo Na emerges, to be greeted by drummers. (A mock chief plays a part in the annual reenactment of chiefly installation among Talensi.)[10] The drummers play "Bandamba," which may be played for any of the highest chiefs, but not "ʒiem." Subsequently the grave site of Pu'Samli substitutes for that of Biyuu, the son of Na Nyagse from whom the name Yo Na is derived. Pu'Samli was a late-seventeenth-century Hausa scholar, healer, and warrior who befriended a young stranger and healed him of yaws. Later the youth, who became Ya Na Zanjina, expressed his gratitude by making Pu'Samli chief of Savelugu even though he was a foreigner (his name refers to a debt "so deep in the stomach" that it can never be repaid). When Pu'Samli died, the people of the town refused to perform his funeral, so his son Zakpalsi Na Abudu pronounced a curse: any Yo Na who did not in the course of his enskinment go to the house site of Pu'Samli for a reading of the Qur'an would die. The site is not a shrine but a place of prayer for Muslims; a white bull is sacrificed there after the reading. Biyuu, still a shrine although it has no tindana and a mosque and a midden are encroaching upon it, has to make do with a kind of afterthought sacrifice that the Yo Na sends after he has settled in his palace.

There are probably other chieftaincies with similar induction procedures. Leaving Dagbon, we turn to Nanun, where, as Peter Skalník tells us, chiefs submit to the authority of "the earth cult," *boxole* (Dagbani *buguli*), and its tindanas, chiefs of four sacred villages.[11] One of these villages is Duuni, whose chief is the Duun'Na; this is the place where Ngmantambu arrived and where he died "before his legendary disappearance into lake Baxri [Bagale]." Upon the death of the paramount, the Bimbilla Na, ritualists from two other sacred villages, Dalaanyili and Binda, perform the funeral together with the Kpandixli, the male custodian of the "god" at Ponaayili (the female custodian is Ponaa). Kpandixli and the Dalaanyili ritualists inspect the grave in pitch darkness to verify that the Na is truly dead and perform "a hoe ritual." The ritualists control the *nam*, which cannot continue without them, and are greatly feared. Skalník does not explain the hoe ritual, but in Dagbon the death of a Ya Na is announced, on the authority of the Kuga Na, by an official who strikes together two circular hoe blades, of the special Dagomba yam hoe called *kuli*, which also means "funeral." The ritual evokes, through a further synonymy, the emotions associated with the death of a Lion of Dagbon: the verb *kuli* means "to be moved by praise-singing."

Besides these ritualists, there are electors, the Na Kpamba, who conduct the investiture. Royal chiefs address these elders, whose titles are said to date from before Ngmantambu, as "grandfather"; the elders are powerful because of the shrines they control, and in fact they "are more sacred and feared than the paramount chief they are selecting." In Nanun, "legitimacy is not connected with power gained by violence." Succession alternates between two royal houses, the Lion House and the Bangle House. The selection itself symbolizes the subordination of the royals to the authority of the autochthonous elders, two of whom hold the candidate tightly and present him to the Juo Na, who sits in the room of the senior wife of the late chief, and say, "We captured your slave." The elders, as autochthons, are not royals, though they may be uterine children of a royal lineage; they are custodians of powerful shrines. By moonlight, the new chief is bathed in powerful herbs and dressed in a chiefly gown and cap. Then he is kept in seclusion for a week. After his outdooring he enters, blindfolded, a hut in Dalaanyili, where he selects a stick that indicates the prospective length of his reign. There is no mention of a special kingmaking object comparable to Gbolon. In Yendi the stick chosen is supposed to be that of the predecessor whom the new Ya Na incarnates.

For Mamprugu we have a much more detailed account of the rituals of enskinment of a Nayiri.[12] The Nayiri is more like a divine king than the others, a being who embodies the "fluid, androgynous forces of naam," whose body is an object so dangerous that it must never touch the ground while he is alive lest his people be cursed. When he is buried, the body is rolled into a grave by the use of medicated instruments so that nobody touches it. The king-elect is seized from his lodging and dragged "like a slave" to the palace. His enskinment is supervised by a commoner Earth priest, the Sagadugunaba, who, much like the Gushie'Na in Dagbon, leaves the capital when it is over and avoids it thereafter. There is an implicit parallel between birth and enskinment: the placenta is said to be the skin on which the guardian spirit of the unborn child sits.[13] At every stage the chief's reluctance and his humility are stressed. He is ritually seated at night on a sacred object (not a block of wood but a stone, which he never sees again) that imbues him with the essential power of kingship and seems to embody the contradiction between human transience and the perdurance of kingship and the state.

After this, although he is already and forever a king, the king's installation is reprised at the shrines of two "senior-elders," in rituals that correspond to what I have called the induction phase in Dagbon.[14] The king is introduced to the people and the princes and then taken to seclusion in the house of a commoner. After some days he "escapes"; a senior elder carrying a rope searches for him to return him to seclusion but accepts a ram in exchange. The king is fed a special stew of forbidden meats, and his name is "inscribed" by the drummers in the genealogy of the kings. Later during his reign, at the Damba festival, the Earth priests who invested him threaten him with spears to show that "they own him." In Susan Drucker-Brown's account, the king-elect is transformed from an aggressive prince into an almost passive, secluded figure who is nevertheless not only the embodiment of *nam* but "the living source" of all its manifestations in Mamprugu. Throughout the process, the interdependence of king and elders, both the court elders and the tindanas, is stressed.[15]

Among Talensi too, the most solemn of the rites that induct a new chief of Tongo must be carried out by the Gbizug tindana, keeper of the most sacred fetish of Tongo chieftaincy, upon which neither the chief nor his clansmen may set eyes. "The Chief speaks of it with an awe which is almost terror," writes Meyer Fortes.[16] "Without the blessing of the Earth, a chief's mystical powers are void. Thus the final phase of his investiture is his ceremonial reception by the tendanas of the community, who present him to their earth shrines. . . . Thereafter he must send animals to them to be sacrificed to the Earth." On his death, a chief is buried secretly by a tindana.[17] Is this relationship of interdependence between chief and tindana merely an imitation, an echo, a borrowing by a famously "stateless" people from the neighboring kingdom? Or does it represent a different degree of development from the same cultural base from which Nanun, Mamprugu, and Dagbon also developed?

Dagbon at the Beginning

Jean Bazin observes that in the absence of a direct reference "the past can be found as a trace, a vestige perhaps scarcely discernible to divergent interpretations, but a witness, nonetheless, in itself and by itself, of its own earlier existence."[18] In Dagbon the researcher, urged to accept each informant's assertion as the truth, may be able to discern hints of historical sequence in the welter of inconsistent statements.

The received history of Dagbon, backed by chiefs, drummers, and scholars, describes chiefs and tindanas as representatives of two distinct social strata, two populations of different origin, even of different evolutionary levels. In chapter 3, as a first approximation, I wrote that there are two kinds of tindana, those subject to chiefs (as the history requires) and independent tindanas, who offer an alternative history. I have shown that local traditions closely related to particular chieftaincies, as at Kumbungu, also offer alternative accounts of not only history but chieftaincy itself. I shall now argue that chiefs and tindanas can be so much alike that it is difficult to tell them apart and that not only originally but still today they are essential components of a single system of government expressed differently in the three Dagbamba kingdoms.

Traditional history in Nanun, unlike in Dagbon, is relatively hard to come by. A British officer inquiring into it in 1931 was obliged to make do with H. A. Blair's informant in Yendi, Malam Halidu.[19] This relative void is consistent with the principle that the more hierarchy, the more "history." In his early essays on Nanun, Skalník accepted with some reservations the historicity of the invasion story of the foundation of the Dagbamba states and the idea that their organization was "traditional," or early modern. Although he quoted Birgitta Benzing's suggestion that a hierarchy of Earth priests facilitated the establishment of the kingdom of Dagbon, he proposed that "the original dichotomic opposition between the immigrant concept of naam (power, office) and the autochthonous concept of tenga (earth, land) most probably reflecting original violent conflicts between the two groups, became transformed with time into a dual unity, bolstered by the interconnected ideology and political system." Alliance between immigrants and tindanas came to be represented as marriage between the chief and the tindana's daughter.[20]

In later work, after observing rituals in Nanun, Skalník writes about the inadequacy of the concept of the traditional state: "The logic which constantly isolates politics from economics, and looks for boundaries between religion and kingship, has too facilely led modern investigators to the conclusion that African leaders and the institutions they personified were of a political nature, comparable to western political institutions. . . . These African institutions were of a nature fundamentally different from that of the political institutions of the modern world. Perhaps they could be compared to the institutions which existed in European antiquity or middle ages, but those institutions of the European past have been equally misunderstood and misinterpreted by modern Westerners."[21]

In Nanun, "unlike in modern states, there is no monopoly of power. Indeed, there is no power as such, rather, authority is diffused in a symbolic network of checks and threats with ritual sanction. . . . All Nanumba share the belief in kali (tradition) and this makes their social integration possible. Through this belief a consensus about the procedures of naam is achieved and permanently renewed."[22] This critique is apt also for Dagbon, its history, and its constitution, although in modern times the role of tindanas is minimized in the "official" account and underlined only in alternative and local versions. Skalník's language—"there is no power as such, rather, authority is diffused in a symbolic network of checks and threats with ritual sanction"—is also reminiscent of Fortes's description of Talensi: there is no tribal government, but a "mystical" interdependence of chief and tindana. The radical contrast between "states" and "acephalous" societies breaks down.

In Nanun as in Taleland, tradition says that the immigrant chiefs arrived peacefully and were welcomed by the indigenes.[23] "The Duuni people and inhabitants further in the interior received Nmantambu and his people on condition that he respected their customs. The most important was that he could 'rule' only if he was confirmed in office by earthpriests and that he, as chief, submitted himself to mortuary rites and enskinment rituals. . . . Thus the deceased Bimbilla Na is not dead, and the naam cannot continue in the body of a new paramount chief without the performance of the naakuli, a ritual funeral."[24] Although this statement is about Nanun, it succinctly describes the central issue in the Yendi conflict from 2002 on.

Martijn Wienia's recent ethnography of Nanun indicates an intimate relationship between chiefs and tindanas. New settlements create both new chieftaincies and new tindana positions. In at least one example, both the chief and the tindana are said to be descendants of the one "big man" who founded the settlement.[25] In Mamprugu also, the founding myth indicates that the immigrant king, the Nayiri, was invited in by the Gambarana (the chief of Gambaga), who is one of four tindana-chiefs who have an important role in the funeral-installation sequence for the Nam. Later, the chief proved stronger, "so now they are different and fear each other"; there is no story of slaughter. In the Mamprusi funeral sequence the most important roles are those of the most senior tindana-chief, the Sagadugunaba, and the senior female chief, the Pwaanaba (comparable to the Nanuni Ponaa and the Dagomba Gundo Na). The Tarana, the most senior of the king's titled elders, comparable to the Kuga Na in Yendi, announces the successful candidate after consulting diviners and dresses the new king in a gown and hat. The kingmaking object on which he is seated, which no one may see, is too dangerous to describe and is usually hidden in a cave, according to Rattray. The Nam is spoken of as an external force that catches the king, who formerly was "dragged like a slave."[26] These descriptions are enough to establish the common elements of *nam* in the three Dagbamba kingdoms: similar rituals by which powerful shrine keepers make chiefs.

In the course of a conversation at Yong Duni in June 2010, the following dialogue referred obliquely to ongoing political disputes in Tamale: "Who is more powerful, the chief or the tindana? The chief is more powerful by day, the tindana by night." At night a slave is transformed into a chief; at night tindanas stay in the house to receive messages from the dead. The mystery of power is occult. But in Dagbon, unlike in Mamprugu and Nanun, power is said by tradition to have been achieved by a conquest that pushed aside, if it did not entirely exterminate, the tindanas. To investigate this paradox we must revisit drum chant, or at least the canonical redactions of it.

Tamakloe prefaces his *Brief History of the Dagbamba People* with a king list, beginning with Na Nyagse, that has been followed by all historians of Dagbon. In the body of the book, however, he mentions earlier "kings" who also appear in oral traditions. His account complements the detailed genealogy of the royal family that Benzing obtained from a drummer in Choggo (Tamale) in 1966 (the drummer is remembered as Adam Bonsurum, Choggo Tampaha Na). This genealogy has the great merit of including the names of many of the wives and mothers of the nobility; in 2011 another Tamale drummer, the Zo-Simli Lun'Na Yakubu, approved of its accuracy.[27] The genealogy begins with the well-known figures of Tohazie, "the Red Hunter," and his son Kpogonumbo but continues with a generation omitted by Tamakloe: Kpogonumbo's son Jipopwora, whose wife Yiwogu gave birth to Kuntili, said here to be the first Ya Na. By another wife Jipopwora had the second Ya Na, Gbewaa, whose two wives were Gbanzalun and Katini. Let us pause to look at these interesting names.[28]

Tohazie, Kpogonumbo (*numbo*, "to inspire fear and respect"), and Jipopwora all are described in different versions of tradition as monstrous and are clearly mythological. In September 1958, when the State Council asked the Namo Na, as chief drummer, whether any Ya Nas had been deformed, he said that Jipopwora had one eye, one nostril, one ear, "one natural leg, and the other supernatural (covered with hair like that of a lion)."[29] The name of his wife, Yiwogu, is also the title of a wife of a Ya Na, and it is the name of the village in which Kuntili is a shrine, the grave of Sitobu (see chapter 3). The names of Jipopwora's son Gbewaa's wives, Gbanzalun and Katini, are the titles given to the first and third wives of any Ya Na. "Katini's room," the Katin'du, is the compound in which kings are enskinned and also buried. Gbewaa is given as the second Ya Na in the genealogy and as the grandson, rather than the son, of Kpogonumbo. His son Zirile, by Gbanzalun, is given as the third Ya Na; Tamakloe calls him a king but does not number him among the Ya Nas.

As the story unfolds in Tamakloe's account, other essential figures make their appearance. When Na Gbewaa migrated from Gurma to Pusiga before the founding of Dagbon, Mamprugu, and Nanun, his followers included Gushie'Na, Gulkpe'Na, Tugurinam, Gomli, "and others who were also fetish priests in the service of the king fetish priest."[30] By his first wife, Katini, Gbewaa begat Ngmantambu, who became the ruler of Nanun; Sitobu, founder of Dagbon; the first Sunson Na; and the first Karaga Na. By Gbanzalun he had Zirile, the first Kuga Na, Nanton Na, Sang Na, and Tohagu, the founder of Mamprugu, all leading chiefs of Dagbon and its neighbors. His youngest and favorite son, Kufogo, was treacherously killed by his older brother Zirile, a deed that moved Gbewaa to disappear into the ground. Zirile had no descendants, but it was he who instituted the offices of Gundo Na, Zohe Na, Balo Na, and Mba Dugu, whose holders play important roles in the succession rituals of the Ya Nas. Arriving in Bagale, Sitobu invested his son Nyagse with the royal insignia as the first Ya Na (number 5 in Benzing's genealogy),[31] to the annoyance of his own brothers, who went away to their respective domains of Sunson, Karaga, and Nanun. (Nanun is a separate kingdom, but Sunson Na is one of two chiefs who must be present when a Ya Na is buried; Karaga became a gate skin to Yendi.) Kuga Na remained and was appointed "fetish consulter" to Na Nyagse.

Thus, although the received history focuses almost entirely on the dynasty, ignoring the "fetish" component, a stable though neglected tradition asserts that nearly all the principal figures in the kingdom's ritual establishment, the Original Elders, were in place before the conquest began, as Benzing argues, and as Davis does for Mamprugu.[32] Mahama writes: "They are very few, but the most powerful in the affairs of State. . . . The special privileges and reverence for some of them are

```
              Tohazie
          "The Red Hunter"
                │
      Kpogonumbo = Sinsabga
                │
         Yiwogu = Jipopwora = Sovare
           │                   │
        Kuntili      Katini = Gbewaa = Gbanzalun
      "First Ya Na"        │                │
       (Benzing)           │                │
  ─────────────────────────┘      ──────────┘──────────────
  Sitobu, Ngmantambu, Sunson, Karaga   Zirili, Kuga, Nanton, Sang, Tohagu, Kufogo
    │
  Nyagse
  "First Ya Na"
  (Tamakloe)
```

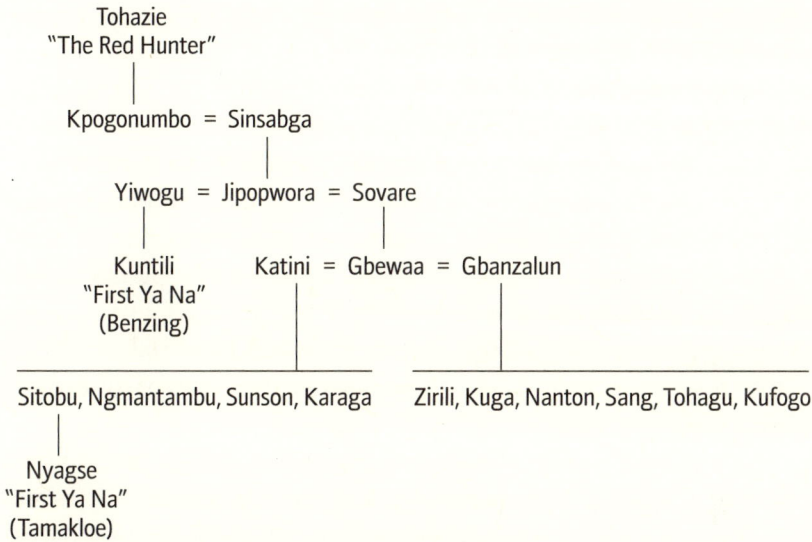

Fig. 10 Genealogy of the early kings, after Benzing.

certainly due to the history of their origins and their intimate association with the Skin and spirits of departed Ya Nas more than the inherent values of the Skin they occupy."[33] Whereas the *lieu de mémoire* of the dynastic history is Yogu (the grave of Na Nyagse), that of the predynastic history is Yiwogu ("grave of Sitobu"), which today goes unmentioned in "official" tradition. The complete story confirms the impression gained from the rituals of *nam* that in the beginning Dagbon was much like Nanun and Mamprugu and that it was formed by a process much less violent than the official Yendi version describes. Although Na Nyagse may have been a historical figure, it may be more to the point that he was a stranger to the polity, as so many African kings were, and that, as the rituals of *nam* indicate, his was a form of limited government, conditionally accepted.

Answers to the question whether the Original Elders are tindanas are ambiguous, probably because of the need to maintain a distinction between the tindanas who belong with the royal establishment and those who were killed off, not to be mentioned again. Yet, as we have seen, there are still tindanas in Dagbon, and their role with respect to some important chiefs is similar to that which at least some of the Original Elders still perform with respect to the king. In Mamprugu, although royal gate shrines are distinguished from earth shrines and the Tarana asserted that he had no connection with Earth priests, in fact both he and Sakpari are referred to as Earth priests, *tindandima*.[34] The question what to call the Original Elders is only meaningful if we assume a radical contrast between chiefs and tindanas rather than the sort of politico-ritual reciprocity that Skalník describes. Clearly they are what remains of a ritual structure and process by which, as in Mamprugu and Nanun, *nam* was created and still is, in the sense that for most people chieftaincy is not just an office but an embodiment of a special, occult power. (In the Mosse kingdom of Yatenga, despite the structural similarity of the relationship between the chief and the tindana, the rituals of royal investiture are quite different from those in Dagbon.)[35]

Traditional chieftaincy is compound. It includes secular factors such as wealth in followers and horses, the title and the respect and perquisites that go with it, but also an essential component derived, literally at night, from the ancestral dead, through the mediation of shrine keepers. This is the "dangerous" element celebrated in drum chant, not to be lightly spoken of. It was realized above all in warlike exploits and in competition with other chiefs for hierarchical advancement. The opposition between the domains of night and day is fundamental to the powers attributed to chiefs. Night is the time of the dead, from whom *nam* is derived; it is also the domain of tindanas, who create *nam* at night, and of women, who are considered to be more in touch with the occult than men are, which is why central figures in the empowerment of the kings of Dagbon, Mamprugu, and Nanun are the Gundo Na, the Pwaanaba, and the Ponaa, respectively.

In the twentieth century, as warfare ceased and modern government sought to coopt chieftaincy, Islam, Christianity, and education ("enlightenment") came to dominate public discourse; it was scarcely possible any longer to articulate once-powerful beliefs. In most contexts, the Gushie'Na, the Ga Na, and the Gulkpe'Na now function as secular "divisional chiefs," although both Cardinall and Blair describe the Gushie'Na as a tindana. A key development in the secularization process (discussed in chapter 2) occurred in 1948, when the Abudu faction of the royal family attempted to replace divination as the selection method for a Ya Na with a Selection Committee that was to make the decision by majority vote; simultaneously, it reduced the installation ritual to mere ceremony, although deposition remained "taboo."

The development of Dagbon as a relatively centralized kingdom with a stronger emphasis on chieftaincy and hierarchy than we find in either Nanun or Mamprugu can be explained as the result of its much more central position, since 1700, in the savanna trading network, especially the Mande and Hausa connections and the link to Asante through Salaga.[36] So in Dagbon even more than in Mamprugu the chief proved stronger than the tindana, at least "by day," so that "now they are different and fear each other." It need not be assumed that in fact chiefs were always royals, descendants of Na Gbewaa and Na Nyagse; examples of aggrandizement and promotion by commoners, together with an analysis of the process, are presented in chapter 5.

The ritual humiliation of kings-to-be as "slaves" is found in Africa from east to west, in conjunctive contrast with conquest stories that stress the kings' absolute and violent power. John Yoder, for example, writes of the incoming king of the Kanyok, in Central Africa, that he is led by a rope, like a slave, and confined in a small hut, both to reenact the original chief's accession and to remind him that he rules by consent of the people.[37] The character of the king as stranger and slave expresses an ambivalent attitude toward power itself, even in statelike formations.[38] As historians abandon the state as the necessary backbone of history, they increasingly recognize the universality of this ambivalence. The view of state formation that prevailed in the 1960s now seems naïve, as though conquest and kingdom building were just regular evolutionary developments, to be taken for granted.

Shrines and Disappearing Chiefs

In the previous chapter I distinguished between territorial and dynastic shrines based on the story that shrines have been there forever, whereas chiefs arrived more recently. Additional information undermines that distinction, since not only are some shrine keepers chiefs but some shrines, though not dynastic, are animated by the spirits of past kings. Shrines, of course, have histories, but tindanas, unlike chiefs, do not need to remember them unless, as in the Upper West Region in modern times, attempts are being made to establish hierarchies among them.[39] In Dagbon we find only suggestions of what may have been the history of some shrines.

The shrine to the original Ga Na, introduced in chapter 3, is at least as much a shrine to Na Nyagse as to his eunuch chief, the first Ga Na.

Kpung Tamale Su'gon, in a hamlet north of Savelugu, though not dynastic, is effectively a shrine to Ya Na Luro, who died in 1660. Known for controlling rain, it includes the shrines Gbewaa and Nyohi, a pair regarded as a married couple (there may be a second female shrine). The female shrine, Nyohi, is in the bush, near a river that is the source of its power; its keeper is a man, but he was away when I visited in 2010, and the tail belonging to him hung in the entrance hall of the tindana of Gbewaa. To approach Nyohi, a client goes through Gbewaa (a name that can refer to any Ya Na). Gbewaa is unusual; it is a small, well-built house like that for a chief's grave, and like the shrine at Ga it stands on a low mound, perhaps a house site, under a baobab. If the house needs repairs, they must be done at night.

The tindana is a young man. Throughout our meeting he said nothing except at the end, when he fetched kola nuts and said that he and his elders were grateful for my visit and my interest in tradition. This farewell was courteous but insincere, since in fact the elders present, or at least the Kambon'Na who spoke for them, were disinclined to reveal anything of interest. Specifically, when I asked about Na Nyagse, he said that it was a heavy matter that would require more *kola*, but when I handed some over, the story I heard was trivial: that Nyagse had come to Kpung Tamale but had been defeated by tindana power, no details. I also heard that there are three gates, that a diviner chooses the successor from the due gate, that the chosen one does not want the job because he is not allowed to farm or to go to market and therefore has no income except what he gets from clients. On the other hand, he seemed to have plenty of clients, to judge by the stack of sheepskins and cowskins on the floor and another collection hanging on the wall. Job seekers, contestants for chiefly office, candidates for Parliament, "even a presidential candidate" (unnamed), come here to seek the backing of the shrine.

In fact the secrets not to be revealed are common knowledge even as far away as Tamale, with several variants in circulation. On the way back to town, the Wulana, who had introduced us to the tindana and who had remained throughout our nondiscussion, approached me with two others, eager to talk. The succession, which the elders explained by drawing in the dirt with sticks, is as at Yong Duni. It is not a gate system at all but a sequence of men whose mothers were oldest daughters (*pakpon*) to a past tindana. In lively discussion the elders wove together what seemed to be three originally unrelated stories. The origin of the shrine was that a malam came by the village of Yiwogu, which is the dynastic shrine to Na Sitobu, but was not well received there, so he passed on to this place, where the inhabitants had been warned by a diviner to expect a stranger and therefore welcomed him. Yiwogu, realizing that a mistake had been made, asked the malam to return, but he refused. Since then there has been a joking relationship between the two villages, each being entitled to raid the other for loose livestock, and so on, on certain occasions. The malam had with him his Qur'an and would pray. Not understanding Islam, the people thought the book was magical. After the malam's death they enshrined it as a fetish, and that was the origin of the shrine. (A story of an original malam is also told in connection with some other shrines.) Malams, such as Pu'Samli, settled in this part of Dagbon in the early eighteenth century; in the 1960s the library of an Islamic scholar in Kpung Tamale comprised twenty-one volumes, and a similar collection belonging to al-Hajj Husayn in Savelugu comprised forty-three.[40]

The second story was that the great warrior king Na Luro, of the mid-seventeenth century, asked the tindana in Gushie, a village further north, toward Diare and Yogu (not to be confused with Gushiegu), to pour a libation of millet beer (*pito*) at the shrine there, giving him millet seeds and telling him to plant them; they would grow and mature in a single day, so that the tindana could brew the *pito*. The tindana took calabash seeds from his hat, saying that they would grow and within one day spread vines everywhere so that he could have a calabash for the *pito*. They parted on bad terms, the tindana saying that the chief would never return to Gushie. This is one of a group of stories in which tindanas compete with chiefs to show who has the greater magical power.

In the third story Na Luro asked one of his wives to cook food for his mother's brother, who was visiting, but the woman refused, so he beat her (see chapter 2 for a longer version). She cursed him, saying, "What kind of man are you to beat women, when you do not know where your predecessor's grave is?" She was referring to the death of Na Dariziegu in a war with Gonja. Enraged by the challenge, Na Luro went to war and defeated the Gonja king Kalosidajia in one of the most famous battles in the history of Dagbon but was himself wounded by a javelin. He died at Kpung Tamale on his way home, never making it as far as Gushie. It is said that a body wearing a war shirt was found and identified as his. (In fact he died at Kafaba, which is a short distance southwest of Salaga in Gonja country.)[41] His grave is a shrine of sorts, in the custody of the

Kpung Lana, who was described as a tindana when I visited him but is one of the elders of the Yo Na, the chief of Savelugu. There are no signs of sacrifice at this "shrine," there is no taboo on visits by royal princes, and the Savelugu District Assembly has made it a tourist site. As at Yiwogu, the only taboo is that no chief from elsewhere passing through, not even the Ya Na, may be accompanied by drumming, except that as he traverses the domain a single drummer may sing the praises of Na Luro.

At Gbewaa, before his death, Na Luro decreed that the head of Kalosidajia should be deposited there, together with the recovered arm of Na Dariziegu. In other versions, part of the body of the recalcitrant cook is among the relics, or else the ashes of her burned body and that of the Gonja king were used to plaster the walls of the shrine. Na Luro's relics are kept inside, along with the Qur'an, although only the tindana may enter, and even he is obliged to enter backwards, so no one has seen them. The relics include the curved sacrificial knife, *sua goŋ*, with which Na Luro cut off the Gonja king's head. This knife, in the form of lightning, strikes those against whom it is directed; people swear by it that they are telling the truth. (Tamakloe mentions "the thunderbolt of Tamale" as a powerful oath.) A curved knife with remains of sacrifice adhering to it hangs in the roof of the tindana's reception hall. Na Luro, like any Ya Na, may be called Gbewaa. This is, therefore, a shrine to the more violent aspects of triumphant chieftaincy.

Additional light is thrown on the Gbewaa shrine by a letter written in 1949, one of a long series of efforts by the Dakpemas of Tamale to protest against the imposition on Tamale of the Gulkpe'Na. Dakpema Alhassan Dawuni took the opportunity of the death of Gulkpe'Na Iddi to ask that his successor reside in Yendi, not Tamale, where he was regarded as a stranger. He wrote that Na Gbewaa had come to Tamale with his wives, Kakpag'Dakpema, Voga, and Nyohi. The senior wife was seduced by the Tutingli tindana; they ran away into the bush, where he built a house for her. He said that when they died the two of them should be buried in one grave, and so it was. The second wife, Voga, died and was buried at Katariga, and the third wife, Nyohi, was buried at Kpung Tamale (see map 4 on p. 74). Na Gbewaa's "son" Bimbiem was buried at Kumbungu, Gbewaa himself at Yong Duni. "All these graves became our fetish or earthly gods." Na Gbewaa's first son, Na Nyagse, left for [the original] Yendi, where he became Ya Na. He left his cousin Gulkpeogu to look after Gbewaa's grave. Near Yendi Gulkpe'Na has his own village, where he has his own fetish, but since Gulkpe'Na Iddi settled in Tamale his fetish has overpowered all the local fetishes—the Tamale fetish, the Kpatia tindana, Yo [Biyuu] at Savelugu, Batanga at Nanton, Katariga, and Bimbiem—with the result that "we cannot worship our fetishes and this cause drought and starvation. We suffered badly from the claws of Gulkpe'Na Iddi." Two colonial officials supported the Dakpema's appeal, but the Ya Na summoned the Dakpema to Yendi and forced him to admit that he had added as signatories to his letter elders who knew nothing about it.[42]

Tutingli, Katariga, and Yong Duni are among the principal shrine places in Tamale. Kakpariga ("Kakpag," or Kakpar'yili) is the place of the tindana called Guma Na, whose own traditions tell a story of a relationship between him and the runaway wife of a Ya Na with whom he is identified to the point of being called "the Ya Na's wife" and as such is obliged to go to Yendi and cook at the enskinment of any new Ya Na. Nyohi has already been mentioned as the female shrine at Kpung Tamale Su'gon. The elders at Katariga deny that Voga is the empowering spirit there, possibly to conceal a secret. Bimbiem, in the village of Mbanaayili, near Kumbungu, is the name of a shrine to the "son" of Na Nyagse who was made the first Kumbun'Na in place of the slain tindana. At Yong Duni they say that the shrine Gbewaa is the place where Na Nyagse, repelled by the power of the Dun'Na, "disappeared into the ground, though that is not where his grave is." Other shrines are similarly empowered. Tulebi, in the village of Fazihini, east of Yong Duni, is the place where a stranger mysteriously disappeared into the earth. Later it was revealed that although he had committed a particularly horrible crime and was running away, he was a son of a Ya Na and in fact the first Gulkpe'Na (see chapter 5). Likewise, Biyuu, the name of a shrine in Savelugu, is the name of the son of Na Nyagse who replaced the tindana there. Thus not only do chiefs derive power from shrines but some shrines that are not dynastic nevertheless incorporate the powers of the earliest royalty. There is parallelism here with royal shrines ("les boli d'État") in the kingdom of Segu in Mali, which were strengthened by the blood of exceptional human victims (conquered chiefs, famous warriors), thus intensifying the development of individuation by singularity that constitutes their divinity.[43] Taken as a whole, traditions concerning shrines suggest, as one would expect, that they too have histories and have not simply been there forever.

Tradition records that Gbewaa and Ngmantambu, the founders of Dagbon and Nanun, also "disappeared." Other disappearing chiefs who become the animating spirits of territorial shrines are reported from Buganda, far away but still within the area of the Niger-Congo languages. Neil Kodesh situates his description of them amid a critique of traditional historiography. The founding hero Kintu (which may be a generic term for such figures) arrived from elsewhere, killed the tyrannical ruler "Bemba the Snake," and embarked on a journey toward the place where he built his capital. After many years he disappeared, following a dispute with the founder of the Otter clan, but his spirit endured through acts of commemoration performed at his shrine. "The image of Kintu as a wandering conqueror-king dominates the master narrative running through most written versions of Ganda history. . . . Because Buganda eventually emerged as a centralized kingdom, scholars have been tempted to view the narratives surrounding its purported founder as necessarily describing the beginnings of this centralizing process." Further scrutiny of recollections concerning Kintu reveals that there were two different Kintus, not only the first king but one who was a powerful spiritual force central to local healing cults, which historians have relegated to the supposedly apolitical and ahistorical category of religion. In the discursive universe shared by Ganda intellectuals and colonial officials, stories about snakes and shrines were discarded or merged with recently introduced European themes.[44]

The parallel with Dagbon could scarcely be closer. It is reasonable to assume that during his many years of service with German and British colonial officials Tamakloe absorbed prevailing European thinking about chiefs and was aware of their debates on the subject. Both he and the elders of Yendi surely knew that tindanas and religion were not supposed to figure in the future of British Dagbon. By 1928 the pressure in favor of "territorial and secular leadership" was already such that in conversation with Rattray the Gambarana in Mamprugu said, "Ah, in olden days [before the British] I was something. When a Na died, myself, the Bokodana, and the Sadagudana used to meet and appoint the new Na and drag him when appointed into the Ba'yureda [spirit room] where he had to remain for seven days."[45] Rattray himself was so convinced of the distance between secular, administrative chiefs and priest-kings that he could only see the enskinment ceremonies in Mamprugu as "an attempt to supply the religious bond otherwise lacking between Rulers and subjects."[46]

The Careers of Big Men

Evidently there are other histories than the official, top-down one. Even though little of them can be recovered, there is enough to indicate a much more organic historical process in which commoners and royals, immigrants and autochthons, participated in complementary rather than simply hierarchical relations proceeding from conquest. The mosaic picture of Dagbon to be gathered from tindanas today suggests a frontier internal to the kingdom. Although there were no doubt invaders, and Na Nyagse may well have existed as a real historical figure, the development over time of the hierarchy of chiefs may have been due in part to the ambition of local "big men." Even the official history makes it clear that the kingdom was formed in a milieu in which several of the most important chiefly and priestly figures were already in place when Na Nyagse arrived.

The concepts of chief and tindana form a pair in the north, even among "stateless" peoples, although, as Goody says, the relationship is not the same everywhere.[47] It was formerly a cliché that chiefs are chiefs over people, whereas tindanas are chiefs over land. A number of chiefs told Rattray that "the people belong to me, the land belongs to the tindana." In Cardinall's opinion, the land question was "closely connected with the religion of the people and does not concern the ruling chiefs who claim the bodies of their subjects not the soil."[48] The terms themselves are not clearly segregated in that *tindana* may also be *na* and a chief is an "owner," *lana*. In the Guan language of Gonja the word *wura* applies very broadly, to Earth priests and compound heads as well as chiefs. Among Talensi, the people of Nkoog, who are Namoos, said to be immigrants, have both a chief and a tindana, and the chief of Biun, though also a Namoo, is himself the local tindana.[49] Among the Kasena of Burkina Faso, just across the Ghanaian frontier, stories of origin always feature the respective ancestors of the chief and the master of the earth in such a way as to produce the simultaneous appearance of an inhabited space and its two principal authority figures.[50] Near Bolgatanga a local tradition tells of an original settlement by two brothers, of whom the older became Earth priest, entrusted with religious affairs, while the younger became chief, entrusted with political responsibilities. In more recent times, soothsayers would identify the next priest, whereas candidates for chief allowed the Mamprusi paramount to enskin them.[51] An ambitious headman among the Kasena or the Builsa could acquire *nam* from a Mamprusi chief and become a chief himself by means of gifts and obedience. "The *naba* [chief], gratified at this recognition, rewarded his visitor with a present of 'medicine', conferring thereby some of the magic which had enabled him to attain so lofty a position." The acceptance of a portion of earth from the *naba*'s compound delegated power. This is not much different from the distribution of *nam* within Mamprugu itself.[52]

Among Konkomba the term *onekpel* applies to the senior man of a kin group that occupies a district. It is said of him that "he holds the people." Of an owner of the earth, *otindaa*, it is said that "he holds the people, he holds the Earth too." Some districts are jointly occupied by two descent groups, with some division of labor between the two: *onek-pelanib*, or the elder's people, and *otindanib*, the owner of the earth's people, said to be the earlier settlers in the district.[53] In the context of the conjoined activities of war, looting, and trade, local leaders could become chiefs, copying the style of their aggressive neighbors if no local precedent existed. The Sisala, in the Upper West, recognized the role of the *sipaalaara*, "one who goes first," exercising economic and military power, who collaborated with the Earth priest, the *tinteeng-tina*. As the slave trade impinged on Sisala villages, linked mostly by kinship, war leaders emerged to defend their people, in the process taking on many of the characteristics of their enemies, including their appearance. The role of chief existed as a model to be followed by those who could. These leaders had more of everything—wives, wealth, cattle, horses, housing— than others did, financed their operations by extracting tolls and raiding, adopted talismans, guns, and protective garments as the Dagbamba did, built defenses, forged alliances, and became involved in local and long-distance trade.[54] On the other hand, those who resented the exactions of chiefs might insist on their independence, as most Konkomba do today.

It is possible to imagine the hierarchy of Dagbon developing as secular power became available, when horses, the principal means of destruction, could be imported in exchange for slaves, given also that Yendi was favorably situated in relation to long-distance trade. Using horses in raiding, the owner could garner more slaves, but horses were most effective in large numbers. They could not be stockpiled, and therefore their deployment favored alliances among warrior horse owners, who could collectively field cavalry squadrons supported by bowmen on foot. The kingdom in turn gave rise to the myth of its own foundation by a single act of conquest, synthesizing a process that included not only invasion by warrior groups but also the aggrandizement of ambitious men. This process, in which big men promote themselves by taking on the trappings of chieftaincy, is reported from all over Ghana. In the history of Dagbon, insofar as it can be reconstructed, the process has been part of the development of the hierarchy and as such has continued in recent times.

In the twentieth century, war was eliminated and trade was completely reorganized, but chieftaincy acquired new bases of support and new prestige. The Konkomba, the Kusasi, the Kasena, the Dagara, and many other peoples of the north felt that they needed to escape the stigma of statelessness inherited from colonial anthropology and indirect rule. As new sources of power became available, ambitious individuals presented themselves as chiefs and as heirs to deep traditions of chieftaincy.[55] Scholars have generally regarded such careers with condescension as inauthentic, a perversion of custom, at the same time implying their acceptance of the claims of "authentic" chiefs, which may be equally though less obviously invented.

Among the Konkomba, David Tait described a "chief," the Kpaliba Na, who lived to some extent like a Dagomba, dressed like one, kept a horse, and wore Dagomba talismans, though he had no authority. Among the Talensi, where by 1925 Yanii had become the preeminent earth shrine, its guardians were able to accumulate ritual power with the support of the colonial state. Building on the rising local and national prestige of Yanii, an astute local entrepreneur, Tengol, became wealthy and powerful by monopolizing the pilgrim traffic. He legitimated his authority by representing himself to Rattray as a descendant of Mamprusi royalty, although he admitted that he was a British chief; this process, say Jean Allman and John Parker, "was not unlike that which brought paramount chieftaincy to people who had never before known chiefs."[56] Meyer Fortes, always a believer in the authority of tradition, described Tengol's story as a "blatant subversion," a function of "overweening conceit" (Blair's "hubris"). Fortes recognized that "nowadays," when the Hill Talis are rent by factions, myths may be fabricated, but he believed in a precolonial condition of social integration, a time when myths of origin were true.[57] The long history of another "British chief," the Tamale Dakpema, to be described in the next chapter, reveals some of the mechanisms by which political promotion could be effected.

5   Tamale
The Dakpema, the Gulkpe'Na, the Bugulana, and the Law of the Land

The history of Tamale in the twentieth century, especially the story of the Dakpemas, is particularly revealing concerning the relationship between tindanas and chiefs in the context of colonial and postcolonial government and the tangle of political opportunities opened in the north by colonial rule. In the mid-seventeenth century Dagbon was occupied by the Gonja, who overran Kasuleyili, Kumbungu, Yogu, Savelugu, Nanton, and Galiwe, among other places, but apparently not Tolon (or Tamale, which did not exist as such at that time). After about 1714, when the Gonja were defeated, chiefs subordinate to Yendi took their place, but neither the boundary of the territory nor sovereignty over it as a unit was clearly defined until the twentieth century. The major local chieftaincies Bamvim and Sagnarigu, in what became Tamale, were certainly extant by 1800 and are probably much older, but Na Abudulai created the chieftaincy of Lamashegu only in the 1860s. These skins are open only to princes. In northern Tamale, as it is now, the chieftaincies of Choggo and Kanvili, founded by minor royals at some generational distance from Yendi, date from the mid-eighteenth century. The Yo Na of Savelugu, holder of a gate skin, took advantage of the confusions of early British rule to assert his authority over Tolon, Kumbungu, and Nanton but lost his bid when indirect rule "restored" the structure of the kingdom.

The British created Tamale in 1907 out of a cluster of indigenous villages with a total population of 1,435 to be their military and administrative headquarters in the north. The center of what is now a city of more than 400,000 still conforms to their original layout. Old Tamale, the territory of those who regard themselves as the real natives (tiŋbihi) of the city center, became the adjoining suburbs of Changli and Kakpar'yili. The name Tamale is a British term for which several Dagbani originals have been proposed, inconclusively. When Major Morris, newly handed the job of organizing the Northern Territories, arrived in what became Tamale in 1905, he found, or was offered, a man to be his go-between with the local population, whom he called the king of Tamale but who was already known locally as the Dakpema. Although some of his descendants claim that *dakpema* means "senior man in Dagbon," in fact it means literally "market elder" and denotes one who collects market tithes on behalf of a tindana, in this instance the Tamale Bugulana. As market elder, he probably had the job of receiving strangers. The Tamale market, already important when the British arrived, is one of six that constitute, in sequence, a cycle of market days and thus a six-day "market week"; the others are at Tolon, Savelugu, Tampion, Nyankpala, and Kumbungu.

The Dakpema whom Major Morris encountered in 1905 and made king of Tamale was Nsungna, probably the descendant of a refugee who some generations earlier had arrived in Tamale under a cloud and had been taken in by the Bugulana and given responsibility for the market. An undated manuscript note in the British political files for Tamale says that the Dakpema was a poor man with no following, but there are reasons to disregard this assessment. The British idea of a chief at the time was someone who looked the part: wealthy, with horses, impressive clothing, and many wives. Nobody in Tamale looked like that. Nsungna's great-uncle Azim, however, had already turned the Dakpema position into one of some influence. It was he who persuaded Ya Na Abudulai (1864–1875) to create the Lamashegu skin for a friend of his, a minor aristocrat, and who arranged for neighboring chiefs to give him pieces of land. Hence the name, which was originally *ilayimshe*, "cobbled together," or so traditions tell us.

Popular opinion in Tamale is unanimous that the British came to Tamale because Nsungna went to the former headquarters at Gambaga to invite them, but according to Colonel Watherston, the first chief commissioner, "The Dagomba Chiefs are a very much better class than can be found elsewhere in the country, and it was mainly due to this that the new headquarters have been moved to Tamale, situated as it is in a thickly populated part of the country under the King of Savelugu."[1] In February 1907 the acting colonial secretary laid down the principles for the European quarters: they should be away from bush or swampy land, have a good water supply, and not be near native buildings. He asked for a report containing "particulars as to the ownership of the surrounding land and the possibility of preserving segregation."[2] Captain O'Kinealy surveyed the site for the new station; his map indicates the villages of Dohinayili, Changli, Bulpiela, Sagnarigu, Nangutigu, Salamba, and Tishiegu as having a good water supply. The buildings were to be built at an estimated cost of £8,935. In July, after official approval of the new site, the government requisitioned land without much regard for indigenous ownership. The chiefs were convened and told to provide the labor in return for presents proportionate to the amount. The commissioner was instructed, "in order to enlist their hearty cooperation in the work, to point out the advantages of having a whiteman in their midst" and to inform them that everything would be done to uphold their authority. For the construction, in local stone, skilled labor had to be brought in from the south.[3]

The new headquarters was officially opened on 10 April 1908. The chiefs present included Nsungna the "Chief of Tamale," Mahama of Savelugu, Bukari of Sagnarigu, Yisifu of Nanton, Suleman of Choggo, Naena of Kanvili, and Yahaya of Kasuleyili. Chief Commissioner Watherston's speech, in "simple language," declared the end of "bow and arrow" conflicts and urged the people to engage in trade and commercial agriculture. The festivities included horse races, exercises, and dances by the different "nations." Such numbers placed a strain on local resources, but the chief of Tamale "rose to the occasion and carried through everything extremely well." The new buildings with their staircases excited great interest; the chiefs were urged to copy the sanitation measures. Choggo Na Naena was made subordinate to the chief of Tamale (the Dakpema) and in due course was given only "a small locket" as his badge of office, rather than a large one like the Dakpema's. He protested that as chief over thirteen villages he was more important, but in vain.[4]

Two years later, progress was still slow as officials bickered about the design and cost of the buildings, now estimated at £15,000. The medical officer complained that the servants' quarters still had grass roofs, "which harbor mosquitoes in a most remarkable manner," and that in the officers' quarters, which lacked ceilings, "I do not consider it safe to sit during the hottest time of day without a helmet" (it was believed at the time that dangerous rays could pierce the thatch).[5] Labor was short, since not too much could be withdrawn from the production of food, already in short supply because of the number of troops and other government employees. By this time laborers were paid fourpence a day. When the chief of Tamale presented a bill for roofing grass for officers' quarters, five hundred loads of grass and three hundred sticks for £3 15s., the officer in charge alleged that in fact no such amount of grass had been delivered and that the cost was excessive. In 1913 Accra refused to pay for an officers' club, saying that there were not enough officers to warrant the cost. Northern officers' complaints about the hardships of their life and the unfairness of their treatment continued into the 1950s.

By 1909 Tamale had ceased to be a cluster of villages and had become a town, inhabited by its indigenous owners but also by Hausa and Mamprusi ex-soldiers from the north, Yorubas from Nigeria, British officers, and southerners in their employ. In 1913 the Twi speakers, numbering more than fifty, formed the Foreigners' Arbitration so that they could settle disputes among themselves and not be subject to the jurisdiction of local chiefs.[6] The Public Works Department and the police headquarters were located where they still are. The government opened a school with fourteen pupils. Official bungalows extended along the ridge leading eastward to the office of the chief commissioner, where the offices of the Northern Region minister now are. Non-native Africans paid rent of 10s. for their houses, half of which went to the Dakpema. The rate of growth is revealed by his income, which increased from £1. 12s. 6d. in 1909 to £11. 12s. 6d. in 1920. Hausas and Yorubas were traders, each group in its own ward; the Yoruba headman complained that his people paid higher rents than the Hausas. Already there were difficulties in collecting rents and identifying tenants correctly.

Tamale continued to expand in the 1920s, as the British strengthened their administrative control and made efforts to increase commercial agricultural production. A plan to build both an inner and an outer ring road, advanced in 1926, was still incomplete at the end of the century. The following year, Governor Guggisberg, expressing concern about economic development in Tamale, said that it was inevitable that a Northern Territories railway would pass through Tamale within ten years. That has not happened yet either, though it is still talked about. The Europeans complained that there was no money for the upkeep of the separate European and African clubs and continued to compare their miserable allotment with the generous amounts available for such purposes in Accra. By then the European population numbered nearly forty, and there was a somewhat greater number of African officials.[7]

The Gulkpe'Na

Dakpema Nsungna served the British well and prospered until he died in 1922. In 1928 British policy turned toward greater reliance on indirect rule, meaning that indigenous institutions would be called upon to carry out more of the functions of government.[8] To "restore" the authority of the Ya Na over Tamale, Commissioner Blair wanted to bring in a representative from Yendi, and the Ya Na sent the Gulkpe'Na to be the "divisional chief" (a European term and concept), although in Yendi his responsibilities concerned the rituals of succession and there was a taboo against his coming west more than three times. It appears that the Gulkpe'Na was the only figure in Yendi with any kind of connection to Tamale. The story sold to the British was that he was the divisional chief of Tamale and happened to be away in Yendi at the time of the German conquest and the partition of Dagbon.[9]

Yendi tradition, in Tamakloe's version, says that Na Nyagse, having killed the fetish priest of Tamale, left his son Tulebi as the chief of the place. Alone among the sons of Na Nyagse, Tulebi did not care for his assignment and moved instead to Zagyuri, leaving the Dakpema in charge, while creating a new title for himself and continuing "to exercise the jurisdiction of Tamale District."[10] This story makes no sense; it is remarkable that anyone ever took it seriously. There was no Dakpema then, and "Tamale District" did not exist in the fifteenth or even the nineteenth century. The story answers the question why only in Tamale there is a "chief" not appointed by Yendi. It emerged after 1907, probably in 1928, because Tamale had become a place of importance, with the Dakpema as its "king," and Yendi needed to have a presence there.

According to local tradition in Tamale, the original Gulkpe'Na was the keeper of the shrine Tulebi, near Zagyuri, a village that now lies near the northern edge of metropolitan Tamale. The Tulebi shrine still exists. Local elders say that any new Gulkpe'Na must go there at the time of his enskinment as divisional chief of Tamale for a sequence of rituals performed by the elders of the nearby villages of Sahakpeligu, Fazihini, Wayamba, and Yong Duni. The shrine itself is said by the elders of these villages to be the place where a runaway son of Na Nyagse whose name was Tulebi and who was the original Gulkpe'Na disappeared into the ground (see chapter 4). The shrine is now in the charge of the Kukuo Na, an elder of Fazihini who is neither a tindana nor a bugulana. It is probable that at one time Tulebi, with the Gulkpe'Na as its tindana, was superior to Yong Duni and the other villages mentioned, where the shrine Gbewaa now takes precedence.

The Gulkpe'Na was no ordinary shrine keeper but one of a cluster of important figures connected with the ritual management of royal succession, the Original Elders, who were obliged to relocate in the second half of the seventeenth century. Because of the Gonja invasion, the last Ya Nas of the First Kingdom were forced to abandon their capital at Yogu or Yenn'dabari, on the White Volta, and move, in effect, the entire kingdom east to the Oti River. One of Na Zangina's successors, after defeating Gonja, established a new capital at a Konkomba place renamed Yani (in English called Yendi). In what Phyllis Ferguson calls the Second Kingdom, towns in the parts of western Dagbon out of which the First Kingdom had grown were refounded nearer the new Yendi.[11] Certain court officials also moved: the Kuga Na, the first officer of the kingdom, from Diare to Kuga, a village east of Yendi; the Gulkpe'Na, from Zagyuri to a small village called Gulkpeogu, near Yendi; the Gushie'Na, from what is now Kasuleyili, west of Tamale, to modern Gushiegu. Like the Gulkpe'Na, the Kuga Na was strictly limited as to the number of times he might return to his original place.

The principal function of the Gulkpe'Na before he became a divisional chief was related to the death and enskinment of Ya Nas. According to inquiries made in 1967, the Gulkpe'Na is the keeper of the royal walking stick, "the stick which makes the holder the most powerful person in Dagbon." If the king should fall ill, the Gulkpe'Na comes from Tamale to Gulkpeogu to supervise the handing over of the stick to a new Ya Na, after which it is purified by sacrifices and kept in a special room inhabited by the souls of dead kings and tended by the Gulkpe'Na's principal wife.[12]

The Dakpemas fought the Gulkpe'Na's intrusion; Nsungna's praise-name says, *Be ye ni Tamali pala tiŋa; timi bi boli ba Tamali ka be kana, ti ye nzila kpe ka be labi be ya,* "They say Tamale is no town; we did not invite them to Tamale, and we will still be here when they return to their homes."[13] In 1931 a successor, Lagmbu, wrote to the district commissioner that in the traditional history of Dagbon "it has never occurred that the chief of Yendi has interfered with the business of Gukpeogu, the Tamale area. This area has never been under the rule of any prince of Yendi."[14] Since this declaration contradicted the idea of an integral Dagomba state in which the British had so much invested, the district commissioner came down heavily on the Dakpema, obliging him to retract his assertion and apologize. Illiterate himself, he denied having written the letter and blamed it on his court clerk, J. S. Kaleem. Kaleem was a recent graduate of the elite southern school of Achimota, where presumably he had picked up insubordinate tendencies. The British accepted Lagmbu's excuse and punished Kaleem by exiling him as a teacher to Yendi.

In January 1932 the first Gulkpe'Na to arrive in Tamale died; he was "universally said to have died from the effects of a fourth visit to Tamale which we compelled him to make." The district commissioner consulted the Ya Na, who said that a rule of avoidance between the Gulkpe'Na and the Dakpema (as tindanas) was only operative if the former actually entered Tamale itself and set eyes on the Dakpema. The Ya Na suggested that the Gulkpe'Na make his headquarters outside Tamale, at "his traditional estate" in Zagyuri. By February 1932 the district commissioner had persuaded the Gulkpe'Na to build a house at Zagyuri. In due course he would build his court at Choggo, still far enough away from Tamale (as it was then). "This superstition," the district commissioner wrote, "can be carried too far; the people and their beliefs should be moulded gradually." In April he reported that the newly appointed Gulkpe'Na had been persuaded to come to Tamale, "although very frightened of the local fetishes and taboos," to take over the reins of government from the Dakpema. "The controversy about the Dakpema's status is settled," the commissioner declared. "This takeover was facilitated by the Dakpema unfortunately having a stroke from which he is still suffering. The Gulkpe'Na has set up his tribunal, which is operating very well with the help of a Dagomba able to read, write and keep simple accounts."[15] In his October 1933 "Progress Report, Dagomba Native Administration," the commissioner described the Gulkpe'Na's administration as probably the most forward in Dagbon. Money flowed to the treasury from the tribunal, and "Tamale was fortunate that Town Rents were an excellent source of revenue." Of the total revenue, 10 percent went to the Ya Na, who also received 25 percent of town rents; 50 percent went to the government; and 25 percent went to the Gulkpe'Na, a most satisfactory arrangement for all concerned.[16] In 1938 Gulkpe'Na Iddi was given a three-inch medal because "he has done sterling work since he has been in Tamale."[17]

Modern Tamale

Although the chief commissioner believed in 1932 that the problem of the Dakpema's relationship to the Gulkpe'Na had been solved, tension between them continued. As collectors of rents and taxes, successive Dakpemas received a salary. Besides their government emoluments, they derived power and authority from control of increasingly valuable land in the center of town. They created a court on the chiefly model, complete with its own elders, drummers, malams, praise-singers, and warriors. The Dakpema installed not only subordinate tindanas but also chiefs; at various times villages switched their allegiance from him to the Gulkpe'Na and back again. Together with court titles and ceremonies, the right to grant settlement rights to strangers was and is a marker of chiefly status and a source of power and wealth. In 1957, continuing his fight for recognition as the chief of Tamale, the Dakpema disputed the right of other chiefs and tindanas to collect taxes on behalf of the government and caused outrage in Yendi by trying to appoint his own chief butcher. Disregarding the contrary opinion of the government agent, the State Council declared "That all of you Tindanas have no connection with Chieftaincy in Dagbon. That you are all guardians of the Fetish as you are all aware," and resolved "That all Tindanas in general have no right to install a Chief or the Head of a Community (But can do so only to minor Fetish Priests under you by way of 'Tail Enrollment' and not by Wearing of Gown, which the latter denotes Chieftaincy)."[18]

Undaunted, in 1962 the new Dakpema, Alhassan Nyuwogu, installed Malam Seidu Dagomba as his imam (principal Muslim cleric). "I am in charge of Changani, Ward H and Ward F," he said, "but in these areas other malams get to weddings, funerals and the like before Seidu, depriving him of his daily bread." The district commissioner replied that the Dakpema was a fetish priest, not entitled to install subchiefs, and that the imam of Tamale was installed by the Gulkpe'Na; any duplication, he said, would disrupt the unity of Muslims. The Gulkpe'Na drew his authority from Yendi, but the Dakpema had the advantage of deep and extensive political and marital alliances in Tamale, so the rivalry continued. Meanwhile, the Tamale Bugulana, though still nominally the Dakpema's superior, faded into the background.

The rapid expansion of Tamale after World War II was both a modernizing success and an administrative nightmare. There was great demand for more copies of maps, but the extreme shortage of linen meant that backed copies could not be provided. Official planners trying to survey new wards to provide housing, water, sanitation, and roads to the growing population constantly found their plans overtaken by the onrush of private enterprise. In 1945, for example, the village of Salamba was to be moved to a new, planned site to make way for an airstrip, but people paid no attention to the rules and were already building there, locating their houses as they saw fit. Plans for housing developments in straight lines and durable materials ran counter to tradition and convenience. The provision of urban and commercial facilities in the center of town required that houses be demolished, a process that continued fifty years later. There was some tension between local people and outsiders. In 1947 leading Muslims, plus the Magajia (the town's senior woman), wrote that they did not mind if the land of their fathers in the center of town went for public uses such as a hospital, but they resented handing it over "for aliens to build stores."[19]

Householders at this time were usually listed by place of origin or "tribal" name, for example, Mumuna Dagomba, Seidu Kumbungu, Bigu Zamberima, Sgt. N. Moshi, Yahya Mamprusi, James Lagos. Lagos built a house that did not follow the approved plan: the sanitary inspector complained that it lacked windows on the inner walls, that the sanitary buildings were not set apart, and that the roof was thatch instead of iron. By 1947 almost all plots within the old town boundary had been allocated. Surveys were to be carried out for plots in Changli, Tishigu, Dohinayili, Nyanshegu, Salamba, Nangbitigu, Mohiyabili, and Bulpiela; they should not infringe too much on existing compounds. Thus the separate villages surveyed by Captain O'Kinealy in 1907 gradually became absorbed into the modern town, although in the minds of their original inhabitants they retained their character as villages, each with its chief, and as "home."

In 1950 Tamale was approved as a planning area, and not a moment too soon. The commissioner of lands wanted to revise the plans, which were too conservative and did not provide for enough public buildings and services. The expansion of Tamale, he pointed out, was much more rapid than had been anticipated in 1946. Food shortages were blamed on inadequate rainfall but also on the drift of educated people to town, causing a decrease in supply and an increase in demand. Yet even then the population numbered fewer than 40,000, little more than one tenth of what it became in 2007 (estimated at 350,000).

In 1952, giving up on indirect rule, the British instituted in Tamale an Urban Council, whose Achimota-educated chairman, Ebenezer Adam, repeatedly wrote directly to Accra demanding money for municipal improvements. "Tamale," he wrote, "is the Capital of the Northern Territories and is growing by leaps and bounds in size to be a real metropolis of the North. The town stretches about four miles or more on every side from the Central Market and Commercial Area. In line with the largeness of the town is the population." "The housing position in Tamale," the chairman declared, "is deplorable. The center of Tamale is a first class Slum. The people still live in centuries-old swish [adobe] round buildings with thatched roofs, and the town is daily being invaded by strangers."[20] The council thought that Tamale should emulate southern cities by building housing estates, as in Accra and Kumasi. In Tamale the government provided quarters only for civil servants, most of whom were southerners. The demand for housing was great; the village of Katariga would have to move, as would parts of Malleshegu, Zagyuri, and Dungu. By this time the problems of modern Tamale were well developed, chief among them uncertainty over titles to land. Disputes were frequent. Even the government's own title to Old Tamale as Crown property since 1922 rested on shaky legal ground, being "a matter of expediency" rather than statute.[21] The chiefs, members of the hierarchy of Dagbon, and the tindanas, particularly the Dakpema, asserted rights of ownership in the modern sense, including, effectively, the right to sell land, although according to law an owner acquires leasehold, not freehold.

In 1959 the Kukuo Na, a village chief, complained that the Lamashe Na, chief of Lamashegu, in south-central Tamale, and a prince, had "sold" land belonging to him. The government agent forwarded the complaint to the Dakpema: "I understand that by custom you are the proper person to go into this land dispute." The Dakpema replied, "Lamashe Na was wrong in selling 60 foundations without informing me or the owner, and even warned people not to tell. I want you to damage the houses or charge the owners severely."[22] The matter was bucked to the Ya Na, who said (not surprisingly, since the Lamashe skin is in his gift) that the land belonged to the Lamashe Na. Both parties were dead by May 1961, when officials decided, with the dispute still unsettled, to let sleeping dogs lie. In 1968, when the Dakpema had been trying to get compensation for lands taken over for urban development, the State Council of Dagbon, made up entirely of high-ranking chiefs, ruled that only the Gulkpe'Na, and not any lesser chief or the Dakpema, was entitled to compensation or could execute leases. Despite this and other decisions, the Dakpema continued to be hotly embroiled in land issues, but the tendency of the government in Tamale to treat the Ya Na as the final arbiter of land disputes, for lack of another, added to the king's power and made his title more than ever an object of competition among royals. In such situations the chiefs recognized by Yendi were fully in accord with the law of the land, which did not mention tindanas.

The Law of the Land

Problems related to land tenure are among the most serious that Ghana faces. Indiscipline reigns in the land sector, characterized by multiple sales of the same tract, encroachments, indeterminate boundaries, insecurity of title, multiple agencies with overlapping authority, bureaucratic incompetence, a long history of patchwork solutions, and endemic conflicts that often degenerate into violence, occasioning loss of life and considerable public expense.[23]

The history of land tenure and its modern problems is intimately bound up with that of chieftaincy. From 1894 to 1912 the Gold Coast government attempted to control access to land, but a combination of chiefs, educated professionals, and European interests eager to keep government at bay insisted that all land was community property, thus keeping the government's hands off without specifying who could act for the community. A model of African land tenure emerged in which the chief managed land as a trustee on behalf of the community.[24] Behind this model lay a much older anthropological view that all Africans were divided into tribes, each headed by a chief whose authority rested on ancestral values and unquestioned tradition. As K. S. Amanor remarks, "In policy circles, it is often assumed that traditional institutions preceded modernization. The customary is often defined in terms of an idyllic Arcadian past, which was characterized by communal and egalitarian values, based on group solidarity and rooted in spiritual and moral values."[25] In fact, although there is nominal continuity with the past, modern chiefs are effectively products of modern times. Over the years, the more market-oriented governments were, the greater their interest in maintaining the "traditional" systems. Anything else was said to violate the right of private property.[26]

Land tenure in the north differs from that in the south because, among other factors, agricultural and mineral resources are richer in the

south; from the early nineteenth century the south had an internation-
ally connected entrepreneurial class that opposed government control of
land; the north did not have the export-oriented cocoa economy and its
political entailments; and government policy toward the north was much
more restrictive.[27] In 1902, when the Northern Territories were made a
protectorate, the chief commissioner was authorized to take any land for
government purposes without compensation. In 1931 a new ordinance
vested control of all northern lands in the governor of the Gold Coast.
In practice, however, most of the north was undisturbed by development
because the government intended that it should be primarily a labor reserve for the south and that education there should be restricted.[28]

Government reports from 1925 on pointed to the problems of the
land sector, first the contradictions between the idea of collective ownership, the increasing commercialization of land, and the fact of private ac-
cumulation, particularly by chiefs, and second, the disconnect between
"customary" law, itself uncodified (and uncodifiable), and the law of the
courts, based on British law, but nothing was done. (In 1936 Blair tried to
codify the law of Dagbon but failed, finding that in practice a chief could
do as he pleased.)[29] In practice, the administration of the Northern Territories muddled through, recognizing both that the "native authorities"
were not well equipped for land management and that in much of the
north legitimate interests in land were held not only by chiefs but also
by tindanas. Given the evidence of increasing interest in land as a source
of revenue even this early, it is not surprising that in 1928 Rattray's informants, the elders of Yendi, told him that the tindanas had been killed
"because they would not run away and because they declared that the
land belonged to them."[30]

After World War II, as preparations were made to replace indirect
rule with modernizing Native Authorities, northern officials respond-
ing to a memorandum from the commissioner of lands conducted an
extended discussion among themselves in which the legacy of anthropological views of priest-kings, intercultural misunderstandings about
land ownership, and the ambiguity of land as territory and as property
are clearly displayed.[31] The acting chief commissioner wrote, "It is probable that the day is not far-distant when all Tindanas will have lost to
the Native Authorities the right to dispose of land." He cited the view
of the district commissioner for Kete Krachi that, given present trends,
religious control of land would have a stultifying effect and continued, "It

is interesting to note that in Western Dagomba the Tindana has already disappeared, for he was eliminated by the conquering Dagombas when they overran the autochthonous inhabitants." In fact, as we know, the tindanas in Western Dagbon were still present and active. Later in the document another official writes, "The Tindana is becoming an anachronism and is being replaced by the Native Authority; but the Native Customary system of land tenure should not be upset even if the Tindana himself does descend to the status of an interesting anthropological relic." The author agrees with another that a tindana would not be able to cope with the formalities of granting land ownership (surveys, etc.) and worries that "a dishonest tindana might one day dispose of the people's birthright for a mess of potage." It did not occur to him that a dishonest chief might do the same.

The document quotes a "categorical statement" made by the Ya Na in council in 1937: "The Ya Na holds the ultimate control over all land in Dagomba. . . . Tingdanas are respected and revered by chiefs . . . but have no executive authority." This statement was primarily an assertion of sovereignty motivated by a feeling that Dagbon was being invaded by strangers. It went on to say that families might take up vacant lands without asking permission but that strangers must ask the chief. "Land cannot be alienated to a non-Dagomba by sale or long lease. . . . The whole conception embodied in the phrase 'sale of land' is completely foreign to Dagomba ideas; there were strictly speaking no proprietary rights on land." The document quotes Blair as having said, "Land is not owned in Dagbon. Even the Ya Na would not dream of claiming such a proprietary right over land." It also quotes him as having said that "a Dagomba would say, the chief owns the land. This is typical of the gradual divorce of ordinary life from religion, which is in history generally associated with an outworn cult."

These local concerns and misunderstandings were overtaken by national events. The Northern Territories Council (NTC) was originally formed in 1946 as a forum in which chiefs, as "natural leaders of the people," could learn modern perspectives, but by 1953 a majority was made up of their educated and ambitious sons, whose prime concern as independence approached was that the north should not find itself in neocolonial subordination to the more developed south.[32] They objected to the Land and Native Rights Ordinance of that year, arguing that control of land should not revert from the governor to individual chiefs but to the

NTC, on the ground that chiefs had caused trouble in the Gold Coast Colony by alienating land to non-natives. The Gonja State Council, on the other hand, was eager that land should revert from the government to the state councils (i.e., the chiefs) and not to the NTC, a "political body" (and therefore untrustworthy), whereas "land was the lawful property of the Paramount Chiefs before Her Majesty took over the administration of the Gold Coast."[33] Again at independence in 1957 the NTC urged that the governor's prerogatives should not pass to the independent government, controlled by southerners, and argued in vain that the control of land should be returned to chiefs; tindanas were not mentioned in this debate.[34] The commissioner of lands commented that the ordinance was intended to protect northern lands from the infiltration of non-natives from the south and from neighboring French territories and added, surprisingly, "Land in the Northern Region [i.e., the erstwhile Northern Territories] is not 'stool land' but is under the control of the land priest, who is quite separate from the ordinary chiefs."[35]

While bureaucrats dithered, the state of affairs on the ground in Tamale is suggested by the indignant tone of Ashetu Dagomba, who with the help of a licensed letter writer wrote extensively in August 1958 to the regional commissioner and others: "I am not certified [satisfied] with the bad practice and treatments given me by The District Valuer, Tamale, hence I sent tremendous letters objecting to his dicision. . . . Later on, I sent a Reminder, there is no any responsibility [response] there from any of them, made me to believe that there is a MOTIVE behind the Plot. . . . I beg to state that I have had the above Plot for over 12 years of which I am even having my ruin house on it." She was told that her ruin was on Crown land.

After Ghana became an independent republic in 1960, Nkrumah's vision of a command economy produced the State Property and Contracts Act, followed in 1962 by the Administration of Lands Act, which effectively made the president the landlord of the north.[36] His scheme of mechanized, state-owned farms was a disaster, but it introduced the idea of modern, capital-intensive farming. The 1969 constitution, intended to restore the status quo ante, could be read as defining so-called public lands in such a way that there were no skin lands in the north, although it also provided that all stool and skin lands should vest in the appropriate stool in trust for the subjects of the stool.[37] There was plenty of room for confusion, and the letter of the law did not have much effect in a time of

tumultuous political and legal changes. Local chiefs disregarded the reg-
ulations of the Lands Department, preferring to lease land to strangers
"traditionally," which in practice often meant treating community land
as personal property.[38] Regional intelligence reports described rampant
irregularities in the Lands Department, where government lands were
being sold to rich individuals at fantastic prices, the proceeds going into
private pockets. Poor people who had managed to acquire a plot might
be told that it had been confiscated to become a "sanitary area."[39] In the
late 1960s military officers, high civil servants, and former Convention
Peoples Party politicians with money to spare rushed to invest in rice
farming, taking advantage of abundant land in the north and the government's willingness to provide subsidized inputs and services.

Confusion reigned. In September 1968 the Dagomba Traditional
Council ruled that only the Gulkpe'Na should be paid for lands in Gulkpeogu, but in May 1970 the Choggo Na, the Lamashe Na, the Wurshe
Na, the Dakpema, the Bomaha Na, and the Tua Na were among the
chiefs still making claims. In July 1970 the council ruled once again that
only the Gulkpe'Na should be paid compensation, he being the divisional
chief, who "appoints sub-chiefs." In March 1971 Ya Na Mahamadu Abdulai wrote to all divisional chiefs, complaining that some of them were
"fond of leasing large quantities of skin lands to foreigners [southern-
ers] for some insatiable compensation." Skin lands, he declared, were not
to be sold. In June 1971 the Dagomba Traditional Council informed the
regional administrative officer that "all traditional lands are vested in the
Ya Na who only apportions them to the various chiefs to look after" and
that all money paid in respect of such lands must go to the council "for
the future development of the Traditional Area." The following month,
the Gonja Kpembewura Jawulla exemplified the prevailing confusion
when he wrote, "Please I want to know whether I should sell the land [to
certain rice farmers] or should I release it to them on probation of years."
He noted that traditionally, "before someone come to beg for a piece of
land from a chief he has to give some drink or pay some money, give
some animal." In October 1975 Gulkpe'Na Abudulai Bukari complained:
"I have been informed by the Senior Lands Officer, Tamale, that neither
by myself nor by any of my sub-chiefs can I give my skin land to anybody
for building purposes. I have further been told that the Government has
taken all my land from me. I am surprised at this. Neither me nor any of
my Elders and Sub-chiefs can accept this situation. How can I be a chief

if I have no land? . . . To accept that situation is to accept the destruction of the very skin I sit on."[40]

This helplessness of chiefs in the face of government ended when they in effect merged with the government. In 1972 the National Redemption Council (NRC) of General Acheampong overthrew President Busia while he was abroad. Later that year the NRC enforced the Ollenu Committee's recommendation that Yakubu II Andani should be reinstated as Ya Na in place of Na Mahamadu Abudulai, setting the stage for strong personal alliances between military officers and Andani politicians.[41] The NRC's policy of economic self-sufficiency—Operation Feed Yourself—included subsidized, large-scale rice farming in the north. Chiefs could become rice farmers and could make land available to their friends in government, who could arrange for fertilizer, bank loans, and import licenses for machinery and would on occasion facilitate smuggling the crop to neighboring countries to avoid the government's own price controls. "The Ya Na [Yakubu] exercised considerable influence in the distribution of resources by nominating or endorsing officials at key establishments concerned with the development of rice farming in particular, and of regional development in general." In fact, he began to distribute lands soon after his enskinment, defying both the Lands Commission and the district chief executive of Yendi.[42] Dakpema Alhassan, a big rice farmer himself, was influential in allocating land to the Cotton Board, of which he was chairman. The politician and Andani partisan Ibrahim Mahama, who acquired land for two rice farms and a cattle ranch, explained to an interviewer "the importance of chieftaincy connections to successful business operations in the North." The whole scheme was hastily conceived, badly executed, riddled with corruption and short lived, but it made fortunes for a few at the expense of many (there are several large rice harvesters rusting in Tamale) and greatly strengthened the Andanis after years of Abudu dominance, though it did nothing for food production. Angry peasants, feeling that they were entitled to a share of the profits from their lands, burned some rice farms. The program collapsed in 1979, when it became apparent that profits depended on government subsidies and graft.[43]

Since many chiefs, often in alliance with members of the military regime in power at the time, were themselves active in commercial farming, a new distinction had to be drawn between skin lands and the personal property of a chief, his own farm. Once upon a time, a chief appointed to a skin arrived with his entourage and the wives he had already acquired. It was the responsibility of his dependents to build and repair his palace and to farm his land; when he died or was promoted, his successor would move into the palace. Now, often with the help of political connections, it became possible for a chief to invest in commercial farming as a private enterprise. In June 1976 the Dagomba Traditional Council decided that the family of a deceased or deskinned chief must vacate his palace and any farm land he was using, though several officials found this rule "obnoxious, if not useless."[44] Can a chief not own land for himself and his family? Is his family to be abruptly displaced? The Gushie'Na has many rice farms; may he give one to the head of state (as he probably did), and if so, why not to any one else? Could his successor take it back?

The reaction against Nkrumah's policies eventually led to the constitution of 1979, followed by that of 1992, which returned nationalized lands to their previous owners, without spelling out who they were. The phrasing hints at underlying confusion:

(3) For the avoidance of doubt, it is hereby declared that all lands in the Northern, Upper East and Upper West Regions of Ghana which immediately before the coming into force of this Constitution were vested in the Government of Ghana are not public lands within the meaning of clauses (1) and (2) of this article.

(4) Subject to the provisions of this Constitution, all lands referred to in clause (3) of this article shall vest in any person who was the owner of the land before the vesting, or in the appropriate skin without further assurance than this clause.[45]

The reference to skin implies that chiefs are envisaged as owners, although, as we have seen, in Dagbon it is only chiefs and their spokesmen who are sure that the term *skin* excludes tindanas. Subsequent clauses effectively leave it to the Lands Commission and related agencies to sort out who owns what. The constitution says that lands vested in the state have reverted to "the appropriate stool on behalf of, and in trust for, the subjects of the stool in accordance with customary law and usage," raising the question which stools or skins were appropriate. In the south, "the chief" is the paramount, but the kingdoms of the north have elaborate structures of chiefs differing in rank and function. What level of chief is entitled to allocate land and enjoy the proceeds? In Dagbon, is the Ya Na to be "the chief"? Successive Ya Nas certainly thought so, but the struggle that ensued is not over yet. Will the Gulkpe'Na's thumbprint suffice to execute leases in Tamale "on behalf of and in trust for the subjects of the various skins."[46]

This is the background to the long-running struggle between the Gulkpe'Na and the Dakpema over who should be recognized as the chief of Tamale.

The Career of a Big Man

Succession rules for chiefs and tindanas were discussed in chapter 3. In chapter 4 I argued that although there were no doubt immigrants in the early (and later) history of Dagbon, chieftaincy in the kingdom at its inception resembled that described for Nanun in modern times, a ritual authority conferred on chiefs by agreement rather than conquest. I also suggested that as the kingdom grew, ambitious "aborigines" could become chiefs and later be assimilated into the dominant narrative. The rest of the story of the Dakpema and the Bugulana shows how such aggrandizement might come about, in the context of developing competition and confusion related to land.

Dakpema Richard Alhassan, installed in 1967, was an educated man with progressive ideas, never afraid to speak his mind. As a devout Muslim, he initially refused the summons of the tail, since it carries responsibilities for pagan shrines, but he was persuaded to obey tradition, delegating care of the shrines to his elders. He proudly admitted that his grandfather Nsungna had been a "British chief."

In September 1968, repeating a story that was well known but not publicly discussed until 2010, Bugulana Azimdow, with the help of an amanuensis, wrote to the Regional Administrative Office as follows: "I, Bugulana of Tamale, installs the Dakpema, for my grandfathers started the Dakpemaship and this was how it came about. One morning when I [i.e., one of his predecessors] came out from my room, I saw a stranger lying in my hall. I asked him where he came from. The stranger said, 'I was driven away from my village.' I asked him what he did and [why he] was driven away. He said he had some medicine which kills people. After his explanation I said I would not drive him away but rather ordered my men to dig a hole to bury the secrets. Even still, it is in existence behind the Dakpema's house. . . . This man was staying in my house. That time there was nothing like the market ticket. I used to go and collect little of things sold for the market. So I told this man to be doing that and one day he was beaten at the market. From then, I gave him a tail which shows that he is representing me. There I named him Dakpema. And now he says I am not more greater than him. . . . Now he receives a government salary for this. Give the salary to me to buy hen and perform my fetish."[47] There was no follow-up to this letter; the Dakpema survived, as his predecessors had done.

As chief of Tamale for forty years, Dakpema Alhassan built a favorable personal reputation and a formidable political apparatus. In constant rivalry with his neighbor the Gulkpe'Na, he exercised powers derived from his family's long history of intermarriage with other families in the town, playing the parts simultaneously of chief and tindana (though strictly speaking he was neither) and claiming authority over land. The Ghanaian constitution recognizes only chiefs and not tindanas as owners of land, qualified to sell it, but the city authorities found it expedient to avoid trouble and allow Alhassan to assert himself as a "landowner." As a chief, he enskinned subordinate chiefs, yet as a tindana and a chief he remained independent of Yendi. As an ally by marriage of the Andani family, however, Dakpema Alhassan benefited from that family's strong links with the National Redemption Council of General Acheampong. Between 1974 and 1979 leading Andani chiefs provided support to the Acheampong regime in the Northern Region and shared in the temporary boom in rice farming. Abudu chiefs and farmers participated in the same corrupt arrangements, but to a much smaller extent because their political position after 1974 was so much weaker. Dakpema Alhassan became a big rice farmer himself, but as a rising political figure, he also benefited from gifts and services offered to him by other ambitious farmers eager to have him as a patron.[48]

In 1974 the Gulkpe'Na was a supporter of the Abudu cause who would not accept the deskinment of Na Abudulai. Refusing to play his appointed ritual role vis-à-vis the new Ya Na, Gulkpe'Na Alhassan Iddi was deskinned by Na Yakubu and replaced by Abudulai Bukari, a rice farmer related to the Andani family. By 1990 Abudulai had fallen ill and had begun to lose control of his elders, whom the Dakpema, in letters to the Ya Na, accused of disturbing the peace. "We Tindamba want to play our roll [sic] as landowners within our areas of jurisdiction and Gulkpe'Na interrupts us." The Gulkpe'Na, he said, had been sent to Tamale in 1932 only to assist Dakpema Lagmbu in court. Since that assistance was no longer necessary, he should go back to his village, Gulkpeogu, near Yendi, where his people had need of him. Not surprisingly, nothing came of this suggestion.[49]

Abudulai died in 1996 after a long illness. His son, as regent, should have conducted his funeral within a year so that a new Gulkpe'Na could be enskinned, but he was still managing to postpone the event when Na Yakubu was murdered in March 2002. Thereafter no enskinment could take place except as part of a general political settlement in Dagbon, which had not yet been reached in 2011. As a regent, however, he was unable to make the appointments and to exercise the authority of a regular chief; and he acquired a reputation for selfishly disposing of lands in Tamale as the city grew and buildings multiplied.

Dakpema Alhassan died in 2008. His successor, Alhassan Dawuni, installed in 2009, assumed even more of the trappings of chieftaincy. His ambition and his disregard of the "humble" behavior appropriate to the newly appointed annoyed everybody. He set up a barrier in front of his palace that was guarded by hostile young men. These men interrogated those who wished to enter, even members of other Dakpema gates, who thereafter refused to have any more to do with him. He appointed a Diema Na, "entertainment chief," who broadcast on local radio statements deemed insulting. The talk of the town attributed the Dakpema's bad behavior to the fact that the tail should have gone, not to him, but to his older brother, who is a doctor in Germany. At a town hall meeting convened by the mayor in 2009 he seated himself at the high table, infuriating the other chiefs, who were seated in the audience. A little later that day, after the Bugulana poured the libation at a celebration of National Farmers Day, Dakpema Dawuni declared that only he was entitled to that spot in the limelight. Whereas Dakpema Alhassan had always been respectful of his ritual superior, his successor told the sellers in the market to disregard the "immemorial custom" whereby "prohibited" chickens (those of a certain coloration, inadvertently brought there by their owners) were surrendered to the Bugulana. Dawuni had drummers sing his praises as chief of Tamale on Mondays and Fridays, but when the Bugulana tried to respond with borrowed drummers, the Dakpema forbade them. The Bugulana then swept aside forty years of discreet compromise in Tamale by addressing a letter, thumbprinted by the representatives of all five Bugulana gates, complaining to every authority from the regional minister on down that the Dakpema had "maliciously crowned himself as Chief of Tamale and further threatened the elders that he will seize the crown tail of Bugulana so that Bugulan'yili will be erased from the tradition of Tamale." He went on to explain that the Dakpema was merely the descendant of a refugee whom a Bugulana of long ago had taken in.[50]

The regional minister asked the regent of Dagbon and the Kuga Na to investigate the dispute. The Kuga Na summoned the "fetish priests" of Tamale to Yendi, where he met first with the Guma Na and the representatives of the Dun'Na, the Tutingli tindana and the Katariga tindana. The Guma Na, who is installed by the Dakpema, who in turn is installed by the Guma Na, was the only one to assert that the Dakpema was superior to the Bugulana; the others all told the story of the disreputable refugee. The Dakpema responded with irrelevant stories of the Bugulana's failure to observe certain courtesies. The argument about who was chief of Tamale became heated, to the point that "the Dakpema walked out of the hall of the Kuga Na without any goodbye. The meeting ended uprootly at 3:30 pm." The Kuga Na advised the regional minister that the Dakpema "is a fetish priest and he should not be treated as a normal chief."[51] The Dakpema rudely replied that the Bugulana might be a fetish priest but that he, as Dakpema, was "a Tindana (Landowner)," recognized as such by successive Ya Nas and by the colonial government. He went on to argue that only members of his family could possibly know the truth of his family history and to offer an unconvincing story to the effect that the predecessors of the Bugulana were newcomers appointed by a past Dakpema.[52] The Bugulana, "Spiritual and Traditional Chief Fetish Priest of Tamale," retorted that if the Dakpema was enskinned by the Guma Na, he should go to Kakpar'yili to look for land. His wording reveals the heart of the matter: "The issue is simply, Guma Naa does not own Tamale land [i.e., land in the center of town where both Dakpema and Bugulana live]." The Bugulana then announced that he had withdrawn from his *dakpema* responsibility for "enskinning landed chiefs within my jurisdiction" and for "allocating plots to settlers for building or development."[53]

Scrambling to produce tradition useful to their cause, the parties concerned and the town's gossip mill churned out fragments of information not usually available that suggested something of the real history of Tamale. Not surprisingly, they indicate that until well into the nineteenth century southwestern Dagbon was a frontier area in which Dagbani speakers mingled with Gonja, intermarrying and even forming military alliances that crosscut "ethnic" boundaries. Shrines might stay put, but the composition of their clientele changed as groups in search of better land or better treatment migrated from a Gonja chiefdom to a Dagomba one, or vice versa. Partisans of the Dakpema vied with those of the Bugulana in arguing over whose village was the heart of the original Tamale and whose shrine was the original major ritual focus. It became clear that the Dakpema's principal ally was the Guma Na, the tindana of Kakpar'yili; that the tindanas of Katariga, Tutingli, and Yong Duni were on the side of the Bugulana; and that these alliances were results of processes over time in which some shrines, or the offices associated with them, had come into existence as offshoots of others already in existence. The Yong Dakpema, for example, in the village of that name south of Tamale proper, clearly thinks of himself as a client of the Tamale Dakpema, whereas his neighbor the Yaguyili tindana is linked to the Tutingli tindana and the Bugulana. These alliances were in existence in the 1960s (and presumably much earlier), when the Bugulana enskinned the Tutingli and Katariga tindanas and the Dakpema and the Guma Na enskinned each other.

Bugulana Abdul-Rahman Alhassan and his grandsons, newly stimulated by the conflict to think about the traditions of his office and to collect supporting documents, reflected one day in July 2010 on the rise to power of the predecessors of their opponent, the current Dakpema. We have already seen that in the mid-nineteenth century Dakpema Azim seems to have been a person of influence, but the real builder of the dynasty may well have been Nsungna in his heyday as Dakpema from about 1880 to 1922. Nsungna may have been the first Dakpema to be buried in the special tindana grave of the Bugulanas. This violation of tradition, according to the present Bugulana, had serious consequences in the form of bad weather and bad harvests; the Bugulana family had been obliged to make a new mausoleum in Changli. (There are, of course, alternative stories about who did what and when.)

The grandsons pointed out that the pakpon succession rule for the Bugulana office constantly diffuses power through women, the daughters of successive holders. Potential successors are grandsons, that is, oldest sons of oldest daughters of any officeholders still remembered; thus, the number of gates can vary. For the Tamale Bugulana tail there are currently five gates, that of the holder and four waiting their turn; "formerly there were three, but the family expanded." In fact these are not gates in the usual sense but lines of daughter's sons (see chapter 3 and fig. 5

on p. 87). These men belong to their father's families, that is, to the families of the men to whom previous officeholders happened to marry off their daughters, "so the incoming Bugulana might not even be a Dagomba." In contrast, the grandsons explained, the Dakpemas, in their move to become chiefs, had adopted an agnatic rule whereby the successor was always the son of a previous Dakpema. The prestige of the office and powers accumulated in connection with it therefore remained "in the family." Moreover, Nsungna had reduced the number of gates from four to three and ensured that two subordinate chiefly titles were permanently vested in each of the surviving gates, thus reducing the likelihood of internal conflict. In this instance the gates are the normal divisions of a Dagomba family. Testimonies from other sources, including supporters of the Dakpema, suggested that three of these six titles were those of the formerly independent keepers of the shrines Tinzamni, Kpambeogu, and Jem (which is at Changli), which the Dakpema had coopted in the course of building up his position. A note by District Commissioner Rutherford marginal to a memorandum about the elders of the Dakpema's court supports this suggestion by indicating that in 1930 the succession rule for the Tinzam'Na was still "matrilineal."[54]

To continue our discussion with the Bugulana and his grandsons, understanding the political weakness of the pakpon succession rule, Bugulana Azimdow deliberately violated it in 1965, insisting on becoming the successor of his father, Aleji. This same Azimdow was the author of the 1969 letter to the authorities (quoted above) denouncing the Dakpema as nothing but a descendant of a refugee who had usurped the Bugulana's prerogatives. Azimdow's innovation, however, outraged both conservatives and the shrine itself. Moreover, he was reputed to own noxious medicines that turned on him, "so he died early." After his death the succession reverted to Nagumsi, the grandson of Aleji to whom it should have gone in the first place.

Evidently, the political advantages to be obtained by manipulating rules of succession and coopting uterine kin are well understood in Dagbon, despite the dogmas of tradition and descent. This dynamism is not incidental but intrinsic to the political system, suggesting to us how, in Matthew Schoffeleer's words quoted in chapter 3, an elite, or parts of one, may rise to power from within the society rather than simply by conquest. Similar strategies are employed in Gonja.[55] As long as the powers and rewards of a given office are modest, ambition will be satisfied by

a rule of rotation such that each gate, or line, succeeds in turn. In Foshegu, a village of moderate size founded in the first years of the British
occupation, the position of "chief," or village headman, is of so little interest that there are no clearly defined gates. Of the five successors to the
founder, three had only a matrilateral relationship to him. In 2011 four
old men contested for the vacant skin, but none of them had any clear
claim based on pedigree.

As competition tightens, gates may be eliminated, as has happened
repeatedly in the history of the kingdom. In the eighteenth century, the
line of Na Tutugri and Na Zanjina, the founders of the new, eastern capital, eliminated the descendants of all the other sons of Na Luro. In the
nineteenth century, as the drum history records, the fighting continued:
"And in Na Kulunku's time, the troubles of Dagbon started, for he drove
out the sons of Na Andani and succeeded his younger brother Mohama.
This deed of his roused the wrath of the dead chiefs, and they sent discord amongst the Dagomba."[56] As recently as June 1947, upon the death
of a long-serving Karaga Na, leaving a gate skin vacant, Sunson Na Adam
wrote to the district commissioner for Yendi asking for it, pointing out
that to qualify he had performed the funeral custom at a cost of £150. In
his view there were three royal families, those of Andani, Abudulai, and
Kworli Na Mahama, all sons of Na Yakubu; if he were not given the gate
skin, the line of Na Mahama would be forever excluded from Yendi (see
fig. 4 on p. 55). There was no reply to this letter, and Mahama's line was
indeed excluded, although the family still insists that there was never a
rule of alternation and that they still have a right to succeed to Yendi.[57]
The accession of Mahamadu Abudulai, son of Abudulai III, in 1969 and
that of Yakubu Andani, son of Andani Mahama, in 1974 both threatened
to institute a rule of primogeniture that would exclude all royal collaterals from the Nam of Yendi. Any such concentration has provoked at-
tacks from excluded factions in the form of actual violence or, in modern
times, litigation, or some combination of these, and still does.

In "patrilineal" terms, the uterine grandson is "mother's family child,"
but the children of princesses do not hesitate to describe themselves as
members of the royal family. The uterine relationship therefore offers a
choice—inclusion or exclusion—and gives the system political flexibility.
Distinguished figures who describe themselves as princes of the royal
family by maternal connection may nevertheless be called "slaves" by
their enemies. In frontier situations matrifiliation is one of the mech-

anisms by which outsiders, such as the Konkomba in eastern Dagbon, may be incorporated into the dominant group.[58] A uterine grandson is not entitled to succeed to his grandfather's skin, although he can expect to be given a subsidiary title and other benefits in return for support. It would help if his father's mother was a princess. Such deals are essential to the political strength of the royal family; the Abudu and Andani factions are made up of uterine supporters as well as princes and their agnates. At least twenty-seven titles are reserved to royal uterine grandsons. For five others succession alternates between women and men, as it does for some tindanas. If his grandfather's title is not an object of strenuous competition, a uterine grandson whose abilities seem greater than those of agnatic rivals may be chosen to succeed. Subsequently his sons may feel entitled to contest for the same title and gradually form a new gate in the family. This is fully consistent with the bilateral nature of the family. Sometimes a family's gates (lineage segments) may be described as the descendants of, say, three wives of the same man, a formulation that assimilates uterine to agnatic filiation. The same fudging of the "rules" occurs in Mamprugu and Gonja.[59]

The supposed contrast between the matrilineal succession of tindanas and the patrilineal succession of chiefs is an anthropological artifact. Of course, ambition, ability, and family politics alone will not bring about much aggrandizement in the absence of real power derived from access to trade, horses, the British administration, or, since 1957, control of land and access to the resources of the national government channeled through the political parties. These new resources shape what perhaps should be called the Fourth Kingdom, but their distribution and exploitation are taking place in a national rather than a local or regional arena.

Chiefs in the National Arena

In the 1960s scholars generally agreed with the nationalist government of Kwame Nkrumah that chieftaincy would and should fade away in modern, rational and democratic times.[1] Many Ghanaian intellectuals still think so, but the facts and the weight of public opinion are against them.[2] All over the country fierce passions and actual violence related to succession disputes testify to the importance most people attach to chieftaincy, even though fewer and fewer of them have much knowledge of things traditional. In eight years all efforts by the government and peacemaking NGOs failed to reduce tensions between the Abudu and Andani factions in the Yendi dispute, which had already been going on since 1948, before the murder of the Ya Na in 2002. Most of the northern peoples who were said not to have chiefs now claim that they did have them or should have them. Kusasi activists in the Upper East now speak of the Kusasi Kingdom.[3] In July 2009 Dagara, from the Upper West, organized what they told me was the first northern festival in Accra. They explicitly intended it not only to counter the slanders of southerners and show that northerners have chiefs and therefore culture but also to make the same claim vis-à-vis the kingdoms of the Northern Region. Accra provided a politically neutral space in which various northern chiefs and ethnic representatives could appear without seeming to challenge one another, as might have been the case in a northern venue.

Chieftaincy North and South

Debate about the future of chieftaincy has always been corrupted by the assumption, general among the southern intellectuals who dominate it, that chieftaincy is the same everywhere in the country. Maxwell Owusu says that during the colonial period "the Akan paradigm of state-craft was, with some local modification, adopted by nearly all other ethnic groups in the country," but it would be more accurate to say that the Akan model was thrust upon them.[4] Beginning in 1960 the government, preparing for its "war" on the chiefs, sent repeated requests to northern officials for the names of paramount chiefs and queen mothers, lists of chiefs per unit, stool name, clan name, and date enstooled. The Dagomba state secretary was among those who had trouble replying to these questions. In Dagbon there are chieftaincies reserved to women, such as the Gundo Na, but no queen mothers nor anyone with a similar role, and nobody has a stool name or a clan name.[5] The fundamental difference is that whereas in the south chiefs are made by men, who can depose (destool) them, northern chiefs are made by the spirits of past chiefs, mediated by diviners and priestly officials, and can therefore be deposed (deskinned) only by natural or violent death. "Chiefship in Ashanti was based on the lineage system. Each lineage was a political unit, and the lineage head represented it on the council. The chief was chosen from one of the lineages by the heads of the other lineages. Kin-right and popular selection were combined. . . . As the fundamental principle was that only those who elected a chief could destool him, a destoolment required the consent of the elders." Chiefs might be destooled for repeatedly rejecting advice, for breaking a taboo, for disgraceful behavior, for becoming physically unfit, or for less substantial reasons, so that destoolment was and is a constant feature of the political process.[6] According to Owusu, the southern chief's role is primarily that of a patron; his responsibility is to provide material prosperity for his people. The perception that he is failing in this or using his position to benefit himself is ground for destoolment and therefore a source of constant political instability.[7]

In Dagbon the term *chieftaincy* covers several varieties. The summary of the chieftaincy structure I give here is a deliberate simplification and does not attempt to resolve contradictory statements by various authorities. Royal skins are open only to the children and grandchildren of past kings, who by self-description are invaders imposed on the aborigines. Princes compete for one of more than a hundred royal skins by sending in a "burial kit," a combination of ceremonial items and valuables, to the managers of the funeral of the last incumbent of the skin in question; by cultivating the Ya Na, as well as his wives and elders; and by making gifts at shrines, paying malams for prayers and charms, sometimes even importing magical experts from afar.[8] They should also make themselves known to the people of the chief's village by attending funerals and other events. Princes are supposed to begin with one of the lesser royal skins and compete for higher ones until they reach the limit of their eligibility, governed by the principle that none may rise higher than his father. In Gonja the competition is much less intense, in Mamprugu perhaps more so. Those who are never enskinned, and they are many, because important chiefs usually have many wives—the late Ya Na had twenty-six—become effectively commoners, although they may acquire nonroyal skins available through their mother's family. The Ya Na may appoint whom he likes, at the risk of alienating other competitors. The nominee's future subjects have no direct say in the appointment, although if they are sufficiently unhappy, they may violently refuse him entry to the palace. There is no equivalent to the organized representatives of the interests of "commoners" known in the south as *asafo* companies.

At the next level, the Ya Na through a similar process appoints the *worizohenima,* "counselors," of whom there are twenty-seven, according to Ibrahim Mahama. Of these, three are of such importance that they are enskinned, like the Ya Na himself, in the Katin'du. In addition, members of this estate may acquire titles reserved to them as counselors of royal titleholders.[9] Chiefs at this level enskin lesser chiefs. In Tamale, the Gulkpe'Na, for example, appoints the Choggo Na and the Kanvil'lana, who in turn enskin village chiefs without first having to get the Ya Na's approval. The choice of the next headman of an ordinary village probably depends on which of the contestants pays more to the investing chief.

Royal chiefs and important worizohenima newly appointed to skins take over the palaces, the subchiefs, and the land of their predecessors. Their business as chiefs is to be as grand as possible and to advance to higher positions. Their role is essentially predatory and even today may be partly based on violence. Cardinall, contrasting them with Akan (southern) chiefs, wrote that "the chiefs are not monarchs restrained by their people from evil-doing, but actual despots." Today they "multiply aggressive strategies for achieving higher status, power and economic control."[10] If a subordinate chief or village headman refused to perform a customary duty such as repairing a house in the chief's compound, he would be compelled or removed by force. Mahama describes it as a "fundamental lapse" that the constitution of Dagbon does not provide for the deskinment of a chief by peaceful means and supposes that it was once unimaginable that a chief might refuse to do what was customary and reasonable.[11] Although a chief would be wise to remain on good terms with his people, he is not responsible for their material well-being and cannot be deskinned simply because they are dissatisfied with it.

So much for the so-called constitution. In historical reality, colonial officials manipulated the selection process for higher skins, including that of Yendi, retaining the right to depose any chief. In postcolonial times litigation and political alliance with the party in power replaced traditional violence as the mechanism of deposition, although in 2002 some Abudus still asserted that the killing of the Ya Na was a traditionally legitimate act of warfare, not a crime. In 1974, deskinment was institutionalized when, on the recommendation of the Ollenu Committee, Ya Na Mahamadu Abudulai was deposed and replaced by Ya Na Yakubu Andani, who then himself deskinned certain Abudu chiefs who could not accept the innovation. Politics similarly trumps tradition elsewhere in the north. In 1957 in Bawku, a principal market town of the Upper East, when the chief, the Bawkunaba, died just as Nkrumah came to power, the Nayiri of Mamprugu appointed a successor, but the Kusasi nominated one of their own, said to be a descendant of the original owners of the land. A government inquiry supported the Kusasi, and Nkrumah gave the Kusasi Bawkunaba autonomy as a paramount, at the same time punishing the Nayiri and other Mamprusi chiefs for their adherence to the Northern People's Party in opposition to his Convention Peoples Party. When Nkrumah was overthrown and the Nayiri's authority was restored, he appointed a new Bawkunaba, who promptly deskinned and replaced all the subordinate chiefs enskinned by his predecessor, with the result that throughout the district there were now rival chiefs. By 2010 Bawku had been under curfew for several years while violence continued. As Christian Lund remarks in his detailed account, all this was odd in two respects: traditionally Mamprusi have no provision for deskinment, and the Kusasi, who in the past had no chiefs, were framing their claims in chieftaincy terms.[12]

The national constitution of 1992, reacting to Nkrumah's attempt to reduce chieftaincy to a condition of picturesque irrelevance, guaranteed "the institution of chieftaincy, together with its traditional councils as established by customary law and usage," and denied Parliament the power "to confer on any person or authority the right to accord or withdraw recognition to or from a chief for any purpose whatsoever."[13] In practice this radical separation is impossible to maintain: the government has a responsibility to keep the peace and punish criminals; factions in chieftaincy disputes regularly file suit in the nation's courts; and the leading chiefs derive much of their power from their partnerships with the dominant political parties. Constitutionally mandated political pluralism enables chiefs to barricade themselves behind a wall of more or less fictive tradition and hold successive governments hostage, as President Kufuor complained in June 2008 after a meeting with the then Bawkunaba. The constitutional privilege of chiefs increases the desire of the "stateless" to have similar leverage.

National and regional Houses of Chiefs are supposed to settle matters of succession but are largely powerless to do so. In February 2008 the press reported that the National House of Chiefs, resuming the project of the indirect rulers of 1930, had completed research on the lines of succession in twenty-one stools or skins of the hundreds in the country in an effort to stem the flood of disputes plaguing the chieftaincy institution. In January 2010 it was reported that the Nanumba Traditional Area had been without a paramount chief since the death of Bimbilla Na Abarika Atah II in 2001. In this instance the dispute was not between two gates, as usual, but between two members of the same gate, themselves front men for two of the kingmakers, each of whom claimed primacy in the enskinment of a new Bimbilla Na. For eight years raging violence occasioned loss of life, with burning of houses, farms, and other valuable properties. Although relative peace then prevailed, the level of mistrust was such that most women and children and some of the businesses that had fled the area were yet to return. The chief executive for Nanumba North complained that the district spent half its budget in security and on the transportation, feeding, and accommodation of the leaders of the two feuding parties whenever they appeared before the judicial committee of the Northern Region House of Chiefs, which is mediating the matter in Tamale but has found no solution.[14]

Officially chiefs are forbidden to enter politics themselves or to endorse a candidate for office. In practice the rule is flouted by most chiefs. Voters tend to follow their chief's indications, although for both chiefs and politicians such support may be a mixed blessing in that what pleases one faction may offend the other. Often enough, however, the chiefs use their power quietly. Civil servants accused of corruption and threatened with dismissal, for example, may appeal to the local chief, who telephones the regional minister to have him dismiss the case. Officially the political parties deny any intention to intervene in chieftaincy disputes should they win the election, and in fact it is not in any government's interest to stir up trouble, but in practice parliamentary candidates are expected to indicate, covertly or otherwise, which chiefly faction they support. In Dagbon it is therefore generally assumed that membership in the National Democratic Congress indicates support for the Andani faction, whereas the New Patriotic Party is identified with the Abudus. In October 2007 a columnist wrote, "Elections year 2008 is not here yet, yet some irresponsible politicians and individuals are already, covertly and overtly, making misguided statements and promises to Dagombas regarding the Dagbon chieftaincy issue in an attempt to win their favor and votes."[15]

Partly, no doubt, because colonial policy reinforced any existing sense of tribe, Ghanaians are intensely proud of their ethnic identity and of the chiefs who represent it. The shifting identities of the past are no more. Public speakers seize every opportunity to declare the importance of ethnic cultures, although the relationship between them and a posited national culture is problematic. Culture is a new and foreign concept that tends to be realized in the production of artifacts and events that appeal to tourists, above all the spectacular festivals of chieftaincy, which are income-generating development projects, tournaments of ethnic pride, and occasions for furthering what Lentz calls "the cultural work of ethnicity."[16] Commercial interests sponsor festivals. Damba, commemorating the birthday of the Prophet, was celebrated at Yendi in 2001 under a banner advertising Star Beer. At the sacrifice of a white bull, as the animal's throat was cut I was told (in English), "Photograph this! It's our culture!"

Arhin Brempong gives a national list of festivals (none of them in Dagbon) and notes that the invention of new festivals is more prolific in areas of new paramountcies, "in which the need to assert separate identities and validate the newly acquired paramount or higher status is urgent."[17] Ethnicity, formerly known as tribalism, is the idiom of segmentary politics in the modern state. Its demonstrations, confrontations, and riots tend to take place in urban areas, where the necessary resources can readily be mobilized and there will be photographers and journalists at hand. "Ethnicised political competition can be seen, at least partly, as an attempt by various groups to solicit the recognition of rights and status by national and other levels of government." Despite constitutional pluralism and the indignation of losing parties, to win is to have the government recognize the justice of one's claims. All governments value this role.[18]

In actuality, traditional chieftaincy in Dagbon, rich with pride and pageantry, is in rapid decline. The patrimonial relationship between a chief and those who farm his land withers as the land is sold and farmers adopt urban occupations. As education spreads, more chiefs, especially those of higher rank, may themselves be educated, but there are fewer retired farmers willing and able to hang about the palace to play the constitutive roles of the chief's entourage. Educated professionals entitled to succeed to a skin may decline it, preferring to remain in Accra or overseas, deputing most of their duties to their elders.[19] Since 1945 all the big chiefs have had houses in Tamale, if not also in Accra, where some who are business people, military officers, doctors, lawyers, bankers, professors, or civil servants may spend most of their time. It is increasingly expensive to keep horses, without which the pageantry of chieftaincy and its associated festivals is greatly diminished. The lack of a solution to the succession crisis in Yendi means that more than fifty titles are vacant, while the related tension continues. The temporary palace of the regent in Yendi is protected by barbed wire and sandbagged army posts. Most of the traditional functions of chiefs have been taken over by modern institutions, so that it is now a serious question what role can be found for them. The fundamental issue is not institutional incompatibility between "tradition" and "modernity" but that of the control and allocation of land, where both *land* and *control* have assumed modern meanings.

Land, Chiefs, and Class Formation

In January 2010 President Atta-Mills announced the formation of a commission on constitutional reform, charged with consulting public opinion on the matter. Hearings were held all over the country. The place of chieftaincy in the constitution is a topic that has been under discussion among intellectuals for years.[20] Progressives declared that chieftaincy was outdated, undemocratic, and an impediment to development. In March 2008 the deputy speaker of Parliament, commenting on the difficulty of passing the chieftaincy bill pending before the House, said that chieftaincy was an anachronistic institution and that most cultural practices were artifacts that belonged in museums.[21] This perspective fails to allow for the intensity of ethnic identification and of popular support for the chiefs who represent it, although Abotchie lamely explains that Ghana "is still a nation in transition from traditionalism to modernity."[22] The conservatives declared that because chiefs have overwhelming power over their subjects and are revered by them as repositories of knowledge, it is essential that "this age-long institution" be kept intact so that it may be "the centerpiece for mobilizing people for communal development."[23] This perspective harks back to a model, borrowed from the fantasies of indirect rule, of the chief as high-minded paternalist, but it also reflects serious disquiet about modern "democratic" politics.

In the introduction to the second edition of his excellent book on the abuses of power that led to the fall of Nkrumah, published in 2006, Owusu, a consultant to the committee that drafted the constitution of 1992, says that the committee introduced several innovations intended to enhance the prospects of political stability, especially "alternative approaches to the notion of 'winner takes all' in general elections." In his foreword to the second edition, E. Gyimah-Boadi remarks that the constitution "seems to have been largely written to regulate the affairs of a society of virtuous citizens with virtuous leaders" and that it also provides an endless "litany of patronage-reinforcing provisions and omissions," outweighing the intended effect of the alternative approaches.[24] The president is free to create deputy ministers and special commissions. These lucrative positions go to the governing party's representatives in Parliament, who therefore are inclined to support the executive rather than the interests of their constituents. "Winner takes all" was still alive in 2010, made explicit at one of the constitutional commission's seminars when a founding member of the NPP, Kwame Pianim, argued that reform was unnecessary, saying that "if the NDC wins, let it come and give contracts to its people. After four years, the NPP will also come and give the contracts to its people."[25] The political youth groups who cause so much local violence have the same expectation of the political process. In March 2010 NDC youths in Yendi asked the government to dismiss the municipal chief executive, who belonged to their own party, or they would kill him. They were incensed because he allegedly had awarded contracts to people who were not party members. The deputy youth organizer complained that he had been given no contract, although as a party official he was qualified to receive one, having worked hard for the NDC's electoral success. "The mayor should give the contracts to party people so that after 15 years, we can finance the party," he said, taking the long view.[26]

Conservatives would like to have a political system that is more responsive to public than to partisan desire, confers stability, and seems less like a foreign import. Owusu exemplified this view in a response to the Acheampong regime's "historic proposal" for a Union Government based on "the tradition, values, and indigenous political beliefs, ideals and practices of Ghanaians."[27] He argued that Ghanaians are not very interested in ideology but are committed to achieving economic mobility. Their modernity "aspires to privilege through high-status seeking and is desirous of well-paid and materially comfortable, mostly white-collar, occupations. . . . This modernist orientation has created structural instability, making drastic political change inevitable" as political elites are seen to do very well for themselves but fail to meet popular aspirations.[28] "Insatiable materialism" has replaced the ideal of harmonious social relationships, but in "what is left of Ghana's indigenous social and political institutions" people still value "integrity, honor and corporate responsibility."[29]

Any participant can testify to the appeal of consensual village democracy, but one is only likely to find it where wealth and the likelihood of attaining it are scarce. Owusu quotes Rattray's praise for democratic accountability in Asante, though even Rattray had to admit that many of the chiefs he knew were autocratic and corrupt.[30] Insisting on the traditional unity of chief and people, Owusu refers to the "average chief," who commands respect and loyalty and enjoys a modest lifestyle little different from that of workers and peasants; he thus elides what can be a vast difference between chiefs great and small.[31] Likewise, the invocation of customary procedures of negotiation, compromise, and consensus glosses over differences of power and political resources.[32] The elision of difference and challenges to it are central to contemporary debates and position papers about land reform and tend to conceal the process of class formation that follows when land and labor become commodities. "Class" is not realized in differences of wealth, which are found in all but subsistence economies, but in differential access to the means of production and social reproduction—education, health care, the law, the modern political system. Nowadays, despite all the talk of tradition, titles are increasingly available to the highest bidder. Because the Houses of Chiefs, to which succession disputes are referred, are underfunded, plaintiffs must pay not only their own but the judicial committee's expenses.[33]

Attempts at agrarian reform began in 1985, when the Food and Agriculture Organization sponsored a seminar. In this and subsequent discussions two main positions emerged, according to Edward Aryeetey and his colleagues. The radical position, calling for state control of land, recalled earlier colonial and socialist policies now widely discredited. The incremental approach, the only one that had a hope of success, argued for modest improvements in the customary land tenure system, represented as flexible and potentially progressive. This approach has been favored by international agencies since their conversion in the 1980s to neoliberal views, in which government is seen as bureaucratic and unfavorable to entrepreneurship; it was thought that room for initiative should be returned to "the people." Advocates of a radical, state-based overhaul of land tenure tend to be top civil servants and people able to influence those in power, whereas advocates of the incremental approach tend to be educated and well-connected chiefs, including many of the active participants in "workshops" summoned to discuss reform.[34] Paramount chiefs and their allies in government and among the educated elite re-define customary tenure in their own interests. Arhin Brempong points out that the phrase "in accordance with customary law and usage," added to the constitution in 1979, "permits super-ordinate authorities to claim and control access to the revenues" that would otherwise have accrued to the heads of village communities.[35] The civil administration regularly appeals to the paramount chief (the Ya Na, for example) for a reading on questions of tradition, on the unjustified assumption that he uniquely knows its rules and speaks for the interests of his people. In fact, the "customary," together with "traditional chieftaincy," is a colonial invention, resulting from collaboration between indigenous leaders and the officials who identified and supported them under the policy of indirect rule. In the north, educated people of every kind, especially chiefs, are fewer in number, so there are fewer people able to participate in and influence the workshops and other exploratory discourses in which land reform is worked out, but the north is not isolated from national trends.

The model of the chief as trustee on behalf of the community necessarily raises questions as to the boundaries of the community, tends to obscure its internal differentiation, and distracts attention from the distribution of power. In the official view of land tenure today, the chief holds allodial (sovereign) rights; all other members of the community, including lesser chiefs, have only usufructory rights, which may be abrogated by the chief at will. Rattray's work on Asante was crucial to the development of this perspective and to the romantic view of chiefly paternalism associated with it.[36] The market economy transformed land into wealth for allodial holders, who make themselves into landlords, selling land for private gain regardless of the impact on members of the traditional group. In most discussions, the holder of allodial title is generically referred to as "the chief," although there is some official recognition that in parts of the country where there were no chiefs in the past it might be held by a *clan* or *family*—vague terms of colonial origin. Many "ethnic" conflicts, north and south, are grounded on the claims of those who say they are firstcomers and owners against those whom they characterize as immigrants and "strangers."[37] When such disputes are referred to Houses of Chiefs in the north, the stateless find themselves like rabbits in a den of lions.

In parts of the Upper West and the Upper East, colonial rule transformed clan heads into what became hierarchies of chiefs. These chiefs now claim allodial rights at the expense of both tindanas and individual farmers, with what Steve Tonah calls disastrous results as the state, the chiefs, and the tindanas struggle for control over increasingly scarce land and communities split into hostile interest groups. Some tindanas, newly motivated by the rents to be obtained, have introduced "traditional" religious practices to bolster their claims.[38] In the south, where—though there is no issue of tindanas—both chiefs and the educated and professional class (often including chiefs) are wealthier and more powerful than in the north, the Lands Commission faces situations in which official institutions and procedures are often ignored and chiefs and judges create "customary law" that differs from the real thing.[39] "There is no certainty that once acquired a piece of land would not have other parties claiming the same land," writes Stefano Boni. "The most serious problem is that there are no clearly known or established processes, procedures and definitive rules of thumb that authoritatively establish a claim to acquisition and ownership of any piece of land as there are always some unknown parties and procedures for securing land."[40] Confusion invites corruption and generates violence: "Since the main aim of the chiefs is to maximise financial returns within the shortest possible time, important land uses such as open spaces, playgrounds, schools, markets, refuse dumps, roads, etc. are sacrificed, in order to augment the supply of building plots."[41] Intense competition has given rise in the south to squads of armed "land guards," hired to protect property claims that the law and the police are unable to defend. The press frequently reports outbreaks of violence involving land guards.[42]

The land bureaucracy is complex, including, besides the Lands Commission, the Land Title Registry, the Survey Department, the Office of the Administrator of Stool Lands, and the Land Valuation Board, all under the Ministry of Lands, Forestry and Mines, as well as the Department of Town and Country Planning under the Ministry of the Environment. This summary is already a simplification. According to I. B. Karikari, "The land sector agencies are presently bedevilled with poor remuneration, poor conditions of service and inadequate logistics; lack of transparency in work processes, delays and cumbersome manual procedures; poor records management; perceived corruption; mistrust on the part of customary land owners in land administration generally; lack of technical expertise in new technology available; and lack of effective collaboration and cooperation between the agencies."[43] In 2004, as part of the National Land Policy, begun in 1999 to develop a unified approach to all the problems, the government embarked on a Land Administration Project (LAP), which in turn introduced Customary Land Secretariats (CLS), intended to strengthen the accountability of customary authorities in land management by providing chiefs with administrative support. At first the chiefs were suspicious, fearing that the government would limit their freedom, but it was the policy of the government not to interfere. Phase One of the LAP, funded by international agencies, ended in December 2010. The new, "streamlined" Lands Commission, as reorganized by Act 767 of 2008, incorporated four divisions: Survey and Mapping, Land Registration, Land Valuation, and Public Lands Management. Phase Two, dependent on additional funding, was to include additional legislation, computerized record keeping, and extensive training. Its ambitious reach measured the extent of continuing problems.[44]

In practice, secretariats associated with powerful stools have been used to consolidate central control and to enhance the income of chiefs rather than the rights of users, thus "fueling resentment between traditional authorities and farmers." The government's treatment of all customary transactions as equivalent to leaseholds plays into the hands of centralizing chiefs and makes large numbers of land users effectively tenants on their own lands, while increasing revenue for the Office of the Administrator of Stool Lands and the municipal assemblies. Janine Ubink and her research associates describe this as a "power game."[45]

In Dagbon this sort of game is only just beginning, but it has advanced further in Tamale than in other towns. To acquire land for development, one must approach the chief, negotiate, and pay money and *kola,* also known as "drink money." The significance of *kola* is always ambiguous: on the one hand, it is a sign of respect ("one does not come empty handed to the house of a chief"); on the other hand, it can amount to a bribe, sufficient money to persuade the chief to do what one wants. The paperwork is handled by the CLS, if the chief has one. One then has the land surveyed, and the Land Title Registry draws up a lease. The Office of the Administrator of Stool Lands keeps a land account for each stool or skin and is responsible for collecting and disbursing revenues. The constitution provides that 10 percent of the revenue accruing from stool lands will be paid to the Office of the Administrator of Stool Lands to cover administrative expenses and that the remaining revenue will be disbursed as follows: 25 percent to the stool through the traditional authority "for the maintenance of the stool in keeping with its status"; 20 percent to the traditional authority; and 55 percent to the District Assembly.[46] Chiefs usually feel that drink money is their customary perquisite and do not include it in the reported revenue.

Tamale, the major economic, political, and administrative center of the north, is growing at a dizzying rate. In 1990 the population was 232,243, representing an increase of 38 percent since the previous census, in 1980, which itself showed an increase of 70 percent since the 1970 census. In 2009 city officials estimated that the population was at least 400,000. Much of the land in urban Tamale has been controlled by the government since colonial times. It is administered by the Regional Lands Commission, which is also supposed to determine who owns what. Over the course of the twentieth century, *land* ceased to refer almost entirely to cultivable land and came to be divided, in Tamale as in other cities, into "rural," used for agriculture; "urban," much of which has been appropriated by the government for public purposes; and "periurban," the rapidly expanding zone in which housing is taking over cultivable land. As I have shown, at every juncture since 1930 powerful chiefs have been keenly aware of the promises latent in the commercialization and rentability of land. In rural areas where land is not greatly in demand for the kind of enterprise that generates rents, tindanas and village chiefs are still on the safe side of the expanding commercial frontier. Most of them seem unaware of their vulnerability, the likelihood that what they think of as their traditional patrimony will be taken from them by onrushing capitalism, though one tindana told me in 2011 that some of his colleagues had discussed the formation of an association to defend their "rights."

In Tamale, particularly among Dagbamba, every man should have a farm, ideally, but land is increasingly hard to come by. On the roads to the east and the north, more and more land is being taken up by private estates, plantations of mango trees, cashews, and biomass (fuel) crops. Rice farming has had an unfortunate history in Dagbon, but it is coming back. Between Tamale and Tolon almost all land is under cultivation; some villagers ride bicycles for considerable distances to be able to farm. In Tamale's expanding suburbs, full of half-built houses, someone will squeeze a maize crop into an unfinished compound. On the main roads beyond suburban development but still within the metropolis, "Keep Off" signs indicate where land had been earmarked for a church, a football field, the new campus for the university, a business, a hotel, or a fuel station. In town, a tailor, a blacksmith, or a schoolteacher with sufficient funds will ride his motorcycle perhaps to Galiwe, in the northeast, where land is more plentiful and where a local chief will make available to him a patch for a negotiable consideration. He will work this patch himself at least in part, hiring local villagers to plough, plant, weed, and harvest when there is more work than he can manage. His aim is to provide a few bags of food for his family, with perhaps a surplus to sell. Some families move to temporary huts on farms as far as fifty miles away from their homes, spending the farming season there. Men and some women who are better off will contract with a village for both land and labor with the intention of selling most of the crop. Neither land nor labor is fully commoditized, except in urban and peri-urban Tamale.

As the city encroaches on a village such as Nyanshegu, a survey is carried out: Indigenous inhabitants are secure in their dwellings. Some land may be taken by the state, either compulsorily, with compensation according to current value, or by agreement, with rent. Other surveyed land is divided into plots, which the chief may sell at market rates. According to the constitution, no interest in, or right over, any stool land in Ghana shall be created that vests in any person or body of persons a freehold interest howsoever described, but in practice everybody speaks of buying and selling and acts accordingly. People who acquire residential lots from the chief get ninety-nine-year leaseholds, any portion of which they may sell. In Tamale, according to the clerk in charge of the accounts, in practice that means that the chief gets nothing and 45 percent goes to the Ya Na as "traditional authority," or at least to the Dagomba Traditional Council. "Where it goes after that is not our business; it is supposed to enhance and support the institution of chieftaincy."[47] The government lacks the resources to keep track of who pays what and where the money goes and is reluctant to stir up trouble by enforcing the tax rules, supposing that it had the technical capacity to do so on a large scale. "In order to secure the votes that the chiefs command, government in the short to medium term is unlikely to risk antagonizing the chiefs by requiring public disclosure of land revenues and accountability in their use, in line with government's broader policy of non-interference in chiefly affairs."[48] Admittedly, the apparent rapacity of urban chiefs can partly be excused because their traditional sources of income have been reduced, their government stipends are derisory, and yet they are expected to support the entourage without which a chief is not a chief. As it is, in urban areas they expect the government to pay for the upkeep of their palace buildings.

According to the constitution, there shall be no disposition or development of any stool land unless the Regional Lands Commission has certified that the development is consistent with the development plan approved by the planning authority. In practice, as has been the case since early colonial times, this requirement is often ignored and planning struggles in vain to keep up with free enterprise. Chiefs, including tindanas, refuse the city's requests to restrain their land sales and may sell plots more than once, with resulting litigation and insecurity of tenure. If the buyer puts up a house immediately, the Lands Commission will say that it deals only with disputes about land, not houses, so he is free and clear. A structure is considered to be a building when the walls reach lintel height.[49]

Of what rank must a chief be to count as a landlord? The presumption is that it will be the "paramount" chief, of whom there are many in the south, whereas in the Northern Region there were only four, the kings of Gonja, Dagbon, Nanun, and Mamprugu.[50] In 1993, however, the Ya Na promoted twenty-seven divisional and subdivisional chefs to paramount status, entitling them to seats in the Northern Region House of Chiefs, which until then had long had only twenty members. In so doing, he "revolutionized chieftaincy in the North and added respectability to the Northern Region House of Chiefs."[51] Indirectly, he also shared his "ownership" of land with his most powerful subordinates and introduced a class distinction between paramounts and the rest. In 2010 it was expected that every paramount chief would be endowed with a CLS, but so far the Gulkpe'Na in Tamale has the only one in the Northern Region.

The Customary Land Secretariats are thus part of the process whereby the hierarchy of chiefs is differentiated into those with access to the resources of the state and the "modern" and those without. The functions of the various kinds of higher chief in Dagbon with respect to the traditional state—royal, ritual, military, advisory—are being dissolved into the common status of landlord. Chiefs with some education are in demand as representatives of the traditional sector on the boards of companies, parastatal organizations, and NGOs. Chieftaincy, instead of standing apart as a bastion of traditional values, becomes a factor in the destruction of the social relations that conservatives regard as essentially Ghanaian.[52] Kasanga quotes a report of 1995 on land tenure in Tamale: "In 1979, when the control was reverted to the traditional rulers the divisional and sub-divisional chiefs sought, by various means, to exclude the village chiefs contrary to customary practices. This has met with resistance and has been the source of some of the land administration problems in the municipality. It is therefore not uncommon to find village lands under the guise of lands vested in the State being sold out by chiefs without any consultation with the villagers or the caretaker chiefs."[53]

The problems continue. In July 2009 a Tamale chief sold a piece of land to a developer who promptly cut down the eighteen-year-old tree plantation on which the villagers had been relying for forest products; their only resort was to threaten some level of civil disorder. It is a matter of public scandal in Dagbon that many chiefs, including the late Ya Na, have been selling off land for personal benefit, often enough the same tract to two or three buyers. That opportunity is one of the reasons why competition for higher skins is so fierce. In February 2010 the outgoing minister of the Northern Region in his farewell speech censured traditional authorities in Tamale for selling every piece of available land in their communities to enrich themselves, including government lands allocated for development purposes, thereby discouraging investors.[54]

In Tamale most chiefs are illiterate. They are in much closer touch with their people than the educated usually are, but they may not understand development in the terms favored by development NGOs, nor are they necessarily a force for good. Some of them, chiefs of "villages" in the center of urban Tamale, can be called upon to provide politicians with "macho men" as persuaders in times of need, augmenting their incomes at the same time. The central issue, however, is not that of personal capacity or inclination but the contradictions of law and economic policy, which have yet to be resolved.

Conclusion

This book revises the early history of Dagbon, using a regional rather than a dynastic perspective, questioning but at the same time expanding the corpus of data. It restores the tindanas, including the Original Elders, to their proper place in the constitution, history, and current affairs of Dagbon, at the same time establishing correspondences among the chiefdoms and even some of the "stateless" societies of the north. It shows how political pressures and deliberate agency can shape a single, flexible social organization once thought to be divided into contrasting patrilineal and matrilineal orders. It traces the evolution of northern chieftaincy in terms of the changing significance of land as territory and as economic resource and demonstrates the influence of ideological and political commitments on historiography both scholarly and traditional.

Governments, especially those that are centralized and bureaucratic, work by sorting people out, imposing distinctions, controlling opportunities, fixing identities, establishing boundaries, keeping records. The constitutive oppositions of the received history that defines Dagbon today—immigrant/aborigine, chief/tindana, and so on—have been realized over time as the result of both indigenous and colonial political action. The elimination of the tindanas in the Dagbamba kingdoms was not effected by conquest in the fifteenth century, but has been brought on, in Dagbon especially, by political processes since the British occupation in 1900 and may be completed soon. As the director of the Gulkpeogu Customary Land Secretariat succinctly put it, "When land is being discussed, a tendana has no business there except to pour libation."[1] Identities are no longer inherently fluid and situational but are fought over, decided in court, defined by reference to Tamakloe and Rattray. Boundaries determined by litigation and the Land Information System replace the open frontier.

The stateless, among them the Konkomba, the Kasena, the Sisala, the Dagara, the Kusasi, the Nawuri, the Nchumuru, and many more, practiced what James C. Scott calls "the art of not being governed,"[2] seeking to run their own affairs in their own way, to the annoyance of both the chiefs and the colonial government, but nowadays all of them want chiefs of their own in order to secure their place in modern Ghana. Horses are no longer the basis of chiefly power; chiefs bargain with the political parties for support in factional disputes in exchange for their influence over the voters. "Village democracy" is giving way to class differentiation. Despite these realities, political discourse and political claims constantly hark back to a mythical time defined by a body of "tradition" that is a joint invention of chiefs, colonial officials, and anthropologists.

My reconstruction of what may have been the early history of Dagbon is admittedly speculative, but it draws attention to the inadequacies of the received history and makes use of neglected data. The received history itself evolved over time, as the chief as holder of allodial rights replaced the "chief over people" and the role of tindanas in relation to *nam,* once shrouded in secrecy, came to be dismissed almost entirely by the forces of secular enlightenment and materialism. It is not merely speculative, however, to see chieftaincy as first of all a model of leadership generally known and available in the north and its realization in certain areas as a function of military pressure, horses as the principal means of destruction, access to trade routes, and changing international demands for gold, kola, and slaves.

Early Dagbon, the First Kingdom, situated just east of the White Volta at the intersection of east-west and north-south routes, was a complex of royal villages (Yiwogu, Yogu), warrior villages (Tolon, Kumbungu), those of ritual figures (Kuga, Ga, Gulkpeogu, Gushiegu), other villages, and a traders' caravansary at Yenn'dabari. Gonja, with links to both eastern trade (Kafaba) and western (Wa), was stronger at first, but as the demand for slaves at Kumasi and kola in the Fulani emirates increased from the late seventeenth century on, Dagbon, now centered on the eastern trading city of Yendi, grew stronger. Neither Nanun nor Mamprugu was that well placed for trade, despite the efforts of Zanjina's contemporary Atabia. Competition between emergent states and the difficulty of extending state power permanently over what H. A. Blair called "recalcitrant aborigines" limited the expansion of each.[3]

The end of the Asante connection weakened Dagbon by reducing the demand for slaves and the control that Asante exercised over the western chiefs. A series of internecine wars ensued, rendered more violent by the wide availability of guns. Under the Pax Brittanica, officials undertook to "restore" a kingdom that had lost its function and was no longer shaped primarily by the properties of the region in which it was situated. Migrant labor in the south replaced warfare as the primary dry-season occupation of northern men, and chiefs became stipendiaries.

As performance art, drum chant, the foundational myth or charter of Dagbon, belongs among Africa's great epics. In association with virtuoso drumming and dance it is the central art form. As history it is open to critique, but as a political document it can only be challenged politically. In Tamale, the Dakpema and more recently the Bugulana offered such challenges, though they are unlikely to succeed in the long run. Other shrine keepers in the past seem to have advanced themselves to chieftaincy, although, except in the case of the Gulkpe'Na, their careers can only be inferred.

In the 1920s the predominant figures in colonial rule, such as Blair, endorsed chieftaincy according to their understanding of it. Others, notably St. J. Eyre-Smith, backed to some extent by R. S. Rattray, argued against it in favor of what they saw as a more authentic and "democratic" form of authority, that of the tindanas, which had been universal in the north in ancient times until invasions disrupted it. This challenge anticipated the modern debate over paternalistic and supposedly consensual traditional authority as opposed to conflict-ridden democracy.[4] The new "consensual democracy" imagined by conservatives is that of the chiefs. Opposition to that model comes from "progressives" who point out that a chief selected from a royal lineage by hereditary kingmakers is inherently undemocratic and who cite both the many examples of violent conflict that result and the autocratic misuse of office by many chiefs. In the north the progressive argument has little support. Groups reputed to have no chiefs are eager to assert that in fact they do so that they may face up to not only the power, prestige, and often aggressive presence of the northern kingdoms but also those who say that the north has neither chiefs nor culture.

Meanwhile, under cover of grandiose but largely irrelevant rhetoric about traditional chieftaincy, the revolutionary emergence of a national division between those who control access to land and capital and those who do not proceeds apace. In the south, this development, dating from the first decades of colonial rule, is much further advanced than in the north; it has been the subject of a number of studies by Gareth Austin and others.[5] The National Democratic Congress and the New Patriotic Party, both deeply implicated in chieftaincy politics, take turns at the national treasury, and only a few protests from the splintered remnants of Nkrumah's Convention Peoples Party deplore the effects of neoliberal policies on the progressive immiseration of the poor. In the 1950s, as independence loomed, activists discovered that election to the Legislative Assembly and appointment to political office opened the way to the comforts of middle-class status and more. As the elections of 2010 approached, speeches by both former president J. J. Rawlings and the Asantehene deplored the fact that politics had become the fast track to personal wealth.[6]

In December 2008, as soon as the election result was clear, members of the victorious NDC engaged in an unseemly scramble for jobs, vehicles, and housing, while simultaneously the party took steps to recover the official vehicles, furniture, bathroom fittings, and the like that members of the outgoing NPP had allegedly taken home with them. In an article titled "Historical review of the two political transitions," a columnist pointed out that the same things had happened at the last regime change eight years earlier, listing such issues as the recovery of state-owned vehicles, scandalous ex-gratia payments to outgoing politicians, sacking of civil servants belonging to the losing party, revelations of economic mismanagement and rising debt, awarding of contracts to party members, and harassment of members of the opposition.[7] Someone, paraphrasing Barack Obama, captured the moment as "the audacity of loot." Meanwhile, all over the country, junior party members violently protested that the expected contracts, appointments, and vehicles had not trickled down to them from the leaders whom they had helped to elect. As Richard Rathbone pointed out long ago, most actors fail to recognize that the interests of patrons and their clients may not coincide.[8]

In scholarship as in politics and mythology, it is much more satisfying to deal with a structure of discrete, contrasted elements than with a swirl of unstable entities. In the 1960s, the age of "nation building" in independent Africa, the historian of Europe Hugh Trevor-Roper provoked a scandalized response from Africanist scholars by asserting, in Hegelian fashion, that Africa had no history, merely "the unrewarding gyrations of barbarous tribes in picturesque but irrelevant corners of the globe."[9]

The problem, however, is not listing what is lacking in Africa, or refuting such listing, but how to capture its history and its dynamic realities without imprisoning them in prefabricated boxes or committing them to imagined trajectories. The history of the north has always been one of constant movement, a play of ambition, opportunity, exogenous influence, and intrusion. Tamale constantly outpaces the planners, its population an anthill of private enterprise, every man and, even more, every woman his or her own managing director. In pursuit of entirely modern rewards, chiefs belligerently insist that tradition is sacred and can never be changed, while the ground shifts beneath their feet.

Postscript

In 2012 the Andanis began to try to restart the kingdom by enskinning chiefs, several of them educated and wealthy. The Abudus generally refused to participate on the ground that the Peace Agreement was being violated and that major issues remained unresolved. They looked forward to the national elections in December 2012 in the hope that a change of government would shift the direction of events in their favor. A new Gulkpe'Na was enskinned and subsequently led through the rituals described in chapter 4; in June the Fazihini Kukuo Na assured me that the rituals had been correctly performed and added that Tulebi, as the principal shrine in Tamale, often receives sacrificial offerings from businessmen and politicians. Downtown, banks and high-rises were more and more numerous; traffic jams intensified. The dispute between the Dakpema and the Bugulana died down. As they had done from the beginning, chiefs complained that the town was daily being invaded by strangers.

Appendix

Outline of Ritual Practice in Dagbon

David Tait attributed the vagueness of Konkombas' cosmology to the fact that they had no central organization, but Dagomba ideas are equally vague. In a sense the dead are ever-present, although the royal dead, at least, live in villages of their own, from which drumming can sometimes be heard. The dead are active at night, so that some tindanas are required to be at home after dark to receive communications from them. Territorial shrines are linked to collective concerns for fertility, good weather, and health; dynastic shrines, with chiefly competition, hierarchy, and violence. Herbalists and diviners are consulted to solve individual problems. No public contention or debate focuses on these distinctions.

Dagbamba distinguish between temporal, fabricated objects (*tima*, s. *tim*, offering "protection") and those that are timeless and are alleged to have come into existence autonomously. Timeless objects are "shrines," or *buɣa*. This distinction is not always clear in practice. Within the class of shrines, some, Earth shrines, are specifically local and therefore fixed; others, associated with families and individuals, are physically portable, though they may not move. Discussing a similar distinction observed by the Bwaba in Burkina Faso, Michèle Coquet introduces the useful word *mobilier*, which denotes mobile property that "furnishes" personal and communal life, as opposed to "real estate."[1] Fixed shrines include both local community shrines and those associated with the dynasty (discussed in chapters 3 and 4). Mobile shrines include family shrines, which in practice rarely move, and "medicinal" shrines, which attract individual clients and may be carried from one place to another. All shrines are nominally distinct from ancestors (*baɣayuli*) and their graves and from personal amulets, "protections," and therapies (*tima*). All these forces are more or less dangerous and tricky to deal with. They form a continuum from the most material (amulets) to the most personal (ancestors).

Tima

Herbal cures and fabricated objects that afford metaphysical "protection" against enemies, thieves, and jealous persons are *tima:* amulets (*gurima*) worn under clothes and charms placed to guard houses, infants, or crops, for example. A traditional house is protected by a *binbarigu,* a "trap," buried under the threshold or placed over the lintel, consisting of a medicated chain or a container such as an animal horn, a sewn packet, or calabash full of noxious ingredients. Crops and infants are similarly protected. The highest-ranking female chief, the Gundo Na, gave her colleague the Zo-Simli Na an amulet-loaded staff she had commissioned for her, warning her that it afforded such dangerous protection that if, when in public, she should strike anyone's foot with it, that person would surely die. A purely mechanical trap for vermin such as mice is also a *binbarigu,* but it is not *tim.* Amulets, charms, and other protections are obtained from a herbalist, a shrine keeper (*bugulana;* see below) or a *malam,* an Islamic expert. A malam writes a Qur'anic text on paper, wraps it, and tells the client to take it to a leatherworker, for whom the malam provides instructions such as the color of the leather packet—red, white, or black. It is characteristic of *tima* that they are tightly wrapped, sewn, and contained. Chiefs who speak of themselves as "enlightened" by their education or religious belief describe the leather-bound amulets they wear on their hats and their sticks as merely ornamental, but again the distinction is not always clear.

There is a diffuse general belief in witchcraft (*soyu*), which is not clearly different from the use of *tima* or even from the power of chiefs and tindanas. Both men and women can be witches (*sonima,* s. *sonya*), but men are rarely accused of witchcraft or punished for it. Some men and even some women may brag about their witchcraft power.

Local and Dynastic Shrines

A fixed, local shrine is sometimes distinguished from a portable one by the term *tiŋa,* "territory," or *tiŋbani,* which may be used for both a tract of land and the shrine that may be associated with it, but it falls within the category of buguli. Its keeper, or "owner," is called *tindana* or *bugulana,* terms that are partly interchangeable (cf. the Talni term *tengban* below). Dynastic shrines are also in the charge of tindanas, but they serve the interests of the aristocracy, the *nabihi,* who alone send sacrifices to them, although they may not approach such shrines personally.

Family Shrines

The family shrines in Dagbon are Tia, Wumbee, Jebuni, Jehi, Wuni, Tilo, and others less well known. It is said that every extended family has Jebuni, to which the deaths of family members at home and abroad must be reported, but it will also have at least one other, because they are specialized to some extent. Jehi, for example, is most appropriate for women's concerns, Wumbee for men's. They usually take the form of calabashes or clay pots, thick with the remains of small sacrifices, kept in the personal rooms of the head of the family (*daŋkpema*) and his principal wife. Once a year, all of them are brought out and renewed, but sacrifices are also made as occasion requires. For example, after childbirth a woman is taken to the female shrine to have her head shaved before it, with a sacrifice of a small chicken. After a misfortune, such as his wife's miscarriage, a man should have the head of the family sacrifice a black fowl for the black event that happened and a particolored one to ask the ancestors by name to give him another child. When a successful birth ensues, a large white cock should be offered as thanks.[2] On ordinary occasions libations of milk or millet beer are appropriate. This elementary color symbolism, found all over sub-Saharan Africa, often in more complex forms, is also operative at territorial and dynastic shrines. Although these objects must have been made by someone, they are thought of as having been in existence for as long as the family itself, that is, "forever." Although these "gods" are known all over Dagbon, one does not approach Wumbee, for example, as it is manifested in someone else's family compound. A localized family of smaller span, *doyiri*, may have its own shrines.

To the elders of Foshegu, which is a single-family village founded about 1900, Jebuni and Jehi are shrines "for the family," whereas the place under a particular baobab where annual collective sacrifices are made is a shrine "for the farm," exemplifying the complementary ritualization of time and space discussed in chapter 3. All three components, however, constitute a single community buguli, in their view.

Medicinal Shrines

"Medicinal" shrines are not only portable but, often enough, literally mobile, participating in national networks of problem-solving rituals. A diviner's bag of tokens is also a sort of mobile shrine. The problems include disease, decision making, and all kinds of misfortunes and frustrations.[3] A much-consulted bugulana in Yendi shows his clients a variety of composite objects, telling where each one came from and what it deals with; he will say, "This one is from Kete Krachi and cures what ails you" or "This one is from Asante and will make you rich." Dagbon and other parts of the north export such shrines to the south, a lucrative industry. The most successful franchise is that of Tongnaab in Talensi country.[4] In the Accra suburb of Madina a Dagomba bugulana miraculously changes paper into any foreign currency, among other services. He lives in a house built for him by a grateful client: the shrine induced the U.S. embassy to give the client a visa enabling him to go to America and make his fortune. Such healers compete directly with Pentecostal, or "Miracle," churches that offer the illusory possibility of similar success.[5]

The exotic appeal of the gods of the alien north is balanced, in the north, by the sense that mysterious southern powers can provide protection to northerners, who buy masks and other works of African art produced abundantly in the south for sale to tourists and hotels. These things are taken north to serve as the foundation of protective devices to which gifts can be offered.

Ancestors

Family shrines are distinct from prayers addressed to the spirits of the dead. *Baɣayuya* (s. *baɣayuli*) refers to both the dead and addresses to them. Traditionally, the dead are buried in the compound they inhabited in life. Prayers and sacrifices can be performed anywhere, not necessarily at the grave itself. The dead have knowledge of things seen and unseen; they have "four eyes" and may be able to help, whereas "we are in the dark." A diviner may tell his client that the source of a problem is an ancestor who has some complaint: "he is following you." Alternatively, the diviner may say that the problem derives from a shrine. It is my impression that prayers are addressed primarily to a father or grandfather whom one has known in life.

One family I know makes annual offerings at a tree that they say sprang instantly from the new grave of their great-great-grandfather. Such graves may well be the origin of many local shrines whose connection with a particular lineage has been lost. The "secret history" of a shrine, not to be casually revealed, is usually a story of some vision or miracle that occurred on the spot once upon a time.

Meyer Fortes, describing the Talensi, especially the Hill Talis, contrasts the "cult of the Earth," performed at a *tengban,* with that of the ancestors, performed at shrines called *boɣa* (s. *boɣar*). This last term is cognate with the Dagbani *buɣuli;* in Talni it refers to "a shrine specifically dedicated by or to the founding ancestor of a lineage or clan," but it also refers to the much less numerous shrines to Tongnaab, the guardian spirit or perhaps ancestor of all the autochthonous Tali clans collectively. Fortes distinguished this second sense by the term "External *boɣar.*" Tongnaab shrines, of which there are about a dozen, each addressed by a congregation comprising a group of clans, are tended by ritual functionaries, including both a *tengdaana* (tindana) and a *boɣarana* (owner of a *bɣar;* Dagbani *buɣulana*).[6] These Talni terms are all cognate with Dagbani terms, but whereas in Dagbon a *tindana,* "owner" of a local shrine, may be called *buguluna,* that term also applies to the owner of a portable shrine, either a family shrine or the fully mobile kind that could be called a "medicine." The individual households of an extended family may be quite widely scattered around Dagbon, but there is no equivalent to the Talensi External *boɣar,* presumably because there is no corresponding "external" clan organization; the closest functional equivalent is provided by the shrines of past kings.

A particular idea of heredity or reincarnation (*siɣili*) creates a feedback loop between ancestors and *tima* (except *tima* provided by a malam). A child is traditionally supposed to be a reincarnation of an ancestor. The family should consult a diviner to find out which ancestor, so that the child may carry his or her name; an indication may be that the child is born with teeth or grey hair. As a reincarnation, the child has the nature, the capacity, and even the identity of the ancestor and is addressed accordingly. If the ancestor was a *kpema* (a term that can mean an elder or senior person, a wise man, or a herbalist), the child will be credited with the same exceptional abilities and may be awarded the designation *kpema* regardless of age. The abilities are innate, not a product of study or imitation, and it is even said that the abilities themselves empower the herbs used; "any leaves would do." At his enskinment, in a darkened room a new Ya Na chooses the stick of a predecessor. This is a kind of divination that reveals the identity of the one whom he reincarnates.

Introduction

1. Tamakloe, *Brief History;* the British referred to Dagbon, its people (the Dagbamba), and its language (Dagbani) as *Dagomba.* Tamakloe's manuscript was prepared for publication by A. W. Cardinall.

2. Smith, "On Segmentary Lineage Systems."

3. On the limited sense of the political in classical social anthropology, see Spencer, "Post-colonialism."

4. Leach, *Political Systems of Highland Burma;* Leach, "Frontiers of 'Burma'"; Firth, *Elements of Social Organization.* On the regional approach and Leach's contributions, see Kuper, "Regional Comparison in African Anthropology"; and Scott, *Art of Not Being Governed,* 38, 214.

5. Fuglestad, "Trevor-Roper Trap," 317. For a general critique of the problem, see White, "Politics of Historical Interpretation."

6. McCaskie, "Empire State"; McCaskie, *State and Society,* ch. 1; Mbembe, *Afriques indociles,* 22–27.

7. Staniland, *Lions of Dagbon,* 13–14.

8. Janzen, *Lemba;* Feierman, "Colonizers, Scholars"; Schoffeleers, *River of Blood,* 11.

9. Olivier de Sardan, "Occultism and the Ethnographic 'I'," 14; Appiah, *In My Father's House,* 121. See also Brenner, "'Religious' Discourse"; Shaw, "Invention of African Traditional Religion"; Feierman, "Colonizers, Scholars," 202; and Goody, *Logic of Writing,* 4–5.

10. Paul Landau takes a more radical position in "'Religion' and Conversion in African History," 29.

11. Vansina, *How Societies Are Born,* 76.

12. See also MacGaffey, "Changing Representations."

13. Miller, *Problem of Slavery as History,* 8.

14. Bierlich, *Problem of Money;* Oppong, *Growing Up in Dagbon.*

15. For a good summary of the received history, see www.dagbon.net/history.php.

16. Fage, "Reflections on the Early History"; Staniland, *Lions of Dagbon,* 1–7; Mahama, *History and Traditions of Dagbon,* 1–16.

17. Der, "Traditional Political Systems."

18. Scott, *Art of Not Being Governed,* esp. 26–39. See also Wilks, "Mossi and Akan States," 345.

19. Swanepoel, "Every Periphery Is Its Own Center."

20. Skalník, "Early States in the Voltaic Basin," 472.

1. Colonial Anthropology and Historical Reconstruction

1. Kirby, "Ethnic Conflicts and Democratization"; Brukum, *Guinea Fowl.*

2. Davis, "Continuity and Change in Mampurugu," 160.

3. Wilks, "Medieval Trade Route."

4. Kea, *Settlements, Trade, and Polities,* 198.

5. Mendonsa, *Continuity and Change,* 27.

6. Johnson, "Slaves of Salaga."

7. Der, *Slave Trade in Northern Ghana;* Lovejoy, *Caravans of Kola,* 108.

8. Webb, "Horse and Slave Trade," 221; Law, *Horse in West African History.*

9. Roberts, *Warriors, Merchants, and Slaves;* Klein, "Slavery in the Western Soudan."

10. Meillassoux, *L'esclavage en Afrique précoloniale,* 24.

11. See Kopytoff, "Internal African Frontier"; on "symbiotic" relations, Scott, *Art of Not Being Governed,* 26; and on "autochthons and strangers," Kuba and Lentz, *Land and the Politics of Belonging.*

12. Bening, "Definition of the International Boundaries"; Staniland, *Lions of Dagbon,* 39; Ladouceur, *Chiefs and Politicians,* ch. 1.

13. Bening, "Administrative Boundaries of Northern Ghana."

14. Brukum, "Chieftaincy and Ethnic Conflicts"; Iliasu, "British Administration in Mamprugu"; Sharpe, "Ethnography and a Regional System."

15. Lentz, "Stateless Societies or Chiefdoms?"

16. Maasole, *Konkomba and their Neighbours,* 65.

17. Der, "Traditional Political Systems"; Lentz, *Ethnicity,* 44; Kuklick, *Savage Within,* 269.

18. Lentz, *Ethnicity,* 14–32; Goody, *Technology, Tradition and the State,* 55; Goody, "Political Systems of the Tallensi," 24; Mendonsa, *Continuity and Change,* 21–67.

19. Goody, "Circulating Succession among the Gonja," 143.

20. Goody, "Over-kingdom of Gonja," 186.

21. Wilks, *Wa and the Wala,* 29.

22. De Heusch, *Drunken King.*

23. Kopytoff, "Internal African Frontier," 63.

24. Mahama, *History and Traditions of Dagbon,* 13; Fage, "Reflections on the Early History."

25. Lentz, *Ethnicity,* 263.

26. Goody, "Political Systems of the Tallensi," 24.

27. Wilks, *Wa and the Wala,* 112; Oppong, *Growing Up in Dagbon,* 24. The slaver/enslaved dichotomy has been challenged elsewhere in West Africa; see Hawthorne, *Planting Rice and Harvesting Slaves,* 8–11, and Hubbell, "View of the Slave Trade."

28. Fortes, *Dynamics of Clanship,* 53.

29. McCaskie, "Empire State," 468.

30. On the invasion model, see Leach, "Aryan Invasions over Four Millennia"; Bernal, "Race, Class, and Gender"; Clark, "Invasion in British Archaeology"; Cooper, "Conflict and Connection," 1519; Braudel, "Situation of History in 1950"; and Miller, *Kings and Kinsmen,* 4–10.

31. Goody, "Restricted Literacy in Northern Ghana," 199.

32. Mahama, *Ethnic Conflict in Northern Ghana,* 158.

33. Duncan-Johnstone and Blair, *Enquiry into the Constitution,* 4.

34. Tait, "History and Social Organization."

35. Fortes, *Dynamics of Clanship,* 16; Lentz, *Ethnicity,* 2. For a southern Ghanaian example, see Gilbert, "No Condition Is Permanent."

36. Schlottner, "We Stay, Others Come and Go," 49; Ferguson, "Islamisation in Dagbon," xxii; Skalník, "On the Inadequacy of the Concept," 306–7.

37. Oppong, *Growing Up in Dagbon,* 24.

38. Tait, "History and Social Organisation," 202.

39. Public Records and Archives Administration Department (PRAAD), Tamale, NRG 8/1/129, Stool Lands Boundaries Commission.

40. Skalník, "Outwitting Ghana," 149.

41. Drucker-Brown, "Structure of the Mamprusi Kingdom," 130.

42. Levtzion, *Muslims and Chiefs,* 88–91.

43. Goody, "Over-kingdom of Gonja," 183, 198; Schlottner, "We Stay, Others Come and Go," 53.

44. Ferguson, "Islamisation in Dagbon," 97.

45. Levtzion, *Muslims and Chiefs,* ch. 1; Johnson, "Slaves of Salaga"; Iliasu, "Asante's Relations with Dagomba."

46. PRAAD, Tamale, NRG 8/4/19.

47. Tamakloe, *Brief History,* 16.

48. Duncan-Johnstone and Blair, *Enquiry into the Constitution,* 39.

49. Rattray, *Tribes of the Ashanti Hinterland,* xii.

50. Ibid.

51. Jack Goody, preface to Tait, *Konkomba of Northern Ghana,* xvi.

52. PRAAD, Tamale, NRG 8/2/32, Native Affairs, 1931–33, "Response by Acting Chief Commissioner to the report of the Dagbon constitutional conference of 1930."

53. MacGaffey, "Concepts of Race."

54. Scott, *Art of Not Being Governed,* ch. 4.

55. PRAAD, Tamale, NRG 8/2/32 (NAG ADM 56/1/179); Lentz, *Ethnicity,* 95.

56. Duncan-Johnstone and Blair, *Enquiry into the Constitution,* 39; Scott, *Art of Not Being Governed,* 220–37; Tonkin, *Narrating our Pasts;* Lentz, "Of Hunters, Goats and Earth Shrines."

57. Mahama, *History and Traditions of Dagbon,* 46.

58. Ibid., 23.

59. PRAAD, Tamale, NRG 8/2/32, Feb. 1930. The copy is on flimsy paper and is disintegrating.

60. PRAAD, Tamale, NRG 8/2/28, Dagomba Native Affairs, 1930–32, "Chieftainship and the Dagomba Constitution," unsigned and undated memorandum, evidently written by Blair; Duncan-Johnstone and Blair, *Enquiry into the Constitution,* 17.

61. Wilks, "Mossi and Akan States"; Fage, "Reflections on the Early History"; Ferguson and Wilks, "Chiefs, Constitutions and the British."

62. Ferguson, "Islamisation in Dagbon," 97. I question Wilks's statement that in Dagomba "the political structure was a highly evolved one long before Islam made a substantial impact." Ferguson and Wilks, "Chiefs, Constitutions and the British," 329.

63. Ferguson, "Islamisation in Dagbon," 247.

64. Ferguson, "Islamisation in Dagbon," 23; Law, *Horse in West African History,* 15.

65. Wilks, *Wa and the Wala,* 85–87; Lentz, *Ethnicity,* 265; Terray, *Histoire du royaume Abron,* 93–96.

66. Dittmer, *Die Sakralen Haüptlingen der Gurunsi,* cited in Liberski-Bagnoud, *Les dieux du territoire,* 110–16.

67. Oppong, *Growing Up in Dagbon,* 23.

68. Skalník, "Authority versus Power," 110.

69. Tsikata and Seini, "Identities, Inequalities and Conflicts," 4; Kelly and Bening, "Ideology, Regionalism."

70. Eyre-Smith, *Brief Review,* 40.

71. Republic of Ghana, *Constitution of the Republic of Ghana,* 1992, article 270, par. 2(a).

72. Owusu, "Rebellion, Revolution and Tradition," 377.

2. Drum Chant and the Political Uses of Tradition

1. Staniland, *Lions of Dagbon,* 172–74.

2. Ferguson, "Islamisation in Dagbon," xxi.

3. Mahama, *Ethnic Conflict in Northern Ghana,* 99.

4. Fage, "Some Notes on a Scheme." "Tait A" and "Tait B" were in the Balme Library of the University of Ghana in 1975; in 2010 librarians could find no trace of them.

5. Abubakari Lunna, "History Stories." Benzing lists a number of recordings and transcriptions dating from the 1960s, said to be in the Institute of African Studies at the University of Ghana, Legon, and yet others held privately. Benzing, *Die Geschichte,* 25–30.

6. Salifu, "Names That Prick"; Zablong, "Lunsi Institution of Dagbon."

7. Schlottner, "We Stay, Others Come and Go," 54.

8. Thornton, "Origin Traditions and History," 37; Schlottner, "We Stay, Others Come and Go," 54; Lentz, "Of Hunters, Goats and Earth Shrines," 193; Ferguson, "Islamisation in Dagbon," xxii; Jones, "Jakpa," 5; Boni, "Contents and Contexts." See also Izard, *Moogo,* 15–26; and Staniland, *Lions of Dagbon,* 174. On the unreliability of king lists and the problem of chronology, see Henige, *Chronology of Oral Tradition.*

9. Davis, "Continuity and Change in Mampurugu," 29, 160; Iliasu, "Origins of the Mossi-Dagomba States," 96.

10. Adapted from Salifu, "Names That Prick," 94. Zablong, "Lunsi Institution of Dagbon," gives a longer prose version.

11. Mahama, *History and Traditions of Dagbon,* 36; "Dikala," at Abubakari Lunna, "History Stories."

12. Z. A. Zablong, conversation with author, 17 May 2010.

13. Davis, "Continuity and Change in Mampurugu," 47. See also Lentz, "Of Hunters, Goats and Earth Shrines," 211.

14. "The Story of Tora," at Abubakari Lunna, "History Stories," emphasis added.

15. Duncan-Johnstone and Blair, *Enquiry into the Constitution,* 43.

16. Salifu, "Names That Prick," 7, 20.

17. On Na Luro in Kpung Tamale, see chapter 4; see also Iliasu, "Origins of the Mossi-Dagomba States," 111n. *Timpana,* Akan instruments (*atumpan*), were not introduced in Dagbon until after 1740, i.e., some sixty years later.

18. Abubakari Lunna, "History Stories"; Chernoff, *African Rhythm and African Sensibility,* 206.

19. PRAAD, Tamale, NRG 8/28/26, Local Government, Sept. 1958.

20. Pietz, "Spirit of Civilization," 33.

21. Eyre-Smith, *Brief Review,* 16, 31.

22. Wood, "Machiavelli's Concept of Virtù Reconsidered."

23. Tradition discreetly omits the fact that Na Abudulai was killed fighting the Bassar.

24. Staniland, *Lions of Dagbon,* 168.

25. Kirby, "Peace-Building in Northern Ghana."

26. Drucker-Brown, "Local Wars in Northern Ghana," 88.

27. Locke, *Drum Damba*, 23; Bierlich, *Problem of Money*, 32.

28. Locke, *Drum Damba*, 12.

29. Mahama, *History and Traditions of Dagbon*, 39.

30. Levtzion, *Muslims and Chiefs*, 110.

31. http://www.modernghana.com/GhanaHome.

32. Lambek, "Sakalava Poiesis of History," 122.

33. Staniland, *Lions of Dagbon*, 27–32.

34. Ferguson and Wilks, "Chiefs, Constitutions and the British," 341.

35. Lovejoy, *Caravans of Kola.*

36. Bowdich, *Mission from Cape Coast Castle*, 170, 178, 330–35.

37. Duncan-Johnstone and Blair, *Enquiry into the Constitution*, 51.

38. Mahama, *Ya-Naa*, 5.

39. Holden, "Zabarima Conquest of Northwest Ghana," 73.

40. Ibid.

41. Locke, *Drum Damba*, 125.

42. Ferguson and Wilks, "Chiefs, Constitutions and the British," 342–45.

43. Locke, *Drum Damba*, 126–31.

44. Mahama, *Ya-Naa*, 5–7.

45. Staniland, *Lions of Dagbon*, 18.

46. Mahama, *Ya-Naa*, 7; Anamzoya, "Sociological Enquiry," 91.

47. Ferguson, "Islamisation in Dagbon," 297.

48. PRAAD, Tamale, NRG 8/2/32, Native Affairs, 1931–33, "Memorandum on the proposed Northern Territories Native Administration Ordinance" [1930].

49. Staniland, *Lions of Dagbon*, chs. 3–6, quotation from 104.

50. Ibid., 113.

51. Arhin Brempong, *Transformations of Traditional Rule*, vii.

52. Staniland, *Lions of Dagbon*, 68–74, quotation from 73.

53. Grischow, *Shaping Tradition;* Talton, *Politics of Social Change;* Lentz, *Ethnicity;* Iliasu, "British Administration in Mamprugu."

54. Ferguson and Wilks, "Chiefs, Constitutions and the British," 329.

55. Quoted by Mahama, *Ya-Naa*, 141; see below, in this chapter.

56. Kuga Na Abdulai Braima to Asantehene, 7 Feb. 2007, copy in author's possession; Staniland, *Lions of Dagbon*, vii.

57. Ferguson and Wilks, "Chiefs, Constitutions and the British," 348; Staniland, *Lions of Dagbon*, 110–12.

58. Staniland, *Lions of Dagbon*, 125.

59. PRAAD, Tamale, NRG, file number indecipherable, "District Diaries."

60. Ferguson and Wilks, "Chiefs, Constitutions and the British," 349; Staniland, *Lions of Dagbon*, 120–25.

61. Anamzoya, "Sociological Enquiry," 98.

62. Duncan-Johnstone and Blair, *Enquiry into the Constitution,* 32.

63. Ladouceur, *Chiefs and Politicians,* 183–84.

64. Staniland, *Lions of Dagbon,* 137–47.

65. Ibid., 182, emphasis added.

66. Ibid., 162–76.

67. On the ambiguities of the position of an ex–Ya Na, see Mahama, *Yaa-Naa,* 204–5.

68. Regional Secretary J. E. Bawa to Ya Na Andani Yakubu II, 25 Oct. 1988, N/R Administration, SCR/NR/127/Vol.4/185, copy in author's possession.

69. Brukum, *Guinea Fowl,* 14; see also Lund, "Bawku Is Still Volatile," 604.

70. Mahama, *History and Traditions of Dagbon,* 152.

71. Anamzoya, "Politicization, Elite Manipulation," 21–22.

72. Republic of Ghana, *White Paper;* Mahama, *Murder of an African King.*

73. "Statement issued by the committee of Eminent Kings of his Majesty Otumfuo Osei Tutu II; the Yagbonwura and the Nayiri on the Dagbon chieftaincy dispute," Manhyia Palace, Kumasi, 10 April 2006, copy in author's possession.

74. Dagbon Traditional Council to Asantehene, 6 June 2006, copy in author's possession.

75. Kuga Na Abdulai Braima to Asantehene, 11 Sept. 2006, copy in author's possession.

76. "Final Peace Agreement," news release, 18 Nov. 2007; Andani Royal Family to Asantehene, 28 Nov. 2007, 5 Dec. 2007; "Abudu royal family's statement on the funeral of the late Ya Na Mahamadu Abudulai," news release, 29 May 2008, copies in author's possession.

3. Tindanas and Chiefs

1. White, "Politics of Historical Interpretation," 122.

2. MacGaffey, "Changing Representations"; MacGaffey, "Oral Tradition in Central Africa."

3. Fortes, *Dynamics of Clanship,* 27–28, quotation from 27; Fortes, "Political System of the Tallensi," 255.

4. Izard, *Gens du pouvoir,* 18; Zahan, "Mossi Kingdoms."

5. McCaskie, *State and Society,* 8.

6. Izard, *Moogo.*

7. Jackson, *Kuranko,* 24.

8. "L'incontournable division du travail idéologique dans les représentations du rapport des hommes à la nature et des hommes entre eux." Izard, *Moogo,* 148.

9. Schoffeleers, *River of Blood,* 9.

10. Turner, *Dramas, Fields, and Metaphors*, 185. See also Izard, *Gens du pouvoir*, 19.

11. Fortes, *Dynamics of Clanship*, 184.

12. Feierman, "Colonizers, Scholars," 200.

13. See esp. Liberski-Bagnoud, *Les dieux du territoire*, 39–42.

14. Tait, *Konkomba of Northern Ghana*, 228; Goody, "Political Systems of the Tallensi," 21; Lentz, *Ethnicity*, 22; Kopytoff, "Internal African Frontier," 62–64.

15. Goody, *Technology, Tradition and the State*, 59–64.

16. PRAAD, Accra, NAG ADM, 56/1/91, "N.T. Laws and customs."

17. In Mamprugu, royal gate shrines are distinguished from earth shrines. Drucker-Brown, *Ritual Aspects of Mamprusi Kingship*, 57.

18. Izard, "De quelques paramètres," 71.

19. Eyre-Smith, *Brief Review*, 26.

20. Interview at Gbanga, July 2009.

21. Staniland, *Lions of Dagbon*, 189n18; Lund, *Local Politics*, 60.

22. Bazin, "Retour aux choses-dieux."

23. Brown, *Cult of the Saints*, 86.

24. Bazin, "Retour aux choses-dieux."

25. Ibid., 270; Friedson, *Remains of Ritual*, 87.

26. Brown, *Cult of the Saints*, 88.

27. Singleton, "Speaking to the Ancestors," 327; Kirby, "Cultural Change and Religious Conversion," 64.

28. Gell, *Art and Agency*, 122.

29. Schoffeleers, *River of Blood*, 7.

30. Fortes, "Political System of the Tallensi," 255.

31. Mahama, *Dagbani English Dictionary*.

32. See Peel's nuanced discussion, "Poverty and Sacrifice." Luc de Heusch emphasizes that the meanings and procedures of sacrifice can be quite different in different societies. De Heusch, *Sacrifice*.

33. Kopytoff, "Ancestors as Elders in Africa"; Singleton, "Speaking to the Ancestors."

34. Cardinall, "Customs of the Konkomba," 33.

35. Keane, "Evidence of the Senses," S120.

36. Jay, *Throughout Your Generations Forever*, 37 (quotation), 68–76.

37. Kirby, "Peace-Building in Northern Ghana," 194n.

38. Mahama, *History and Traditions of Dagbon*, 95; Drucker-Brown, *Ritual Aspects of Mamprusi Kingship*; Cardinall, "Customs at the Death of a King."

39. Kuba, "Spiritual Hierarchies and Unholy Alliances," 60; Fortes, "Political System of the Tallensi," 256, 261.

40. Baum, "Slaves without Rulers."

41. Mahama, *History and Traditions of Dagbon*, 24.

42. PRAAD, Tamale, NRG 8/2/28, Blair to Commissioner Southern Province, 9 June 1930.

43. Skalník, "On the Inadequacy of the Concept," 310.

44. Mahama, *History and Traditions of Dagbon*, 17–26; Rattray, *Tribes of the Ashanti Hinterland*, 575–76.

45. Goody, *Technology, Tradition and the State*, 63–64; Allman and Parker, *Tongnaab*, 62.

46. Cardinall, *Natives of the Northern Territories*, 49.

47. Candler, in PRAAD, Tamale, NRG 8/2/32.

48. Goody, "Mande and the Akan Hinterland," 201.

49. Rattray, *Tribes of the Ashanti Hinterland*, 571.

50. Author's field notes from Yenn'Yogu, June 2001. Cf. Rattray, *Tribes of the Ashanti Hinterland*, 583–84; and Mahama, *History and Traditions of Dagbon*, 10, 77–78.

51. Fortes, *Dynamics of Clanship*, plate XIb.

52. Salifu, "Names That Prick," 93–94.

4. Chiefs and Tindanas

1. Izard, *Moogo*, 63.

2. De Heusch, *Pourquoi l'épouser?*, 66–68.

3. Mahama, *History and Traditions of Dagbon*, 26, and other authorities offer, indeed insist on, somewhat different lists. My list was provided by a senior drummer in Yendi in June 2011. Detailed accounts of the ritual for the enskinment of a Ya Na, of which I present only certain elements, are given by Tamakloe, Cardinall, Rattray, and Mahama. Tamakloe, *Brief History*, 67–70; Cardinall, *In Ashanti and Beyond*, 114; Rattray, *Tribes of the Ashanti Hinterland*, 582–86; Mahama, *History and Traditions of Dagbon*, 76–80; Iddi, *Ya Na of the Dagombas*.

4. Cardinall, "Customs at the Death of a King."

5. Tamakloe, *Brief History*, 67; Anamzoya, "Sociological Enquiry," 84.

6. Rattray, *Tribes of the Ashanti Hinterland*, 583–86; Mahama, *History and Traditions of Dagbon*, 76–80.

7. "Authorities" differ as to whether the Kumbun'Na undergoes the Katin'du ritual.

8. Mahama, *History and Traditions of Dagbon*, 96.

9. Chernoff, *African Rhythm and African Sensibility*, 46, 83. "ʒiem" is defined in Mahama's *Dagbani English Dictionary* as "a rowdy dance; as a verb, to show disrespect."

10. Fortes, "Ritual Festivals and Social Cohesion," 156.

11. This paragraph and the next are based on Skalník, "Authority versus Power," 113–14, and Skalník, "Ideological and Symbolic Authority," 90–91.

12. This paragraph is based on Drucker-Brown, "Horse, Dog and Donkey," 77–85.

13. Drucker-Brown, *Ritual Aspects of Mamprusi Kingship*, 101.

14. Ibid., 88.

15. For a different interpretation, see Davis, "Then the White Man Came."

16. Fortes, "Ritual Festivals and Social Cohesion," 151.

17. Fortes, "Political System of the Tallensi," 260.

18. Bazin, "Past in the Present," 60.

19. PRAAD, Tamale, NRG 8/2/35, Nanumba Kingdom.

20. Skalník, "Early States in the Voltaic Basin" 472 (quotation); Skalník, "Dynamics of Early State Development"; Skalník, "On the Inadequacy of the Concept"; Benzing, *Die Geschichte*, 46.

21. Skalník, "Authority versus Power," 110–11.

22. Ibid., 94. See also Schlottner, "We Stay, Others Come and Go," 54–55, which says much the same thing about Mamprugu.

23. Skalník, "On the Inadequacy of the Concept," 328; Fortes, "Political System of the Tallensi," 245; Fortes, *Dynamics of Clanship*, 22.

24. Skalník, "Ideological and Symbolic Authority," 90.

25. Wienia, "Ominous Calm," 135.

26. Drucker-Brown, *Ritual Aspects of Mamprusi Kingship*, 44–48, 95; Drucker-Brown, "Horse, Dog and Donkey"; Rattray, *Tribes of the Ashanti Hinterland*, 557.

27. Benzing, *Die Geschichte*, 219–21.

28. Scholars since Leo Frobenius have observed that all the elements of the story of Tohazie and Kpogonumbo recur again and again in the Sunjata epic of Mali.

29. PRAAD, Tamale, NRG 8, Local Government, Sept. 1958. The Ya Na is known as "the Lion of Dagbon."

30. Tamakloe, *Brief History*, 7.

31. Benzing, *Die Geschichte*, 219–21.

32. Ibid., 46; Davis, "Then the White Man Came," 633.

33. Mahama, *History and Traditions of Dagbon*, 23.

34. Drucker-Brown, *Ritual Aspects of Mamprusi Kingship*, 57.

35. Izard, "De quelques paramètres."

36. Levtzion, *Muslims and Chiefs*, fig. 2.

37. Yoder, *Kanyok of Zaire*, 99; cf. Ceyssens, *Le roi Kanyok*.

38. This issue has been provocatively discussed, though in very different terms in each case, in De Heusch, "Symbolic Mechanisms of Sacred Kingship," and Graeber, *Possibilities*, ch. 4.

39. Lentz, "Of Hunters, Goats and Earth Shrines"; Lentz, "Is Land Inalienable?"

40. Goody, "Restricted Literacy in Northern Ghana," 217.

41. Ferguson, "Islamisation in Dagbon," 132.

42. PRAAD, Tamale, NRG 8/2/93, Native Affairs, 28 June 1949.

43. Bazin, "Retour aux choses-dieux," 272.

44. Kodesh, "History from the Healer's Shrine," quotation from 536.

45. Rattray, *Tribes of the Ashanti Hinterland*, 459.

46. Ibid., 554.

47. Goody, "Political Systems of the Tallensi," 15; Goody, "Over-kingdom of Gonja," 145.

48. Rattray, *Tribes of the Ashanti Hinterland*, xii; PRAAD, Tamale, NRG 8/2/32, Native Affairs, 1931–32, "Extract from a report by Mr. A. W. Cardinall, 20 July 1928."

49. Fortes, *Dynamics of Clanship*, 187.

50. Liberski-Bagnoud, *Les dieux du territoire*, 109.

51. Lund, *Local Politics*, 71.

52. Cardinall, *Natives of the Northern Territories*, 20 (quotation); Drucker-Brown, "Structure of the Mamprusi Kingdom," 118–20.

53. Tait, *Konkomba of Northern Ghana*, 11, 35–36, 228.

54. Mendonsa, *Continuity and Change*, 29–39.

55. Lentz, *Ethnicity*, ch. 2 and passim.

56. Allman and Parker, *Tongnaab*, 100.

57. Fortes, *Dynamics of Clanship*, 24.

5. Tamale

1. Watherston, "Northern Territories," 356.

2. PRAAD, Accra, ADM 56/1/57, 1 Feb. 1907.

3. Ibid., 10 Feb. 1907.

4. Ibid., ADM 56/1/73, 1908.

5. Ibid., 56/1/57, Medical Officer, N.T., 1910.

6. Kimble, *Political History of Ghana*, 535.

7. PRAAD, Accra, ADM 56/1/90.

8. Staniland, *Lions of Dagbon*, ch. 5.

9. Ibid., 107.

10. Tamakloe, *Brief History*, 17.

11. Ferguson, "Islamisation in Dagbon," 35.

12. Iddi, *Ya Na of the Dagombas*, 50.

13. Salifu, "Names That Prick," 73.

14. PRAAD, Tamale, NRG 8/2/32, Native Administration.

15. Ibid., NRG 2/3/1, Native Administration, Dagomba Sub-district.

16. Ibid., NRG 8/2/32, J. E. Miller, Oct. 1933.

17. Ibid., NRG 2/3/1, Report of Native Administration, Dagomba Sub-district, "Distribution of medallions to chiefs," Oct. 1938.

18. Ibid., NRG 8/2/128, Dagomba Native Affairs, 1955–69, Apr. 1958.

19. Ibid., NRG 2/3/1, Native Administration, Dagomba Sub-district, correspondence, Mar. 1947.

20. Ibid., NRG 8/28/26, Tamale Urban Council, Ebenezer Adam to Central Government, Gold Coast.

21. Ibid., NRG 2/7/2, Informal Diaries, Government Agent, Dagomba, in Yendi, to the Chief Regional Officer, 13 Sept. 1954, NTS, Tamale (quotation); Bening, "Land Policy and Administration," 258.

22. PRAAD, Tamale, NRG 8/28/28, Local Government, correspondence, Apr. 1959.

23. E. Aryeetey et al., *Politics of Land Tenure Reform*, 48; Karikari, "Ghana's Land Administration Project"; Brukum, "Chieftaincy and Ethnic Conflicts"; Brukum, "Ethnic Conflicts in Gonja"; Berry, *Chiefs Know Their Boundaries.*

24. Crook, "Decolonization, the Colonial State," 88; E. Aryeetey et al., *Politics of Land Tenure Reform*, 11.

25. Amanor, "Changing Face of Customary Land Tenure," 55. See also Berry, "Ancestral Property," 27.

26. E. Aryeetey et al., *Politics of Land Tenure Reform*, 24.

27. Tsikata and Seini, "Identities, Inequalities and Conflicts," 4.

28. Ibid., 54–56; Amanor, "Changing Face of Customary Land Tenure," 59–60; E. Aryeetey et al., *Politics of Land Tenure Reform*, 10–14; Kasanga, "Land Tenure, Resource Access"; Sutton, "Colonial Agricultural Policy"; Ladouceur, *Chiefs and Politicians*, 44–52; Staniland, *Lions of Dagbon*, 52–56; Grischow, *Shaping Tradition*, ch. 3; Antoine, "Politics of Rice-Farming," 60–80.

29. Staniland, *Lions of Dagbon*, 91.

30. Rattray, *Tribes of the Ashanti Hinterland*, 563.

31. PRAAD, Tamale, NRG 8/1/55, Land Tenure in the Protectorate. The following quotations are taken from a badly decayed document dated 18 August 1948 but lacking a first page.

32. Ladouceur, *Chiefs and Politicians*, 72–96.

33. PRAAD, Tamale, NRG 8/1/148, Land Tenure in the Protectorate, 25 Aug. 1955.

34. Ibid., NRG 8/1/129, Stool Lands Boundaries Commission.

35. Ibid., NRG 8/1/148, 14 May 1957.

36. Bening, "Land Policy and Administration," 254.

37. Republic of Ghana, *Constitution of the Republic of Ghana*, 1969, articles 162, 164.

38. Konings, "Capitalist Rice Farming and Land Allocation"; Ladouceur, *Chiefs and Politicians*, 214.

39. PRAAD, Tamale, NRG 8/3/270, Intelligence Reports Tamale, Aug. 1966.

40. Ibid., NRG 8/1/311, Stool and Skin Land.

41. Nugent, *Big Men, Small Boys,* 74.

42. PRAAD, Tamale, NRG 8/1/311, Stool and Skin Land, 8 Aug. 1974.

43. Antoine, "Politics of Rice-Farming," 53, 204 (quotation); Konings, *State and Rural Class Formation,* 163–236.

44. PRAAD, Tamale, NRG 8/1/311, 2 June 1976.

45. Republic of Ghana, *Constitution of the Republic of Ghana,* 1992, article 257, par. 3.

46. PRAAD, Tamale, NRG 8/1/311, correspondence, 1970.

47. Ibid., NRG 8/2/128, Dagomba Native Affairs, 1955–69, Sept. 1968.

48. Antoine, "Politics of Rice-Farming," 47.

49. "We the thumb-printed Tindanas of Tamale," 13th August, 1990, and "We, the four gates of Tamale indigenous citizens" to Ya Na, 20 June 1995, 10 July 1990, copies in author's possession.

50. Tamale Bugulana to Regional Police Commander, 14 Dec. 2009, "The status of the Dakpema in Tamale," copy in author's possession.

51. Kuga Na to Regional Minister, 3 June 2010, "Status of Buglana of Tamale and Dakpema of Tamale," with minutes of the meeting attached, copy in author's possession.

52. Dakpema M. Alhassan Dawuni to Kuga Na, 4 June 2010, copy in author's possession.

53. Bugulana Abdul-Rahman Alhassan to Chairman, Regional Security Council, 16 June 2010, with copies to the commanders of the army and the air force, among others, copy in author's possession.

54. PRAAD, Tamale, NRG 8/2/32, 15 July 1930.

55. Goody, "Circulating Succession among the Gonja," 156.

56. Duncan-Johnstone and Blair, *Enquiry into the Constitution,* app. 3, "History of the Dagomba," 51.

57. PRAAD, Tamale, NRG 8/2/93, Native Affairs; Anamzoya, "Politicization, Elite Manipulation," 9.

58. This is also the case among the Talensi. Fortes, *Dynamics of Clanship,* 150, 200.

59. Drucker-Brown, *Ritual Aspects of Mamprusi Kingship,* 90.

6. Chiefs in the National Arena

1. Rathbone, *Nkrumah and the Chiefs,* 3.

2. Boafo-Arthur, "Chieftaincy in Ghana."

3. See also Talton, *Politics of Social Change,* ch. 5.

4. Owusu, *Uses and Abuses,* 81; Arhin Brempong, *Transformations of Traditional Rule,* vii.

5. PRAAD, Tamale, NRG 8/2/99, List of chiefs NR 1948–62, 24 Mar. 1961.

6. Busia, *Position of the Chief,* 21.

7. Owusu, *Uses and Abuses*, 223–26.

8. Goody, "Circulating Succession among the Gonja," 155; Davis, "Continuity and Change in Mampurugu," 22, 31; Tonah, "Diviners, Malams, God."

9. Mahama, *History and Traditions of Dagbon*, 24–26.

10. PRAAD, Tamale, NRG 8/2/32, Native Affairs, 1931–32, "Extract from a report by Mr. A. W. Cardinall, 20 July 1928"; Kirby, "Peace-Building in Northern Ghana," 171.

11. Mahama, *History and Traditions of Dagbon*, 81–82.

12. Lund, "Bawku Is Still Volatile," 593–94.

13. Republic of Ghana, *Constitution of the Republic of Ghana*, 1992, article 270.

14. Ghana News Agency, 6 Jan. 2010; Anamzoya, "Chieftaincy Conflicts in Northern Ghana," 219–20.

15. Natogmah Issahaku, "Politicians, Dagbon is no longer your Waterloo," Ghana News Agency, 13 Oct. 2007.

16. Lentz, *Ethnicity*, 252.

17. Arhin Brempong, *Transformations of Traditional Rule*, 90.

18. Lund, "Bawku Is Still Volatile," 588 (quotation), 604–6.

19. Boafo-Arthur, "Chieftaincy in Ghana," 132.

20. Odotei and Awedoba, *Chieftaincy in Ghana*.

21. Ghana News Agency, 27 Mar. 2008.

22. Abotchie, "Position of the Chief," 178.

23. Boafo-Arthur, "Chieftaincy and Politics," 1.

24. Owusu, *Uses and Abuses*, 6, xv; see also Gyimah-Boadi, "Another Step Forward for Ghana."

25. *Daily Graphic*, 20 July 2010.

26. Myjoyonline.com/news, 30 Mar. 2010.

27. Owusu, *Uses and Abuses*, 353.

28. Ibid., 272. On this subject in general, see Nugent, *Big Men, Small Boys*; Price, "Politics and Culture."

29. Owusu, *Uses and Abuses*, 361.

30. Ibid., 361–62; Rattray, *Ashanti Law and Constitution*, 406.

31. Owusu, *Uses and Abuses*, 405.

32. Ubink, "Negotiated or Negated?," 282.

33. Anamzoya and Tonah, "If You Don't Have the Money."

34. E. Aryeetey et al., *Politics of Land Tenure Reform*, 2.

35. Arhin Brempong, *Transformations of Traditional Rule*, 101.

36. Crook, "Decolonization, the Colonial State," 89.

37. E. Aryeetey et al., *Politics of Land Tenure Reform*, 6, 28–29.

38. Tonah, "Chiefs, Earth Priests"; Lund, "Who Owns Bolgatanga?"

39. Boni, "Traditional Ambiguities and Authoritarian Interpretations."

40. E. B.-D. Aryeetey et al., *Legal and Institutional Issues.*

41. Ubink and Quan, "How to Combine Tradition and Modernity?"

42. "Police arrest land guards terrorizing Adenta residents," Myjoyonline.com/news, 4 Feb. 2010.

43. Karikari, "Ghana's Land Administration Project," 2.

44. See "GHANA: Land Administration Project—2," www.ghanalap.gov.gh/.

45. Quan, Ubink, and Antwi, "Risks and Opportunities," quotations from 197 and 198.

46. Republic of Ghana, *Constitution of the Republic of Ghana,* 1992, article 267, par. 6.

47. Clerk in charge of accounts, Office of Stool Lands, Tamale, interview by author, Dec. 2003.

48. Ubink and Quan, "How to Combine Tradition and Modernity?," 209.

49. Abudulai, "Land Rights, Land-Use Dynamics."

50. Kasanga, *Role of Chiefs and Tendamba,* 7.

51. Mahama, *Murder of an African King,* xii.

52. Owusu, *Uses and Abuses,* 395.

53. Kasanga, *Role of Chiefs and Tendamba,* 7.

54. *Ghanaian Chronicle,* 3 Feb. 2010.

Conclusion

1. Interview by author, 29 May 2010, Tamale.

2. Scott, *Art of Not Being Governed.*

3. PRAAD, Tamale, NRG, 8/2/28, Dagomba Native Affairs, 1930–32, "Chieftainship and the Dagomba Constitution."

4. Lentz, *Ethnicity,* 94–103.

5. See Austin, "Capitalists and Chiefs."

6. See Owusu, *Uses and Abuses,* 216, 242.

7. Benjamin Opuku Agyepong, Ghanaweb Feature Article #160136, 8 Apr. 2009, www.ghanaweb.com/GhanaHomePage/NewsArchive/.

8. Rathbone, "Businessmen in Politics." See also Mbembe, *On the Postcolony,* 44–49.

9. Trevor-Roper, *Rise of Christian Europe,* 9.

Appendix

1. Coquet, "Esthétique du fétiche," 113–14.

2. See also Chernoff, "Spiritual Foundations," 264.

3. See Bierlich, *Problem of Money.*

4. Allman and Parker, *Tongnaab,* ch. 4; Friedson, *Remains of Ritual,* 7–9.

5. Meyer, *Translating the Devil.*

6. Fortes, *Dynamics of Clanship,* 107n; Allman and Parker, *Tongnaab,* 43–47.

bugulana, pl. *bugulanima* (*buɣulana,* pl. *buɣulanima*)   Shrine owner.

buguli, pl. *buga* (*buɣuli,* pl. *buɣa*)   Shrine.

Dagbamba   The people of Dagbon.

Dagbani   Language of Dagbon.

Dagomba   Anglicization introduced in colonial times, substituting for *Dagboŋ* (the kingdom), *Dagbamba* (the people), and *Dagbani* (the language).

dakpema   Lit. "market elder." Title of certain shrine keepers.

gate (*dunoli*)   Lineage; title qualifying the holder to compete for a higher title; line of men or women with rights to a tindana position. *See also* skin.

Gbewaa   Founder of the Dagbamba kingdoms; name of any Ya Na; name of certain shrines.

gboŋlana   Lit. "owner of the skin." Oldest son (at a funeral); regent (during an interregnum).

guŋ (pl. *guma*)   Special grave for certain tindanas. See also *siliga.*

kamboŋa (pl. *kambonsi*)   Warrior.

Kambon'Na   Chief warrior.

kola   Customary gift in hierarchical situations; general term for honorific gifts, usually in cash.

komlana   Lit. "owner of water." Favorite wife.

Kpamba   (s. Kpema). Elders; courtiers.

lana   Owner; person possessed of or responsible for something; chief. Always preceded by the object, title, or responsibility that is "owned."

lunga (*luŋa*, pl. *lunsi*)   Tension drum; drummer whose instrument this is; praise-singer.

Lun'Na   Titled drummer and praise-singer.

malam   Muslim cleric.

na (pl. *nanima*)   Chief; king (when it precedes a personal name).

naba   Chief (Mamprugu, Nanun).

nabia (pl. *nabihi*)   Chief's child; prince; royal.

nam   Title; essence of chieftaincy.

pakpon (*pakpoŋ*)   Man's oldest daughter (at his funeral).

sambanluŋa   Special recital of tradition at a chief's palace.

siliga   Special grave for certain tindanas. See also *guŋ*.

skin (*gboŋ*)   Chiefly title.

stool   Chiefly title (southern Ghana).

tail   Horsetail; the office of tindana; the sign of the office.

tim (pl. *tima*)   Medicine; device for healing or protection.

timpana   Talking drums, played in pairs.

tiŋa   Territory; tract of land.

tindana, pl. *tindamba* (*tiŋdana*, pl. *tiŋdamba*)   Shrine keeper, "Earth priest," "fetish priest."

wulana   Chief's spokesperson, linguist.

Ya Na   King of Dagbon.

Yo Na   Chief of Savelugu; entitled to compete for Yendi.

Bibliography

Abotchie, C. "Has the Position of the Chief Become Anachronistic in Contemporary Ghanaian Politics?" In Odotei and Awedoba, *Chieftaincy in Ghana*, 169–91.

Abubakari Lunna. "History Stories." As told to David Locke. wikis.uit.tufts.edu/confluence/display/DagombaDanceDrumming.

Abudulai, S. "Land Rights, Land-Use Dynamics and Policy in Peri-urban Tamale, Ghana." In *The Dynamics of Resource Tenure in West Africa*, edited by Camilla Toulmin, Philippe Lavigne Delville, and Samba Traoré, 107–27. London: International Institute for Environment and Development, 2002.

Allman, Jean, and John Parker. *Tongnaab: The History of a West African God.* Bloomington: Indiana Univ. Press, 2005.

Amanor, K. "The Changing Face of Customary Land Tenure." In Ubink and Amanor, *Contesting Land and Custom in Ghana*, 55–79.

Anamzoya, S. A. "Chieftaincy Conflicts in Northern Ghana: A Challenge to National Stability." In *Contemporary Social Problems in Ghana*, edited by S. Tonah, 209–27. Accra: Yamens, 2009.

———. "Politicization, Elite Manipulation, or Institutional Weaknesses? The Search for Alternative Explanations to the Dagbon Chieftaincy Disputes in Northern Ghana." *Research Review*, n.s., 24, no. 1 (2008): 1–25.

———. "A Sociological Enquiry into the 2002 Dagbon Chieftaincy Conflict in the Northern Region of Ghana." MPhil thesis, Department of Sociology, Univ. of Ghana Legon, 2004.

Anamzoya, S. A., and S. Tonah. "'If You Don't Have the Money Why Do You Want to Be a Chief?': An Analysis of the Commercialization of Justice in the Houses of Chiefs in Ghana." *Ghana Social Science Journal* 7, no. 1 (2010): 1–13.

Antoine, A. "The Politics of Rice-Farming in Dagbon, 1972–1979." PhD thesis, Univ. of London, 1985.

Appiah, Kwame A. *In My Father's House.* New York: Oxford Univ. Press, 1992.

Arhin Brempong, K. *Transformations of Traditional Rule in Ghana (1951–1996).* Accra: Sedco, 2001.

Aryeetey, E., J. R. A. Ayee, K. A. Ninsin, and Dzodzi Tsikata. *The Politics of Land Tenure Reform in Ghana.* Legon: Institute of Statistical, Social and Economic Research, Univ. of Ghana, 2007.

Aryeetey, E. B.-D., Nii A. Kotey, N. Amponsah, and K. Bentsi-Enchill. *Legal and Institutional Issues in Land Policy Reform in Ghana.* Legon: Institute of Statistical, Social and Economic Research, Univ. of Ghana, 2007.

Austin, G. "Capitalists and Chiefs in the Cocoa Hold-ups in South Asante, 1927–38." *International Journal of African Historical Studies* 21, no. 1 (1998): 63–95.

Baum, R. "Slaves without Rulers: Domestic Slavery among the Diola of Senegambia." In *African Systems of Slavery,* edited by J. Spaulding and S. Beswick, 45–66. Trenton, NJ: Africa World, 2010.

Bazin, J. "The Past in the Present: Notes on Oral Archaeology." In *African Historiographies,* edited by B. Jewsiewicki and D. Newbury, 59–74. Beverly Hills, CA: Sage, 1986.

———. "Retour aux choses-dieux." In *Corps des dieux,* edited by C. Malamoud and J.-P. Vernant, 253–73. Paris: Gallimard, 1986.

Bening, R. B. "Administrative Boundaries of Northern Ghana, 1898–1951." In *Regionalism and Public Policy in Northern Ghana,* edited by Y. Saaka, 13–33. New York: Peter Lang, 2001.

———. "The Definition of the International Boundaries of Northern Ghana, 1888–1904." *Transactions of the Historical Society of Ghana* 14, no. 2 (1973): 229–61.

———. "Land Policy and Administration in Northern Ghana." *Transactions of the Historical Society of Ghana* 16, no. 2 (1975): 227–66.

Benzing, B. *Die Geschichte und das Herrschaftssystem der Dagomba.* Meisenheim am Glau: Anton Hahn, 1971.

Bernal, M. "Race, Class, and Gender in the Formation of the Aryan Model of Greek Origins." In *Nations, Identities, Cultures,* edited by V. Y. Mudimbe, 7–28. Durham, NC: Duke Univ. Press, 1997.

Berry, S. "Ancestral Property: Land, Politics, and 'the Deeds of the Ancestors' in Ghana and Côte d'Ivoire." In Ubink and Amanor, *Contesting Land and Custom in Ghana,* 27–53.

———. *Chiefs Know Their Boundaries.* Portsmouth, NH: Heinemann, 2001.

Bierlich, B. *The Problem of Money: African Agency and Western Medicine in Northern Ghana.* New York: Berghahn, 2007.

Boafo-Arthur, K. "Chieftaincy and Politics in Ghana since 1982." *West Africa Review* 3, no. 1 (2002): 1–25.

———. "Chieftaincy in Ghana: Challenges and Prospects in the 21st Century." *African and Asian Studies* 2, no. 2 (2003): 125–53.

Boni, S. "Contents and Contexts: The Rhetoric of Oral Traditions in the Oman of Sefwi Wiawso, Ghana." *Africa* 7, no. 4 (2000): 568–94.

———. "Traditional Ambiguities and Authoritarian Interpretations in Sefwi Land Disputes." In Ubink and Amanor, *Contesting Land and Custom in Ghana*, 81–111.

Bowdich, T. E. *Mission from Cape Coast Castle to Ashantee.* 3rd ed. 1819. Reprint, London: Frank Cass, 1966.

Braudel, F. *The Mediterranean and the Mediterranean World in the Age of Philip II.* 2 vols. New York: Harper & Row, 1972 [1966].

———. "The Situation of History in 1950." In *On History,* translated by S. Matthews, 6–22. Chicago: Univ. of Chicago Press, 1980.

Brenner, L. 1989. "'Religious' Discourse in and about Africa." In *Discourse and Its Disguises,* edited by K. Barber and P. F. de Moraes Farias, 87–105. Birmingham, UK: Centre of West African Studies, Univ. of Birmingham, 1989.

Brown, Peter. *The Cult of the Saints.* Chicago: Univ. of Chicago Press, 1981.

Brukum, N. J. K. "Chieftaincy and Ethnic Conflicts in the Northern Region of Ghana, 1980–2002." In *Ethnicity, Conflicts and Consensus in Ghana,* edited by S. Tonah, 98–115. Accra: Woeli, 2007.

———. "Ethnic Conflicts in Gonja, 1980–94." In *Democracy and Conflict Resolution in Ghana,* edited by M. Oquaye, 67–74. Accra: Gold-Type, 1995.

———. *The Guinea Fowl, Mango and Pito Wars.* Accra: Ghana Universities Press, 2001.

———. "Studied Neglect or Lack of Resources?" *Transactions of the Historical Society of Ghana,* n.s., 2 (1998): 117–31.

———. "Traditional Constitutions and Succession Disputes in the Northern Region, Ghana." *WOPAG—Working Papers on Ghana: Historical and Contemporary Studies Nr. 4.* Helsinki: Univ. of Helsinki, Institute of Asian and African Studies, 2004.

Busia, K. A. *The Position of the Chief in the Modern Political System of Ashanti.* 1958. Reprint, London: Frank Cass, 1968.

Cardinall, A. W. "Customs at the Death of a King of Dagomba." *Man* 21 (1921), note 52.

———. *In Ashanti and Beyond.* Philadelphia: Lippincott, 1927.

———. *The Natives of the Northern Territories of the Gold Coast.* 1920. Reprint, New York: Negro Universities Press, 1969.

———. "Some Random Notes on the Customs of the Konkomba." *Journal of the African Society* 18, no. 59 (1918): 45–80.

Ceyssens, R. *Le roi Kanyok au milieu de quatre coins.* Fribourg: Editions Universitaires, 2003.

Chernoff, J. M. *African Rhythm and African Sensibility.* Chicago: Univ. of Chicago Press, 1979.

———. "Spiritual Foundations of Dagbamba Religion and Culture." In *African Spirituality,* edited by J. K. Olupona, 257–74. New York: Crossroad, 2000.

Clark, G. "The Invasion in British Archaeology." *Antiquity* 40 (1966): 172–89.

Cooper, F. "Conflict and Connection: Rethinking Colonial African History." *American Historical Review* 99 (1994): 1516–45.

Coquet, M. "Une esthétique du fétiche." In *Fétiches: Objets enchantés, mots réalisés,* edited by A. Surgy, 111–40. Systèmes de pensée en Afrique noire, 8. Paris: École Pratique des Hautes Études, 1985.

Crook, R. C. "Decolonization, the Colonial State, and Chieftaincy in the Gold Coast." *African Affairs* 85, no. 338 (1986): 75–105.

Davis, D. C. "Continuity and Change in Mampurugu: A Study of Tradition as Ideology." PhD diss., Northwestern Univ., 1984.

———. "'Then the White Man Came with His Whitish Ideas': The British and the Evolution of Traditional Government in Mampurugu." *International Journal of African Historical Studies* 20, no. 4 (1987): 627–46.

De Heusch, Luc. *The Drunken King.* Translated by R. Willis. Bloomington: Indiana Univ. Press, 1982.

———. *Pourquoi l'épouser?* Paris: Gallimard, 1971.

———. *Sacrifice.* Translated by L. O'Brien and A. Morton. Bloomington: Indiana Univ. Press, 1985.

———. "The Symbolic Mechanisms of Sacred Kingship: Rediscovering Frazer." *Journal of the Royal Anthropological Institute,* n.s., 3 (1997): 213–32.

Der, Benedict G. *The Slave Trade in Northern Ghana.* Accra: Woeli, 1998.

———. "The Traditional Political Systems of Northern Ghana Reconsidered." In *Regionalism and Public Policy in Northern Ghana,* edited by Y. Saaka, 35–65. New York: Peter Lang, 2001.

Dittmer, Kunz. *Die Sakralen Haüptlingen der Gurunsi im Ober-Volta-Gebiet.* Hamburg: Cram, de Gruyter, 1961.

Drucker-Brown, Susan. "Horse, Dog and Donkey: The Making of a Mamprusi King." *Man,* n.s., 27, no. 1 (1992): 71–90.

———. "Local Wars in Northern Ghana." *Cambridge Anthropology* 13, no. 2 (1988–89): 87–106.

———. *Ritual Aspects of Mamprusi Kingship.* Cambridge: African Studies Center, 1975.

———. "The Structure of the Mamprusi Kingdom and the Cult of Naam." In *The Study of the State,* edited by H. J. M. Claessen and P. Skalník, 117–31. The Hague: Mouton, 1981.

Duncan-Johnstone, A., and H. A. Blair. *Enquiry into the Constitution and Organisation of the Dagbon Kingdom.* Accra: Government Printer, 1932.

Eyre-Smith, St. J. *A Brief Review of the History and Social Organization of the Peoples of the Northern Territories of the Gold Coast.* Accra: Government Printer, 1933.

Fage, J. D. "Reflections on the Early History of the Mossi-Dagomba Group of States." In *The Historian in Tropical Africa,* edited by J. Vansina, R. Mauny, and L. F. Thomas, 177–89. London: Oxford Univ. Press, 1964.

———. "Some Notes on a Scheme for the Investigation of Oral Tradition in the Northern Territories of the Gold Coast." *Journal of the Historical Society of Nigeria* 1, no. 1 (1956): 15–19.

Feierman, Steven. "Colonizers, Scholars and the Creation of Invisible Histories." In *Beyond the Cultural Turn,* edited by V. E. Bonnell and L. Hunt, 182–216. Berkeley: Univ. of California Press, 1999.

Ferguson, P. "Islamisation in Dagbon." PhD diss., Univ. of Cambridge, 1972.

Ferguson, P., and I. Wilks. "Chiefs, Constitutions and the British in Northern Ghana." In *West African Chiefs,* edited by M. Crowder and O. Ikime, 326–69. New York: Africana, 1970.

Firth, Raymond. *Elements of Social Organization.* New York: Philosophical Library, 1951.

Fortes, Meyer. *The Dynamics of Clanship among the Tallensi.* London: Oxford Univ. Press, 1945.

———. "The Political System of the Tallensi of the Northern Territories of the Gold Coast." In *African Political Systems,* edited by M. Fortes and E. E. Evans-Pritchard, 237–71. London: Oxford Univ. Press, 1940.

———. "Ritual Festivals and Social Cohesion in the Hinterland of the Gold Coast." In *Time and Social Structure, and Other Essays,* 147–63. London: Athlone, 1970.

Friedson, Steven M. *Remains of Ritual: Northern Gods in a Southern Land.* Chicago: Univ. Chicago Press, 2009.

Fuglestad, F. "The Trevor-Roper Trap, or the Imperialism of History." *History in Africa* 19 (1992): 309–26.

Geertz, C. "Shifting Aims, Moving Targets: On the Anthropology of Religion." *Journal of the Royal Anthropological Institute,* n.s., 11 (2005): 1–15.

Gell, Alfred. *Art and Agency.* Oxford: Clarendon, 1998.

Gilbert, M. "'No Condition Is Permanent': Ethnic Construction and the Use of History in Akuapem." *Africa* 67, no. 4 (1997): 501–33.

Goody, J. R. "Circulating Succession among the Gonja." In *Succession to High Office,* edited by J. R. Goody, 142–76. Cambridge Papers in Social Anthropology, No. 4. Cambridge: Cambridge Univ. Press, 1966.

———. *The Logic of Writing and the Organization of Society.* Cambridge: Cambridge Univ. Press, 1986.

———. "The Mande and the Akan Hinterland." In *The Historian in Tropical Africa,* edited by J. Vansina, R. Mauny, and L. F. Thomas, 190–216. London: Oxford Univ. Press, 1964.

———. "The Over-kingdom of Gonja." In *West African Kingdoms in the Nineteenth Century,* edited by D. Forde and P. M. Kaberry, 178–205. London: Oxford Univ. Press, 1967.

———. "The Political Systems of the Tallensi and Their Neighbours, 1888–1915." *Cambridge Anthropology* 14, no. 2 (1990): 1–25.

———. "Restricted Literacy in Northern Ghana." In *Literacy in Traditional Societies,* edited by J. R. Goody, 198–264. Cambridge: Cambridge Univ. Press, 1968.

———. *Technology, Tradition and the State in Africa.* London: Oxford Univ. Press, 1971.

Graeber, David. *Possibilities: Essays in Hierarchy, Rebellion and Desire.* Edinburgh: AK Press, 2007.

Grischow, Jeff. *Shaping Tradition: Civil Society, Community and Development in Colonial Northern Ghana, 1899–1957.* Leiden: Brill, 2010.

Gyimah-Boadi, E. "Another Step Forward for Ghana." *Journal of Democracy* 20, no. 2 (2009): 138–52.

Hawkins, Sean. *Writing and Colonialism in Northern Ghana.* Toronto: Univ. of Toronto Press, 2002.

Hawthorne, W. *Planting Rice and Harvesting Slaves: Transformations along the Guinea-Bissau Coast, 1400–1900.* Portsmouth, NH: Heinemann, 2003.

Henige, David P. *The Chronology of Oral Tradition.* Oxford: Clarendon, 1974.

Holden, J. J. "The Zabarima Conquest of Northwest Ghana." *Transactions of the Historical Society of Ghana* 8 (1965): 60–86.

Hubbell, A. "A View of the Slave Trade from the Margin: Souroudougou in the Late Nineteenth Century Slave Trade in the Niger Bend." *Journal of African History* 42, no. 1 (2001): 25–47.

Iddi, D. *The Ya Na of the Dagombas.* Accra: Univ. of Ghana Institute of African Studies, 1968.

Iliasu, A. A. "Asante's Relations with Dagomba, ca. 1740–1874." *Ghana Social Science Journal* 1, no. 2 (1971): 54–62.

———. "The Establishment of British Administration in Mamprugu, 1898–1937." *Transactions of the Historical Society of Ghana* 16, no. 1 (1975): 1–28.

———. "The Origins of the Mossi-Dagomba States." *Institute of African Studies Research Review* 7, no. 2 (1971): 95–113.

Izard, Michel. "De quelques paramètres de la souveraineté." In *Chefs et rois sacrés,* edited by Luc de Heusch, 69–91. Systèmes de pensée en Afrique noire, 10. Paris: CNRS, 1990.

———. *Gens du pouvoir, gens de la terre.* London: Cambridge Univ. Press, 1985.

——. *Moogo: L'émergence d'un espace étatique ouest-africain au XVIe siècle.* Paris: Karthala, 2003.

Jackson, M. D. *The Kuranko: Dimensions of Social Reality in a West African Society.* London: Hurst, 1977.

Janzen, John M. *Lemba, 1650–1930.* New York: Garland, 1982.

Jay, Nancy. *Throughout Your Generations Forever.* Chicago: Univ. of Chicago Press, 1992.

Johnson, M. "The Slaves of Salaga." *Journal of African History* 17, no. 2 (1986): 344–49.

Jones, D. H. "Jakpa and the Foundation of Gonja." *Transactions of the Historical Society of Ghana* 6 (1962): 1–29.

Karikari, I. B. "Ghana's Land Administration Project (LAP) and Land Information Systems (LIS) Implementation: The Issues." *International Federation of Surveyors, Article of the Month,* February 2006.

Kasanga, K. "Land Tenure, Resource Access and Decentralization in Ghana." In *The Dynamics of Resource Tenure in West Africa,* edited by Camilla Toulmin, Philippe Lavigne Delville, and Samba Traoré, 25–36. London: International Institute for Environment and Development, 2002.

——. *The Role of Chiefs and Tendamba in Land Administration in Northern Ghana.* London: Royal Institution of Chartered Surveyors, 1996.

Kea, R. A. *Settlements, Trade, and Polities in the Seventeenth Century Gold Coast.* Baltimore: Johns Hopkins Univ. Press, 1982.

Keane, W. "The Evidence of the Senses and the Materiality of Religion." Special issue, *Journal of the Royal Anthropological Institute* 14 (2008): S110–S127.

Kelly, R., and R. B. Bening. "Ideology, Regionalism, Self-Interest and Tradition: An Investigation into Contemporary Politics in Northern Ghana." *Africa* 77, no. 2 (2007): 180–206.

Kimble, David. *A Political History of Ghana: The Rise of Gold Coast Nationalism, 1850–1928.* Oxford: Clarendon, 1963.

Kirby, J. P. "Cultural Change and Religious Conversion in West Africa." In *Religion in Africa,* edited by T. D. Blakely, D. H. Thompson, and W. E. A. van Beek, 57–71. Portsmouth, NH: Heinemann, 1994.

——. "Ethnic Conflicts and Democratization: New Paths towards Equilibrium in Northern Ghana." *Transactions of the Historical Society of Ghana,* n.s., 10 (2006–7): 65–108.

——. "Peace-Building in Northern Ghana: Cultural Themes and Ethnic Conflict." In *Ghana's North,* edited by F. Kröger and B. Meier, 161–205. Frankfurt am Main: Peter Lang, 2003.

Klein, M. A. "Slavery in the Western Soudan." In *African Systems of Slavery,* edited by J. Spaulding and S. Beswick, 11–44. Trenton, NJ: Africa World, 2010.

Kodesh, Neil. *Beyond the Royal Gaze: Clanship and Public Healing in Buganda.* Charlottesville: Univ. of Virginia Press, 2010.

———. "History from the Healer's Shrine: Genre, Historical Imagination, and Early Ganda History." *Comparative Studies in Society and History* 49, no. 3 (2007): 527–52.

Konings, P. "Capitalist Rice Farming and Land Allocation in Northern Ghana." *Journal of Legal Pluralism* 22 (1984): 89–119.

———. *The State and Rural Class Formation in Ghana.* Boston: KPI, 1986.

Kopytoff, I. "Ancestors as Elders in Africa." *Africa* 41, no. 2 (1971): 129–42.

———. "The Internal African Frontier." In *The African Frontier,* edited by I. Kopytoff, 3–84. Bloomington: Indiana Univ. Press, 1987.

Kuba, R. "Spiritual Hierarchies and Unholy Alliances: Competing Earth Priests in a Context of Migration in Southwestern Burkina Faso." In Kuba and Lentz, *Land and the Politics of Belonging in West Africa,* 57–75.

Kuba, R., and C. Lentz. *Land and the Politics of Belonging in West Africa.* Leiden: Brill, 2006.

Kuklick, Henrika. *The Savage Within: The Social History of British Anthropology, 1885–1945.* Cambridge: Cambridge Univ. Press, 1991.

Kuper, A. "Regional Comparison in African Anthropology." *African Affairs* 78, no. 310 (1979): 110–11.

Ladouceur, Paul A. *Chiefs and Politicians: The Politics of Regionalism in Northern Ghana.* London: Longman, 1979.

Lambek, M. "The Sakalava Poiesis of History: Realizing the Past through Spirit Possession in Madagascar." *American Ethnologist* 25, no. 2 (1998): 106–27.

Landau, P. "'Religion' and Conversion in African History: A New Model." *Journal of Religious History* 23 (1999): 8–30.

Law, Robin. *The Horse in West African History.* London: Oxford Univ. Press, 1980.

Leach, Edmund R. "Aryan Invasions over Four Millennia." In *Culture through Time,* edited by E. Ohnuki-Tierney, 227–45. Stanford: Stanford Univ. Press, 1990.

———. "The Frontiers of 'Burma.'" *Comparative Studies in Society and History* 3, no. 1 (1961): 49–68.

———. *Political Systems of Highland Burma.* London: Athlone, 1954.

Lentz, C. *Ethnicity and the Making of History in Northern Ghana.* Edinburgh: Edinburgh Univ. Press, 2006.

———. "Is Land Inalienable? Historical and Current Debates on Land Transfers in Northern Ghana." *Africa* 80, no. 1 (2010): 56–80.

———. "Local Culture in the National Arena: The Politics of Cultural Festivals in Ghana." *African Studies Review* 44, no. 3 (2001): 47–72.

————. "Of Hunters, Goats and Earth Shrines: Settlement Histories and the Politics of Oral Tradition in Northern Ghana." *History in Africa* 27 (2000): 193–95.

————. "Stateless Societies or Chiefdoms? A Debate among Dagara Intellectuals." In *Ghana's North,* edited by F. Kröger and B. Meier, 129–59. Frankfurt am Main: Peter Lang, 2003.

Levtzion, N. *Muslims and Chiefs in West Africa.* Oxford: Clarendon, 1968.

Liberski-Bagnoud, D. *Les dieux du territoire.* Paris: CNRS, 2002.

Locke, D. *Drum Damba.* Crown Point, IN: White Cliffs Media, 1990.

Lovejoy, Paul E. *Caravans of Kola: The Hausa Kola Trade, 1700–1900.* Zaria, Nigeria: Ahmadu Bello Univ. Press, 1980.

Lund, C. "'Bawku Is Still Volatile': Ethnopolitical Conflict and State Recognition in Northern Ghana." *Journal of Modern African Studies* 41, no. 4 (2003): 593–610.

————. *Local Politics and the Dynamics of Property in Africa.* Cambridge: Cambridge Univ. Press, 2008.

————. "Who Owns Bolgatanga? A Story of Inconclusive Encounters." In Kuba and Lentz, *Land and the Politics of Belonging in West Africa,* 77–98.

Maasole, C. S. *The Konkomba and their Neighbours.* Accra: Ghana Universities Press, 2006.

MacGaffey, W. "Changing Representations in Central African History." *Journal of African History* 46, no. 2 (2005): 189–207.

————. "Concepts of Race in the Historiography of Northeast Africa." *Journal of African History* 7, no. 1 (1966): 1–17.

————. "Death of a King, Death of a Kingdom?" *Journal of Modern African Studies* 44, no. 1 (2006): 79–99.

————. "Oral Tradition in Central Africa." *International Journal of African Historical Studies* 7, no. 3 (1975): 417–26.

Mahama, Ibrahim. *Dagbani-English Dictionary.* Tamale: GILLBT, 2003.

————. *Ethnic Conflict in Northern Ghana.* Tamale: Cyber Systems, 2003.

————. *History and Traditions of Dagbon.* Tamale: GILLBT, 2004.

————. *Murder of an African King: Ya Na Yakubu II.* New York: Vantage, 2009.

————. *Ya-Naa: The African King of Power.* N.p.: privately printed, 1987.

Mbembe, Achille. *Afriques indociles.* Paris: Editions Kartala, 1988.

————. *On the Postcolony.* Berkeley: Univ. of California Press, 2001.

McCaskie, T. C. "Empire State: Asante and the Historians." *Journal of African History* 33, no. 3 (1992): 467–76.

————. *State and Society in Pre-colonial Asante.* Cambridge: Cambridge Univ. Press, 1995.

Meillassoux, Claude, ed. *L'esclavage en Afrique précoloniale.* Paris: Maspero, 1975.

Mendonsa, E. L. *Continuity and Change in a West African Society.* Durham, NC: Carolina Academic, 2001.

Meyer, Birgit. *Translating the Devil.* Trenton, NJ: Africa World, 1999.

Miller, Joseph C. *Kings and Kinsmen: Early Mbundu States in Angola.* Oxford: Clarendon, 1976

———. *The Problem of Slavery as History.* New Haven, CT: Yale Univ. Press, 2012.

Nugent, Paul. *Big Men, Small Boys and Politics in Ghana.* London: Pinter, 1995.

Odotei, I., and A. K. Awedoba, eds. *Chieftaincy in Ghana.* Accra: Sub-Saharan, 2006.

Olivier de Sardan, J.-P. "Occultism and the Ethnographic 'I': The Exoticizing of Magic from Durkheim to 'Postmodern' Anthropology." *Critique of Anthropology* 12, no. 1 (1992): 5–25.

Oppong, Christine. *Growing up in Dagbon.* Accra: Ghana Publishing, 1973.

Owusu, Maxwell. "Politics without Parties: Reflections on the Union Government Proposals in Ghana." *African Studies Review* 22, no. 1 (1979): 89–108.

———. "Rebellion, Revolution and Tradition: Reinterpreting Coups in Ghana." *Comparative Studies in Society and History* 31, no. 2 (1989): 372–97.

———. *Uses and Abuses of Political Power.* 2nd ed. Accra: Ghana Universities Press, 2006.

Peel, J. D. Y. "Poverty and Sacrifice in Nineteenth Century Yorubaland." *Journal of African History* 31, no. 3 (1990): 465–84.

Pietz, W. "The Spirit of Civilization: Blood Sacrifice and Monetary Debt." *Res* 28 (Autumn 1995): 23–38.

Price, R. "Politics and Culture in Contemporary Ghana: The Big-Man Small-Boy Syndrome." *Journal of African Studies* 1 (1974): 173–204.

Quan, J., J. Ubink, and A. Antwi. "Risks and Opportunities of State Intervention in Customary Land Management." In Ubink and Amanor, *Contesting Land and Custom in Ghana,* 183–208.

Rathbone, R. "Businessmen in Politics: Party Struggle in Ghana, 1949–57." *Journal of Development Studies* 9, no. 3 (1973): 391–40.

———. *Nkrumah and the Chiefs: The Politics of Chieftaincy in Ghana, 1951–1960.* Athens: Ohio Univ. Press, 2000.

Rattray, R. S. *Ashanti Law and Constitution.* Oxford: Clarendon, 1929.

———. *The Tribes of the Ashanti Hinterland.* 1932. Reprint, Oxford: Clarendon, 1969.

Republic of Ghana. *Constitution of the Republic of Ghana.* Accra, 1969.

———. *Constitution of the Republic of Ghana.* [Accra], 1992.

———. *White Paper on the Report of the Wuaku Commission.* Accra, 2002.

Roberts, R. L. *Warriors, Merchants, and Slaves: The State and the Economy in the Middle Niger Valley, 1700–1914.* Stanford: Stanford Univ. Press, 1987.

Salifu, Abdulai. "Names That Prick: Royal Praise Names in Dagbon, Northern Ghana." PhD diss., Indiana Univ., Bloomington, 2008.

Schlottner, M. "'We Stay, Others Come and Go': Identity among the Mamprusi in Northern Ghana." In *Ethnicity in Ghana,* edited by C. Lentz and P. Nugent, 49–67. New York: St. Martin's, 2000.

Schoffeleers, Matthew. *River of Blood.* Madison: Univ. of Wisconsin Press, 1992.

Scott, James C. *The Art of Not Being Governed.* New Haven, CT: Yale Univ. Press, 2009.

Seligman, C. G. *The Races of Africa.* London: Butterworth, 1930.

Sharpe, B. "Ethnography and a Regional System: Mental Maps and the Myth of States and Tribes in North-Central Nigeria." *Critique of Anthropology* 6, no. 3 (1986): 33–65.

Shaw, R. "The Invention of African Traditional Religion." *Religion* 20 (1990): 339–3.

Singleton, M. "Speaking to the Ancestors: Religion as Interlocutory Interaction." *Anthropos* 104 (2009): 311–32.

Skalník, Peter. "Authority versus Power: Democracy in Africa Must Include Original African Institutions." *Journal of Legal Pluralism* 37–38 (1996): 109–22.

———. "Dynamics of Early State Development in the Voltaic Area." In *Political Anthropology: The State of the Art,* edited by S. L. Seaton and H. J. M. Claessen, 197–214. The Hague: Mouton, 1979.

———. "Early States in the Voltaic Basin." In *The Early State,* edited by H. J. M. Claessen and P. Skalník, 469–94. The Hague: Mouton, 1978.

———. "Ideological and Symbolic Authority: Political Culture in Nanun, Northern Ghana." In *Ideology in the Formation of Early States,* edited by H. J. M. Claessen and J. Oosten, 84–98. Leiden: Brill, 1996.

———. "On the Inadequacy of the Concept of the 'Traditional State': Illustrated with Ethnographic Material on Nanun, Ghana." *Journal of Legal Pluralism* 26–27 (1987): 301–25.

———. "Outwitting Ghana: Pluralism of Political Culture in Nanun." In *Outwitting the State,* edited by P. Skalník, 147–69. New Brunswick, NJ: Transaction, 1989.

Smith, M. G. "On Segmentary Lineage Systems." *Journal of the Royal Anthropological Institute* 86, pt. 2 (1956): 39–80.

Spencer, J. "Post-colonialism and the Political Imagination." *Journal of the Royal Anthropological Institute,* n.s., 3 (1997): 1–19.

Staniland, Martin. *The Lions of Dagbon.* Cambridge: Cambridge Univ. Press, 1975.

Sutton, I. "Colonial Agricultural Policy: The Non-development of the Northern Territories of the Gold Coast." *International Journal of African Historical Studies* 22, no. 4 (1989): 637–69.

Swanepoel, N. J. "Every Periphery Is Its Own Center: Sociopolitical and Economic Interactions in Nineteenth-Century Northwestern Ghana." *International Journal of African Historical Studies* 42, no. 3 (2009): 411–32.

Tait, David. "History and Social Organization of the Konkomba." *Transactions of the Gold Coast and Togoland Historical Society* 1, no. 5 (1955): 193–210.

———. *The Konkomba of Northern Ghana.* Edited by J. R. Goody. London: Oxford Univ. Press, 1961.

Talton, Benjamin. *Politics of Social Change in Ghana: The Konkomba Struggle for Political Equality.* New York: Palgrave, 2010.

Tamakloe, E. F. *A Brief History of the Dagbamba People.* Accra: Government Printer, 1931.

Terray, Emmanuel. *Une histoire du royaume Abron du Gyaman.* Paris: Karthala, 1995.

Thornton, John K. "Origin Traditions and History in Central Africa." *African Arts* 37, no. 1 (2004): 32–37.

Tonah, Steve. "Chiefs, Earth Priests and the State: Irrigation Agriculture, Competing Institutions." In *Ethnicity, Conflict and Consensus in Ghana,* edited by S. Tonah, 113–30. Accra: Woeli, 2007.

———. "Diviners, Malams, God and the Contest for Paramount Chiefship in Mamprugu (Northern Ghana)." *Anthropos* 101 (2006): 21–35.

Tonkin, Elizabeth. *Narrating our Pasts: The Social Construction of Oral History.* Cambridge: Cambridge Univ. Press, 1992.

Trevor-Roper, Hugh. *The Rise of Christian Europe.* New York: Harcourt Brace, 1965.

Tsikata, D., and W. Seini. "Identities, Inequalities and Conflicts in Ghana." Working paper 5, Centre for Research on Inequality, Human Security and Ethnicity, Univ. of Oxford, 2004.

Turner, V. W. *Dramas, Fields, and Metaphors.* Ithaca, NY: Cornell Univ. Press, 1974.

Ubink, J. M. "Negotiated or Negated? The Rhetoric and Reality of Customary Tenure in an Ashanti Village in Ghana." *Africa* 78, no. 2 (2008): 264–87.

Ubink, J. M., and K. S. Amanor, eds. *Contesting Land and Custom in Ghana.* Leiden: Leiden Univ. Press, 2008.

Ubink, J. M., and J. F. Quan. "How to Combine Tradition and Modernity? Regulating Customary Land Management in Ghana." *Land Use Policy* 25 (2008): 198–213.

Vansina, Jan. *How Societies Are Born.* Charlottesville: Univ. of Virginia Press, 2004.

Watherston, A. E. G. "The Northern Territories of the Gold Coast." *Journal of the Royal African Society* 7, no. 28 (1908): 344–73.

Webb, J. L. "The Horse and Slave Trade between the Western Sahara and the Senegambia." *Journal of African History* 34, no. 2 (1993): 221–46.

White, H. "The Politics of Historical Interpretation: Discipline and De-sublimation." *Critical Inquiry* 9, no. 1 (1982): 113–37.

Wienia, M. "Ominous Calm: Autochthony and Sovereignty in Konkomba/Nanumba Violence and Peace." PhD thesis, Leiden Univ., 2009.

Wilks, Ivor. "A Medieval Trade Route from the Niger to the Gulf of Guinea." *Journal of African History* 7, no. 2 (1966): 337–341.

———. "The Mossi and Akan States, 1500–1800." In *History of West Africa,* edited by J. F. A. Ajayi and M. Crowder, 1:344–86. New York: Columbia Univ. Press, 1972.

———. *Wa and the Wala.* Cambridge: Cambridge Univ. Press, 1989.

Wood, N. "Machiavelli's Concept of Virtù Reconsidered." *Political Studies* 15, no. 2 (1967): 159–72.

Yoder, J. C. *The Kanyok of Zaire.* Cambridge: Cambridge Univ. Press, 1992.

Zablong, Z. A. "The Lunsi Institution of Dagbon: An Insider's Description." MA thesis, Univ. of Ghana Legon, 2008.

Zahan, D. "The Mossi Kingdoms." In *West African Kingdoms in the Nineteenth Century,* edited by D. Forde and P. Kaberry, 152–78. London: Oxford Univ. Press, 1967.

Index

Note: In accordance with Dagbani usage, Bugulanas, Dakpemas, Gulkpe'Nas, and Ya Nas are listed under Bugulana, Dakpema, Gulkpe'Na, and Na respectively, followed by their personal names. The offices of Bugulana, Dakpema, Gulkpe'Na, and Ya Na are listed separately. Other chiefs' titles are followed by Na or Lana. If the place to which a chief's title relates is a topic in itself, the two are listed separately—e.g., Bagale, Bagale Na. Italicized page numbers refer to maps and figures.